Border Poetics in German and Polish Literature

Studies in German Literature, Linguistics, and Culture

Border Poetics in German and Polish Literature

Cosmopolitan Imaginations since 1989

Karolina May-Chu

Rochester, New York

Copyright © 2024 Karolina May-Chu

All Rights Reserved. Except as permitted under current legislation, no part of this work may be photocopied, stored in a retrieval system, published, performed in public, adapted, broadcast, transmitted, recorded, or reproduced in any form or by any means, without the prior permission of the copyright owner.

First published 2024
by Camden House

Camden House is an imprint of Boydell & Brewer Inc.
668 Mt. Hope Avenue, Rochester, NY 14620, USA
and of Boydell & Brewer Limited
PO Box 9, Woodbridge, Suffolk IP12 3DF, UK
https://boydellandbrewer.com

ISBN-13: 978-1-64014-169-8

Library of Congress Cataloging-in-Publication Data

CIP data is available from the Library of Congress.

The publisher has no responsibility for the continued existence or accuracy of URLs for external or third-party internet websites referred to in this book, and does not guarantee that any content on such websites is, or will remain, accurate or appropriate.

für Mutti

Literature is built on tenderness toward any being other than ourselves. It is the basic psychological mechanism of the novel. Thanks to this miraculous tool, the most sophisticated means of human communication, our experience can travel through time, reaching those who have not yet been born, but who will one day turn to what we have written, the stories we told about ourselves and our world.

Literatura jest właśnie zbudowana na czułości wobec każdego innego od nas bytu. To jest podstawowy psychologiczny mechanizm powieści. Dzięki temu cudownemu narzędziu, najbardziej wyrafinowanemu sposobowi ludzkiej komunikacji, nasze doświadczenie podróżuje poprzez czas i trafia do tych, którzy się jeszcze nie urodzili, a którzy kiedyś sięgną po to, co napisaliśmy, co opowiedzieliśmy o nas samych i o naszym świecie.

—Olga Tokarczuk, Nobel Lecture / Przemowa noblowska

Contents

Acknowledgments	ix
Notes on Terminology and Translations	xi
Introduction	1

Part I.
Context and Theoretical Frameworks

1:	Entanglements in German and Polish History, Literature, and Culture	33
2:	Border Poetics	63

Part II.
Reading Border Poetics

3:	Disruption: Fictions of Memory by Inga Iwasiów, Sabrina Janesch, and Tanja Dückers	93
4:	Belonging: Defocalized Narratives by Günter Grass, Sabrina Janesch, and Olga Tokarczuk	130

Ends and Beginnings (Not a Conclusion)	170
Bibliography	175
Index	195

Acknowledgments

WRITING A BOOK is a journey, and not an easy one. I am grateful to many people in North America and Europe who have inspired, encouraged, and supported me along the way. First, I would like to thank my friends and colleagues at my home institution, the University of Wisconsin–Milwaukee (UWM), and especially in the Department of Ancient and Modern Languages, Literatures and Cultures. My special thanks go to Jonathan Wipplinger, who has been a wonderful colleague, mentor, and friend from the moment I joined the German Program. I am also grateful to UWM and its Office of Research for providing valuable assistance through the Research Assistance Fund and the Advancing Research and Creativity Award.

I owe a debt of gratitude to colleagues who have offered feedback and guidance at different stages of this book project, from the proposal to reading drafts to stimulating conversations. I especially thank Sabine Gross, Sonja Klocke, B. Venkat Mani, and Marc Silberman at the University of Wisconsin–Madison, where this project began many years ago. Their scholarship inspires me, and they continue to be my models for academic mentorship. I also benefited greatly from the advice of Søren Frank, Ela Gezen, David Kim, and Maria Stehle. I cannot thank them enough for being so generous with their time, encouragement, and constructive criticism.

Jim Walker at Camden House has been an enthusiastic supporter of this project from the beginning, and I thank him and his colleagues, especially Jane Best, for steering this book through the publishing process with great care and patience. The two anonymous peer reviewers offered both encouragement and helpful criticism, and I thank them for their time and their thoughtful comments on the manuscript. I am also grateful to Phil Dematteis and Jacob Watson for helping me fine-tune the manuscript.

The Diversity and Decolonization of the German Curriculum Remote Write-on-Site Group has been instrumental to the completion of this book. In varying constellations, this online community of scholars has created an uplifting and reassuring virtual environment to write together. I thank especially Marisol Bayona Roman, Carol Anne Costabile-Heming, Sarah Hall, Claire A. Ross, Kathryn Sederberg, Rebekah Slodounik, and Holly Yanacek. My virtual spaces have their corresponding ones in the real world. This book was written in apartments, offices, and libraries in Germany, Poland, and the United States. The National Library in Warsaw as well as the library of the German Historical Institute in Warsaw have proven especially productive places to think and write.

x ♦ ACKNOWLEDGMENTS

This book could not have been written without the support of friends and family in various parts of the world. Viktorija Bilić and Anika Wilson have been dear friends, and I cannot thank them enough for keeping me nourished with good food and conversations. For their friendship over the years, I also want to thank Jasmine Alinder, Justin Court, Georg Essl, Christine Evans, Nick Fleisher, Kristopher Imbrigotta, Jennifer Jordan, Catherine Kirchman, Aims McGuinness, Sarah Reed, Jeanne Schueller, Lisa Silverman, Tami Williams, Jason Williamson, Lynn Wolff, and Paula Wojcik. I hope to make up for the inadequacy of these few lines and any omissions in person.

My families in the United States and in Germany have patiently supported me over the years, even when the time spent on this book has meant less time spent with them. First and foremost, I want to thank Winson Chu for being my partner, friend, and favorite travel companion. His love, care, and support have carried me through the ups and downs of this project, and more importantly, life. I also thank my family in Germany, in particular Nicole, Marten, and Larissa, for not giving up on me. Above all, I thank my mother, Jadwiga, who from an early age instilled in me an appreciation for the literary imagination and a desire to travel and see the world from a multitude of viewpoints. This book is dedicated to her.

* * *

This project evolved over many years, and some materials contained in this book have been published previously. I explored the connection between German, European, and world literature in the context of narratives of refuge in "Reading Germany, Europe, and the World in Abbas Khider's Novel *Ohrfeige*" (2020), which appeared in a special issue of *Colloquia Germanica*, edited by Anke Biendarra and Friederike Eigler. The article's theoretical framing has been revised and became part of the introduction to this book. A discussion of one of the novels I analyze in chapter 3 as well as earlier ideas about border poetics were part of my article "Measuring the Borderland in Sabrina Janesch's *Katzenberge* (2010)," which appeared in a special issue of *Monatshefte* (vol. 108, no. 3, 2016), edited by B. Venkat Mani and Pamela Potter (© 2016 by the Board of Regents of the University of Wisconsin System. All rights reserved). My article "Von Grenzlandliteratur zur Poetik der Grenze: Deutschpolnische Transiträume und die kosmopolitische Imagination" appeared in 2016 in a special issue of *Zeitschrift für interkulturelle Germanistik*, edited by Withold Bonner and Sabine Egger. The ideas presented there became points of departure for my theoretical reflections on border poetics. I thank the publishers for allowing me to republish revised versions of these articles here. I am also grateful to Camden House for allowing me to use parts of my analysis of Inga Iwasiów's *Bambino*, presented here in chapter 3, in my "Introduction to the Translation," which was published in 2024 in a special section on *German-Polish Borderlands in Contemporary Literature and Culture* in the journal *TRANSIT*. The issue includes two chapters from Iwasiów's novel in a first-time English translation by Karolina Hicke and me.

Notes on Terminology and Translations

German-Polish or Polish-German

THROUGHOUT THIS BOOK, I refer to "German-Polish" or "Polish-German" literature. This is intended as a thematic orientation. It is literature about topics that pertain to Germany and Poland, mainly the German-Polish borderland in its past and present variations or as a mental construct. This book includes works originally written in German or in Polish by authors who identify as German or Polish or both, or who do not make their affiliations explicit. I alternate the use of "German-Polish" and "Polish-German," but the order of the adjectives indicates no hierarchy of any kind.

Translations

This study relies on sources in German, Polish, and English. For some texts, published translations exist in one or both of the other two languages. Other sources are multilingual, including bilingual or trilingual print publications or websites. Of the major works examined in this study, only the novels by the two Nobel Prize winners, Günter Grass and Olga Tokarczuk, have been translated into the respective other language and into English. There are currently no published English translations of Sabrina Janesch's novels *Katzenberge* and *Ambra*, or of Tanja Dückers's novel *Himmelskörper*. While *Himmelskörper* has been translated into Polish, Janesch's novels have not. For Polish author Inga Iwasiów's novel *Bambino*, published translations in English exist only of individual chapters. If a translation is my own or if an existing translation is modified, this is noted in the footnote. Title translations are offered in parentheses, and they are italicized if they refer to a published translation. Translators are listed in the bibliography.

Introduction

A WALL RUNS THROUGH the middle of one family's house, an Iraq veteran's mind is invaded by traumatic memories, a young woman is kept locked inside an apartment until she finishes telling her story, and a spider inside an amber pendant is the all-knowing and all-feeling narrator of it all. These are just some instances of the real and figurative boundaries in Sabrina Janesch's *Ambra* (2012). The novel tells a German-Polish border story that stretches from the mid-nineteenth century to the present through the lens of one family. Two central characters, the brothers Konrad and Marian Mysza, grow up at a time of heightened nationalism in a village near Danzig. When they are born, in 1911 and 1914, respectively, the area is part of the German Empire. After the First World War, Danzig becomes a Free City within the territory of the newly reestablished Polish state but maintains a majority German population. The shifting political borders also cut through the family, so, when Marian converts to Catholicism and marries a Polish woman, this creates a rift between the brothers. After the Second World War, Danzig becomes part of Poland and is renamed Gdańsk; Marian's family remains in the city, Konrad's is expelled and settles in West Germany. The family's history remains buried until two decades after the end of the Cold War, when Konrad's granddaughter recovers it. She is assisted by the spider narrator, which allows her to go beyond the boundaries of time, space, and individual consciousness. *Ambra* draws attention to the entanglements between political and figurative boundaries, inviting the reader to reimagine these borders and apply a more tender or cosmopolitan view. Borders do not disappear, but they are made visible as arbitrary and changeable constructs and thus appear less divisive, less stable, and less finite.

Such cosmopolitan perspectives appeared plausible during a brief period following the fall of the Berlin Wall in 1989. In the initial post–Cold War years of the 1990s, there was an optimistic feeling that suggested the world was interconnected and that everyone was able to move about freely, either physically or virtually through media and consumption. Even though this kind of freedom was never actually granted to the majority of the world's population, many in North America, as well as in Europe, bought into the pervasive illusion that borders were gradually disappearing. It has long since become clear that borders have anything but vanished. In fact, borders are now "dispersed a little everywhere."[1] They are made present and tangible by an incessant flow of images and information on the internet and social media, but they are also

---

1   Balibar, *We, the People of Europe*, 1.

2 ♦ Introduction

distant and disappear from view quickly—for those, at least, whose lives are not directly caught up in them. This study considers how literature, which, as Olga Tokarczuk says, "is built on tenderness toward any being other than ourselves," can stimulate our cosmopolitan imagination by bringing these borders back into our line of vision and challenging us to engage them critically and productively.[2]

In November 2021, the border between Belarus and Poland became a violent emblem of the global resurgence of borders, only to be eclipsed by Russia's invasion of Ukraine on February 24, 2022. That previous fall, however, the Belarusian government under President Aleksandr Lukashenko recruited migrants from the Middle East and brought them to Belarus's border with the European Union. He used them to manufacture a humanitarian border crisis that has been widely regarded as retaliation against EU sanctions.[3] In response to Lukashenko's actions, Poland fortified its borders, denied the trapped migrants their right to claim asylum, and banned media and aid organizations from an almost 2-mile-wide restricted zone along the 250-mile-long border.[4] These events have also put the strained relationship between Germany and Poland into sharp relief. Poland forms one of the EU's outer limits, but Germany is a desired destination for many of the migrants hoping for safety and a better life. The war in Ukraine and attendant discussions over sanctions against Russia or the supply of weapons to Ukraine have only made these rifts more visible.[5]

Since the end of the Cold War, Germany and Poland have enjoyed remarkably strong ties, but these relations—as well as those between Poland and the EU—have been tense at least since Poland's 2015 parliamentary elections, which brought the national-conservative Law and Justice party (PiS) to power. Subsequent elections shifted the country even further to the right and confirmed its general political direction, including an anti-German and anti-EU stance (which are often equivalent). The EU, for its part, determined after much deliberation that antidemocratic developments in Poland constituted a violation of the rule of law, which resulted in fines and a withholding

---

2   Tokarczuk, "Nobel Lecture," 25.

3   The sanctions were a result of repressive measures and falsifications during Belarus's 2020 presidential election. See European Council and Council of the European Union, "EU Restrictive Measures."

4   See, for example, Wanat, "Poland's Persistent Forbidden Zone"; and Higgins, "Live Updates." Polish filmmaker Agnieszka Holland's 2023 *The Green Border* is a fictionalized account of this situation. It tells a story in which the perspectives of the refugees, Polish activists, and border guards become entwined in the borderland.

5   See, for example, Lüdke and dpa, "Streit um Panzer-Ringtausch"; dpa and tsp, "Update/Scharfe Kritik"; and Łada-Konefał and Kucharczyk, *Der deutsche und der polnische Blick*.

of EU funding in 2021.[6] Acknowledging Poland's geostrategic importance in light of the Belarus border crisis and Russia's attack on Ukraine, the EU softened its stance toward Poland briefly in early 2022, but renewed its criticism only weeks later.[7] Tensions between Germany and Poland increased accordingly. Some observers accused the Polish government of taking advantage of these crises, while others have pointed to Germany's complicity in the developments owing to its failure to take a stronger stance against Russia in the past.[8] Relations between Poland and Germany are expected to improve after the 2023 parliamentary elections brought a new, pro-European government to power.[9] Meanwhile, however, millions of people—from Ukraine and from the Middle East—are still in need of refuge and protection.

At the time of writing this introduction, at the end of 2023, the above events and developments are on the minds of many people in Europe and North America. It is unclear how and when these crises will end, and what the global or regional repercussions will be. As this book makes its way into the world, new borders and new crises will emerge. The details, names, and places will change, but at their very core, the mechanisms and structures, and the devastating effects of borders will be similar. This violent resurgence of borders has been underway for some time. At least since the 9/11 terrorist attacks, it has been difficult to conceive of a weakening of borders, let alone their disappearance. Instead, a widespread revival of nationalism fuels conflicts and exclusion, and parties with antiglobalization programs and isolationist views have been gaining in popularity. Climate change and the resulting environmental crises are accelerating these developments while raising the stakes, and we now live in an age where a staggering 108.4 million people have been forcibly displaced from their homes.[10] Their movements are regulated, restricted, and most often prevented by actors and institutions on various levels from trans- to subnational. We live in an age of borders.

Literature is at times politically instrumentalized to justify divisions, and at other times writers have been consciously involved in reifying borders; for

---

6   European Commission, "Commission Staff Working Document"; and Deutschlandfunk, "Nach der Millionen-Strafe des EuGH."

7   See, for example, Großmann and Kelnberger, "Justiz in Polen"; Gutschker, "Rechtsstaatsbericht"; and Vertretung in Deutschland, "Rechtsstaatlichkeit."

8   Bachmann, "Die polnische Regierung missbraucht die Flüchtlingskrise." Much has been written on the connection (and the disconnect) between the treatment of Middle Eastern and of Ukrainian refugees; see, for example, Zessin-Jurek, "Real Refugees." See also footnote 5 above for more on the disagreements between Germany and Poland.

9   In the October 2023 elections, popular support for the governing PiS party was still strong, but it lost its parliamentary majority to an alliance of pro-EU parties headed by former (and again current) Polish prime minister and former European Council president Donald Tusk.

10   UNHCR, "Global Trends," 2022.

4 ♦ Introduction

example, German National Socialist writers who promoted antisemitic and racist ideologies through their works. This book, however, focuses on literature that pushes back against the divisiveness of borders and on authors who present more-inclusive perspectives in their writing. This kind of literature along with other forms of artistic expression are important venues for advocating transborder connections and criticizing exclusionary boundaries. Many writers use their public platforms to speak out against injustices, and they emphasize the transnational landscape of the ongoing violent conflicts and humanitarian crises. This was, for example, the case when an international group of Nobel Prize winners—Elfriede Jelinek, Herta Müller, Svetlana Alexievich, and Olga Tokarczuk—appealed in an open letter to the EU to find a humanitarian solution to the situation at the Belarusian border, or when writers across the world began to speak out against the war in Ukraine a few months later.[11] Even more, in the literary works of these writers themselves we find calls for transnational and cosmopolitan ways of thinking. These works are not, and cannot be, quick reactions to the constantly changing landscape of current events and news coverage, but they are nonetheless deeply rooted in the contemporary moment. They engage with the present and (often indirectly) counter its simplified and fast-paced narratives. I regard these artistic expressions as part of what sociologist Gerard Delanty has called the "cosmopolitan imagination"; that is, an imagination grounded in a "critical cosmopolitanism" that entails a view of "society as an ongoing process of self-constitution through the continuous opening up of new perspectives in light of the encounter with the Other."[12] Expanding on Delanty and using contemporary German- and Polish-language literature as case studies, this book examines how borders and borderlands can become sites for exercising the cosmopolitan imagination. I refer to the narrative and cultural practice that opens up these new spaces of engagement as "border poetics."

The notion of "border poetics" has been used before, and mainly in two ways, as I explain in more detail below. In short, it is a general descriptor for the literary, that is, "poetic," engagement with borders. At the same time, it has been theorized by Johan Schimanski and others to denote a tool of scholarly analysis to be applied to such texts. In this book, I endeavor to merge these two uses and thereby both hone and broaden the term. I adapt the term "border poetics" to describe a narrative and cultural practice that puts historically and geopolitically specific boundaries in relation to more universal and figurative border experiences, such as those of gender, ethnicity, or class, as

---

11   FAZ.NET, "Schriftstellerinnen zu Belarus." While this letter urging the upholding of human rights was rather uncontroversial, an open letter by German intellectuals protesting Vladimir Putin's aggression against Ukraine but also demanding that Germany not supply weapons to Ukraine, triggered a more critical response. See Oltermann, "German Thinkers' War of Words."

12   Delanty, *The Cosmopolitan Imagination*, 2 and 13.

well as epistemological and ontological boundaries, including those of language, knowledge, and reality. I ascribe this practice to narratives in which "real" borderlands are staging grounds for symbolic border crossings that represent fundamentally human experiences. As border poetics rests on the same productive tension between the particular and the universal that also drives contemporary notions of cosmopolitanism, I argue for viewing border poetics as an idiom of the cosmopolitan imagination. The German-Polish context and the theoretical foundations of my understanding of border poetics are the foci of the next two chapters, but a brief overview of both helps elucidate the idea of border poetics and illustrate why the complexity of contemporary border narratives requires us to constantly refine our existing vocabulary and expand our analytical frameworks for talking about borders in literature and other forms of art.

Stories of Disruption and Belonging

The lands that are today Germany and Poland share a long and entangled history that goes beyond nation-centric definitions based on borders. Centuries of contact among peoples have led to defocalized, multiple understandings of people's ethnic, political, and personal affiliations, although these were frequently challenged by the drawing and redrawing of political borders. Especially Germany's invasion of Poland in 1939 and the violence of the Second World War have made it difficult to come to terms with the notion of a shared past. Thus, for much of the twentieth century, the German-Polish border served as a point of contention, and it was narratively constructed as a dividing line. Even today, the history of German aggression against Poland and memories of traumatic events continue to impact Polish-German relations. This historical legacy has been at the basis of many tensions between the two countries, especially since Poland's political shift to the right in 2015. While these developments are concerning, it is also important to acknowledge that such disagreements often run counter to the views of prominent figures in civil society, scholars, and artists in both countries. A longer historical view shows that despite recent heightened tensions, Germany and Poland have gone through a remarkable—though not always smooth—reconciliation process since 1945 and that they have developed strong neighborly relations, especially after the end of the Cold War and Poland's accession to the European Union in 2004.

The year 1989 serves as an important temporal anchor for this study as the year that marks a radical change in the political nature of the Polish-German relationship. We could consider other major caesuras in the twentieth century that impact the character of borders and our view of them, but for the proliferation of border poetics, the fall of the Berlin Wall holds central significance. There are multiple reasons for this, but most importantly, the end of the Cold War enabled Poles and Germans to develop a more dialogic relationship,

6   ◆   INTRODUCTION

rediscover their intertwined histories within a larger European context, and engage differently with the history of the Second World War and its aftermath. These changes also had an impact on the literary and cultural imagination, and narratives that articulate the borderland as a space of contact and mixing became more prominent. The gradual development of a shared and more diverse space corresponds to the transformation of the border from a hard dividing line into a more porous boundary, and many such narratives use the language of transnational contact and exchange. This approach, however, seems too limited when considering narratives such as the one below, which is part of Olga Tokarczuk's novel *Dom dzienny, dom nocny* (1998; *House of Day, House of Night*, 2002). The setting is the southern Polish region of Silesia, and the episode takes place in the 1990s, near the Polish-Czech border. As is true for much of Silesia, this area was part of Germany during the first half of the twentieth century. When borders were newly drawn after the Second World War, ethnic Germans were expelled from this now Polish region, which was also the case for Peter Dieter, the protagonist of the episode recounted here.

Peter Dieter is an elderly German who has come to visit his former Silesian homeland one last time. The small village that he knew as a child is almost gone, and no trace is left of his parents' house. Hopeful that he may still be able to find some remnants of his past, he tries to reconcile his fragmentary memory with the landscape in front of him. He roams alone through the timbered mountains he knew as a child. But the climb is strenuous, and his heart is weak, and as soon as he reaches the Polish-Czech border, which runs along the mountains' ridge, he suffers a heart attack. He tries to rest and, in a last effort, drags himself to a nearby boundary post. He leans against the pole to gather strength, but he dies shortly thereafter—a piece of chocolate melting in his mouth, one leg on the Czech side, the other on the Polish side. Before long, two Czech border guards find him. It is almost the end of their shift, however, and to avoid overtime, they carry Peter Dieter to the Polish side of the border. Not much later, the scene repeats, and the Polish border guards likewise carry the dead man to the Czech side: "And this is how Peter Dieter remembered his death before his soul departed forever—as a mechanical movement to the one side and to the other side, like teetering on the edge, standing on a bridge."[13]

Peter Dieter's story entails several kinds of real and symbolic border crossings. There is the mountain range: a physical, natural border; but this natural border also coincides with a current political border. It has been suggested that the moving back and forth of the deceased indicates that national borders have

---

13   Tokarczuk, *House*, 97. Translation modified. The original reads, "Tak też Peter Dieter zapamiętał swoją śmierć, zanim jego dusza odeszła na zawsze—jako mechaniczny ruch, w jedną i w drugą stronę, jako balansowanie na krawędzi, stanie na moście"; Tokarczuk, *Dom*, 132.

lost their significance.[14] And while some borders may have become invisible—say, to a tourist on a hike—the border guards' moving of the body in an effort to remove the burden of responsibility for it indeed emphasizes their continued importance.[15] The entire region is also a borderland that throughout history has been claimed by various nations and ethnic groups. All these borders are porous and changeable, and even if some of them no longer exist, they can be classified as "real" borders. At the same time, the real border is intertwined with a figurative border here: the border between life and death. Peter Dieter dies gradually, his consciousness drifting away slowly. As he is dying, his soul hovers in a transitory space from where he observes the fate of his body being moved back and forth.

Borders and borderlands figure in various ways in the literary imagination, ranging from spaces of conflict and violence to sites of peaceful exchange and mixing, and this is true for German and Polish narratives as well as border narratives more generally. Frequently, writers employ contradiction and ambiguity to create a complex and polyvalent picture of the borderland. As we see with the Peter Dieter episode, this complexity is heightened when border figurations go beyond territorial or political demarcations and physical borderlands are permeated by symbolic or universal border crossings. Yet, how do we describe and analyze these highly complex articulations of borders and border experiences? Existing interpretive frameworks of contact, exchange, or dialogue are often insufficient. For example, the idea of geographically or ethnographically defined "contact zones" is crucial in today's understanding of borders. According to Mary Louise Pratt, "contact zones" are "social spaces where cultures meet, clash, and grapple with each other, often in contexts of highly asymmetrical relations of power."[16] Pratt's concept is instructive, not least because such contact zones produce transculturation, a process whereby cultures shape one another through processes of convergence and mixing, and because they unsettle notions of community as "discrete, self-defined, coherent" or "finite, sovereign, fraternal."[17] While Pratt's original concept of the

14   Wagner, "Literarische Grenzüberschreitungen," 179. I agree with Hans-Christian Trepte, also cited by Wagner, that the moving of the body signifies the arbitrariness and artificial character of borders. Trepte, "Zur niederschlesischen Identität," 102–3.

15   Tokarczuk describes a sense of being under permanent observation despite the border's material invisibility in the chapter "The border" (*House*, 71–72; "Granica," *Dom*, 99–100). For a real-life example of the continued significance of this border, see also the accidental 2020 takeover of a Czech chapel by the Polish military in Cameron, "Poland 'Invades' Czech Republic."

16   Pratt, "Arts of the Contact Zone," 34.

17   Pratt, "Arts of the Contact Zone," 36–37. The notion of transculturation originates in the work of Cuban scholar Fernando Ortiz in the 1940s, as Pratt also explains, but it was later fundamentally shaped by Wolfgang Welsch in the 1990s and early 2000s. Antor, "Interculturality or Transculturality," 70.

8   ◆   INTRODUCTION

"contact zone" is useful for understanding complex configurations of spaces and cultures, it is less so when it comes to examining the dynamics between real and figurative border crossings and the narrative practices that facilitate them. Figurative boundaries create different connections and divisions, and they often run counter to the more visible political or territorial or even symbolic "cultural" demarcations and power differentials. By paying closer attention to the figurative boundaries and metaphorical border experiences that are represented in literature, we can gain a better understanding of how borders structure our thinking and thus affect the more or less physical "contact zones" created by borders.

The notion that borders structure our thinking brings me to another reason why 1989 is such an important threshold for this study. Intersecting real and figurative borders are present in all literatures of the world and in different time periods, so I do not claim that the phenomenon that I describe here as border poetics is entirely new. Because the engagement with real and figurative boundaries often stems from a desire to imagine new social models, however, I contend that border poetics does gain prominence as the awareness of the diverse and entangled nature of borders and bordering practices grows. Such an awareness has different timelines in different places and contexts, but as indicated above, in the Polish-German case, it emerged in a pronounced way around 1989/90. This awareness became more acute owing to a fundamental rearrangement of global power dynamics, ideological systems, and local structures resulting from the end of the Cold War. These transformations were ambiguous, to say the least: on the one hand, political and other borders were dissolved, in turn accelerating processes of globalization and transnationalization; on the other hand, the 1990s were characterized by a rise in violent conflicts over the establishment of new national and ethnic boundaries. Within this tension, border studies, in its early stages driven primarily by geographers and historians, transformed into a multidisciplinary field of inquiry for examining borders from different perspectives and as complex structures with material and immaterial aspects.[18]

These changes in our understanding of borders are significant because border poetics can only arise when borders themselves are recognized for their inherent ambiguity. No matter how rigid they seem, borders are not immutable. They are also contradictory and can unsettle the very unit of sameness they purportedly enclose. Borders therefore already contain the conditions for their own destabilization, and border poetics draws attention to this process. Susan Stanford Friedman points to the contradictions of border spaces by articulating a series of tensions that are always already included in the notion of borders:

---

18   Laine, "A Historical View," 15 and 18–23; and Gerst, Klessmann, and Krämer, "Einleitung," 9–17.

Borders are fixed and fluid, impermeable and porous. They separate but also connect, demarcate but also blend differences. Absolute at any moment in time, they are always changing over time. They promise safety, security, a sense of being at home; they also enforce exclusions, the state of being alien, foreign, and homeless. They protect but also confine. They materialize the law, policing separations; but as such, they are always being crossed, transgressed, subverted. Borders are used to exercise power over others but also to empower survival against others. They regulate migration, movement, travel—the flow of people, goods, ideas, and cultural formations of all kinds. They undermine regulatory practices by fostering intercultural encounter and the concomitant production of syncretic heterogeneities and hybridities. They insist on purity, distinction, difference but facilitate contamination, mixing, creolization.[19]

These contradictions apply to real and figurative borders alike, and they make the border a rich trope for describing and analyzing the various phenomena that transpire where places and people as well as figurative and "real" boundaries intersect and entangle.

The expansion of how we understand and study borders coincided with another development: according to David Kim, the rebordering processes of the 1990s also led to a revival of the idea of world citizenship and an expansion of the study of cosmopolitanism. It was a reaction to the worldwide rise of political and ethnic conflicts and the increase in right-wing extremism that sparked a desire for new, globally minded narratives. Initially, the Holocaust emerged as a seemingly universal and "timeless ethical point of reference" for this new cosmopolitanism, but this Eurocentric view was challenged by an urgent demand to also acknowledge silenced histories of colonial violence.[20] While cosmopolitan studies underwent a bifurcation "between Holocaust memory and postcolonial awareness," Kim shows how post-unification German literature has at times produced "cosmopolitan parables" that overcome or at least question this divide.[21] These works provide a more entangled view of global histories of violence, and they encourage a reimagining of world citizenship for the future. I argue that it is within this confluence of a changed understanding of borders and an increased and renewed interest in cosmopolitanism that border poetics emerges as a prominent and distinct narrative and cultural practice.

The rise of border poetics and its expressly cosmopolitan concerns also fit within the novel's most recent developmental stage, which Debjani Ganguly has described as the "contemporary world novel."[22] It begins to emerge "around 1989," by which Ganguly means an extended temporal frame that

19   Friedman, "Migration, Diasporas, and Borders," 273.
20   Kim, *Cosmopolitan Parables*, 35–43, here 35.
21   Kim, *Cosmopolitan Parables*, 25.
22   Ganguly, *This Thing Called the World*, 1.

10 ♦ Introduction

reaches from the 1960s until 2001, specifically 9/11. Within this frame, 1989 functions as a "critical threshold of the 'contemporary,'" and it "illuminates the present through a remediation of the recent past."[23] Ganguly argues that three phenomena in particular have contributed to and continue to shape the contemporary world novel: "the geopolitics of war and violence since the end of the Cold War; hyperconnectivity through advances in information technology; and the emergence of a new humanitarian sensibility in a context where suffering has a presence in everyday life through the immediacy of digital images."[24] Ganguly focuses on how a sense of perpetual global war and the constant presence of death are the driving forces behind the contemporary world novel. War in the post-1989 period is thoroughly global and transnational in character, it is highly medialized, it overwhelmingly affects civilians, and it produces unprecedented humanitarian crises.[25] Border regimes must certainly be viewed as part of the bleak topography Ganguly describes, but in this book, I wish to look more closely at borders to understand how they can also help structure a way of thinking that gestures toward alternatives and, ultimately, a different, more sustainable future.

Still, Ganguly's framing of the contemporary world novel prompts me to emphasize again the violence of borders, as addressed in the first pages of this introduction, and as it shines through in the example from Tokarczuk's novel as well as my brief introduction of the German and Polish context. It therefore bears repeating that border poetics expresses a *critical* cosmopolitanism—it does not ignore or do away with the violence that is embedded in borders of all kinds and that we see unfold in the world every single day. Rather, it draws attention to the exclusions, inequalities, and power differentials that borders enforce and that disrupt feelings of attachment, safety, and home. At the same time, however, it counters this reality by presenting the reader with opportunities to imagine belonging and affiliation differently.

Throughout this study, belonging and disruption will serve as key terms and guiding concepts. Within the context of border poetics, I understand belonging as a feeling of attachment and an affiliation that can be expressed through a variety of everyday practices. Belonging is fluid, changeable, and multiple, and, most importantly, it is something that can be claimed. Disruption, on the other hand, refers to the historical and ongoing violence of borders that interferes with belonging and that must be confronted and worked through. Belonging and disruption are thus in a dynamic relationship that is subject to continuous reevaluation. Gloria Anzaldúa has famously described this tension in her book *Borderlands/La Frontera*: In the United States, Mexican-Americans constantly clash with visible and invisible borders, and this causes both physical and psychological harm. The wounds thus

23   Ganguly, *This Thing Called the World*, 4–16, here 6.
24   Ganguly, *This Thing Called the World*, 1.
25   Ganguly, *This Thing Called the World*, 9–10 and 15–16.

created do not heal—they remain present markers of difference and constant reminders of the injury. What Anzaldúa describes as borderlands are both physical spaces and mental states; they are embodied inflictions passed down through multiple generations. At the same time, they are places of negotiation and engagement with contradictions, and they have significant subversive and empowering potential. For Anzaldúa, a borderland is an "open wound" and a place of collision, but it is also a homeland, a cultural borderland, and a "third country."[26] This nexus between disruption and belonging not only invites but necessitates a cosmopolitan imagination.

Goals of this Book and Previous Scholarship

One aim of this book is to better understand the mechanisms and strategies of border poetics by developing an analytical framework of entangled literary and cultural analysis that draws on the link between borders and contemporary cosmopolitanism. First, I need to further clarify my use of the term border poetics and explain how my understanding differs from previous conceptualizations of the term: the study of the relation between different types of real and symbolic boundaries is not new, and it is present in a number of concepts and discussions in literary and cultural studies. The assumption underlying these examinations is that borders exist not only as physical or political demarcations but that they are constructed and imbued with symbolic meaning. Furthermore, there are borders without physical manifestations, but their immaterial nature makes them no less forceful and their effects no less real. Impulses for thinking about borders in a more encompassing way emanated from reflections on borders—and space in general—as socially constructed, and this scholarship was important for shaping border studies as a discipline in its own right in the late twentieth century.[27] Without necessarily expanding on the specificity of the border or using the term "border poetics," literary and cultural studies have also brought forth multiple notions that have points of contact with border poetics; for example, Homi Bhabha's concepts of hybridity and third spaces, Edward Said's imagined or imaginative geographies, or ideas of geopoetics as articulated by Magdalena Marszałek and Sylvia Sasse or Elżbieta Rybicka.[28] These and other related concepts have led to extensive

26   Anzaldúa, *Borderlands/La Frontera*, 24–25.
27   Gerst, Klessmann, and Krämer, "Einleitung," 9–17. For an overview of the historical foundations of today's border studies, see, for example, Laine, "A Historical View on the Study of Borders."
28   Bhabha, *The Location of Culture*; Marszałek and Sasse, *Geopoetiken*; Rybicka, *Geopoetyka*; and Said, *Orientalism*.

12 ◆ Introduction

scholarship in literary studies that examines the representation of real borderlands and their interaction with symbolic boundaries.[29]

The term "border poetics" itself has been previously applied to describe
narratives with a thematic or formal concern with borders; it is sometimes
invoked in scholarly articles and in book or project titles to refer broadly to
aesthetic representations of fluid or porous boundaries, but often without
discussing the term itself.[30] There are two notable exceptions to this deficit
in theoretical reflection. One is Alexander (Xan) Holt's examination of select
German and Polish literary works written in the first two decades of the Cold
War. Holt focuses on the "counter-discursive capacities of literature" in a
period in which ideological differences between East and West were becoming
solidified, and he draws attention to features such as intertextuality, figurative
language, mapping, and perspective to demonstrate that the "crossing of polit-
ical-geographical dividing lines represented in the content is doubled by the
transgression of formal boundaries in the text."[31] There is not one single border poetics but different strategies and modes of writing that attempt to "come
to terms with, problematize, and reinforce the postwar division of the globe."[32]

The other exception, and the one that relates specifically to my proposed framing and articulation of border poetics in this study, is the Border
Poetics/Border Culture research group that originated at the University of
Tromsø, Norway, and was initiated by Johan Schimanski and Stephen Wolfe.[33]
According to the group, border poetics is a tool, a field of analysis, and a method
to examine various border phenomena that produce a "border aesthetics."[34] As
such, scholars use it to interrogate real and symbolic borders and their varying constellations. The analysis rests on three main assumptions about borders: "1) that narrative and symbolic representation is a central element in

---

29 Monographs include, for example, Görner, *Grenzen, Schwellen, Übergänge*; and
Lamping, *Über Grenzen*. For edited volumes, see, for example, Albrecht, Neumann,
and Talarczyk, *Literatur, Grenzen, Erinnerungsräume*; Egger, Hajduk, and Jung, *Sarmatien—Germania Slavica—Mitteleuropa*; Faber and Naumann, *Literatur der Grenze*; and
Kuczyński and Schneider, *Das literarische Antlitz des Grenzlandes*.

30 See, for example, Karahasan and Jaroschka, eds., *Poetik der Grenze*; Gelberg,
Poetik und Politik der Grenze. For other examples and uses of the term, see Schimanski
and Wolfe, "Cultural Production," 40.

31 Holt, "Cold War Crossings," 25 and 5.

32 Holt, "Cold War Crossings," 247.

33 The network organized a first symposium on the topic in 2004. Since then, the
scholars have held conferences, produced numerous publications, and promoted border research, e.g., through the "Border Aesthetics" Facebook group. See also Schimanski, *Grenzungen*; Schimanski, "Border Aesthetics."

34 "Border aesthetics" rather than "border poetics" appears as a central term in
many of the group's more recent publications. Border aesthetics refers to the global
"cultural production related to geopolitical borders" as well as "the aesthetic or sensual
dimension of borders of all kinds and scales." See Schimanski, "Border Aesthetics."

border formation and experience; 2) that textual or medial borders within or around aesthetic works are related to the borders represented in these works; 3) that figurations of borders in cultural expressions matter for social, political, and historical processes of bordering."[35] Border poetics then, is a "field of cultural analysis" that examines how various expressions of borders negotiate the relationship "between territorial borders and textual frames."[36] Elsewhere, Schimanski and Wolfe further define border poetics as "a set of strategies for analyzing the successful or failed crossings of institutional, national or generic borders" as well as a set of "practical strategies . . . for examining the function of these forms of representation in the intersection between territorial borders and aesthetic works."[37] In short, according to this view, border poetics is a scholarly tool of analysis that is applied to constellations in which territorial borders and their medialized iterations meet and overlap.

I am inspired by this scholarship, especially the notion that border poetics is concerned with various types of entangled territorial and symbolic borders and how they translate into texts.[38] At the same time, I expand this framework in two important ways. First, I propose a shift in perspective from the outside to the inside—from focusing on border poetics as a "category of analysis" to regarding it as a "category of practice," so to speak.[39] Following this shift, I view border poetics as a narrative and cultural *practice*—a form of worldmaking achieved by authors and their texts—and not as an analytical strategy or tool that I apply to narratives about borders and the various constellations of borders and bordering practices within them. Second, my definition aligns with the group's theoretical reflection about borders, but I argue that it is border poetics as a *practice* that makes variously constellated forms of attachment and the movements and border crossings between such affiliations visible. In my conception, then, border poetics can still be viewed as a strategy or tool of analysis, but in this book, I focus on how writers themselves analyze and critique borders and how they translate their critique into aesthetic form.

This shift in attention toward the "architecture" of a text is reminiscent of the move encapsulated in Rebecca Walkowitz's notion of "comparison literature"; that is, works that are affiliated with multiple national, ethnic, or linguistic contexts at once and that challenge singular and clearly defined sites and scales of belonging. For Walkowitz, comparison is not merely a method that scholars apply to texts but a feature already built into the literary text. Arguing that despite its transnational approach, the field of "comparative

35   UiT, "Border Poetics/Border Culture."
36   "Border Poetics," Wikidot.com.
37   Schimanski and Wolfe, *Border Poetics De-Limited,* 10, 24.
38   Schimanski and Wolfe, *Border Poetics De-Limited,* 10–13.
39   Brubaker, "Categories of Analysis and Categories of Practice." Rogers Brubaker makes a helpful distinction here between everyday uses of categories such as ethnicity, race, and gender and their use as categories of sociological analysis.

14 ◆ Introduction

literature often takes for granted that each literary culture is geographically and politically separate," Walkowitz shifts the attention to novels and their "comparative architecture" as part of an "effort to imagine transnational and/or cosmopolitan paradigms that offer alternatives to national models of political community."[40] Questions of translation are an important feature of this architecture, but not in a linguistic sense. Comparison novels are "born translated" because they address the politics and plurality of language through "narrative events" rather than the language itself.[41] In sum, my emphasis is on border poetics as a narrative practice; that is, on how the engagement with borders produces new constellations of belonging by working through issues of exclusion and marginalization. I examine how this engagement could contribute to a reimagination of established borders and bordering processes.

The complexity of the phenomenon of border poetics calls for a multifaceted approach, and my analysis therefore operates within several critical spaces simultaneously, especially transnational approaches to German and Polish studies, European studies, and world literature. These frames of reference overlap and entangle and cannot always be neatly separated, but they all derive from a comparative impulse. Because no perspective can be detached from its location, each of these frames of reference also outlines a specific context and thus a new boundary—albeit a more porous and amorphous one than nation-centered frameworks do—within which the circulation of texts, authors, ideas, and material objects comes into view.[42] Acknowledging the ideological inflections of these particular access points is crucial, but I am interested in seeing how they can challenge and enhance one another in the interpretation of literary works. This study therefore pays attention to the links between these different frameworks and thereby hopes to contribute to a "Literaturgeschichte als Verflechtungsgeschichte" (literary history as entangled history), as proposed by Annette Werberger and inspired by similar strategies in historical studies. Among other things, an entangled literary history considers transnational connections and multidirectional global transfers throughout history and applies multiple perspectives in examining how these connections and transfers are represented in texts.[43]

40 Walkowitz, "Comparison Literature," 567–68.

41 Walkowitz, "Comparison Literature," 570–71.

42 On the importance of considering the location of one's perspective, see, for example, Baumbach, "Rooting 'New European Literature,'" 55–56; and Damrosch, *What Is World Literature?*, 27.

43 Werberger, "Überlegungen zu einer Literaturgeschichte als Verflechtungsgeschichte," esp. 121–31. Werberger notes that it is especially the work of historians who examine histories and cultures across borders under the rubric of *histoire croisée* or *Verflechtungsgeschichte* that provides impulses for similar considerations in literary studies (122). She mentions world literature studies as a promising example of such an entangled approach (124–27).

The objective of such an endeavor cannot be, in Walkowitz's words, to "expand or simply disable literary histories based on the nation" but to allow for multiple "scales" of belonging, ranging from local to global, to exist at the same time and to "imagine new literary histories ... whose object includes not only the production of books but also their translation, circulation, and comparison."[44] As a narrative practice, border poetics attends to many overlapping frames of reference simultaneously, and it thereby both produces and requires a heterogeneous theoretical and practical basis. The broad scope of this study is ambitious, to say the least, and my own background, my spaces of affiliation and belonging, have necessarily shaped this book. Most importantly, my perspective is that of a German studies scholar trained in the United States. Inevitably, there will be omissions, but, as Todd Kontje points out, "German literary critics sometimes speak of filling a gap in one's knowledge of a field (*Bildungslücke*), as if there were a finite number of themes to consider, so that the edifice of our erudition would one day be complete. In fact, however, the field is more like the Internet, infinitely capable of absorbing more data and facilitating endless discussion."[45] It is my hope that by highlighting the connections between what are typically separate conversations, this study, with all its gaps and shortcomings, will be productive and stir new conversations about borders and cosmopolitanism and inspire new areas of investigation in German studies and beyond.

My analysis builds on scholarship that treats notions of the global, European, national, regional, local, and even the personal as plural and flexible concepts and with room for more complex understandings of belonging. In German-Polish studies, the open and collaborative work that enables such views was simply impossible for most of the twentieth century. The idea of the nation served as the main interpretive framework, and dialogue was severely hindered not just by language barriers but even more by political and ideological constraints. By contrast, since the end of the Cold War, scholarship on Germany and Poland has increasingly turned to the intertwined nature of German and Polish literary and cultural relations from a transnational perspective. It often focuses on the dismantling of binary views and on the connections rather than the divisions in the German-Polish relationship, and it seeks to place that relationship within a larger European context.[46] In Europe, the transnational study of Polish-German connections is prominent in and

---

44   Walkowitz, "The Location of Literature," 542–43.

45   Kontje, *Imperial Fictions*, 255.

46   In the areas of history and cultural studies, there is ample evidence of cross-border collaborations, which have often resulted in bilingual or simultaneous German and Polish publications. See, for example, Aust, Ruchniewicz, and Troebst, *Verflochtene Erinnerungen*; Barbian and Zybura, *Erlebte Nachbarschaft*; Hahn and Traba, *Deutsch-Polnische Erinnerungsorte*; and Zybura, *Querdenker, Vermittler, Grenzüberschreiter*. Transnational publications and series also come out of institutes and centers, including the Deutsches Polen-Institut in Darmstadt, the Willy Brandt Center at the University of

16 ◆ INTRODUCTION

across disciplines that include history, sociology, and cultural studies. In literary studies, many scholars have worked toward advancing a more entangled view of the literary imagination, including Marion Brandt, Bożena Chołuj, Sabine Egger, Brygida Helbig, Jürgen Joachimsthaler, Hubert Orłowski, Hans-Christian Trepte, Monika Wolting, Małgorzata Zduniak-Wiktorowicz, and Marek Zybura, to name but a few. In North America, and from a German studies perspective, scholars such as Friederike Eigler, Todd Kontje, and Kristin Kopp have laid important groundwork for the transnational understanding of these literary and cultural borderlands. Randall Halle's scholarship, concerned with transnational European cinema, also provides critical impulses for literary scholars of Germany and Poland.[47] Likewise, newer literary histories offer an expanded view and consider German or Polish literature within the broader context of other European literatures, thereby contributing significantly to a more entangled literary history.[48]

Many literary studies that center on the narrative representation of borderlands aim to show that borders function not only as locations of conflict and division but also as in-between spaces and sites of dialogue and exchange. This is especially the case where questions of memory and postmemory are concerned, and much scholarship focuses on the changes in collective and personal memory for writers of the second and third generations after the Second World War. These transformations have also led to a different engagement with displacement and the idea of "home," or, as I am framing it here, with disruption and belonging. Friederike Eigler and Przemysław Czapliński, for example, demonstrate how works of post–Cold War German and Polish literature, respectively, have shifted in their treatment of "Heimat" and "small fatherlands" from expressing revisionist or nostalgic views toward more self-critical and transnational positions that reflect a changed relationship with past and present borders. Therefore, in both countries, transnational European narratives have emerged that deconstruct established, nation-centered narratives and draw attention to the dynamic and multinodal networks of border spaces.[49] Nicole Coleman has described this changed relationship to "Heimat"

Wrocław, or the Aleksander-Brückner-Zentrum (a collaboration between the Universities of Halle and Jena).

47   See, for example, Eigler, *Heimat, Space, Narrative*; Eigler and Weigert, "German-Polish Border Regions"; Halle, *German Film after Germany*; Halle, *The Europeanization of Cinema*; Kontje, *German Orientalisms*; and Kopp, *Germany's Wild East*.

48   See especially the following two publications: Cornis-Pope and Neubauer, *History of the Literary Cultures of East-Central Europe*; and Joachimsthaler, *Text-Ränder*. German literature is outside the purview of Cornis-Pope and Neubauer, but their literary history is significant because it focuses on "junctures and disjunctures" that cut across national lines. The contributions are not dictated by national frameworks. Rather, they offer an entangled perspective by focusing on political events, literary periods and genres, cities and regions, literary institutions, and real and imaginary figures.

49   Eigler, *Heimat, Space, Narrative*, e.g., 8, 27–28; Czapliński, "Mythic Homeland," 360–65.

in German authors as a move away from the insistence on a political "right to return," expressed in Germany in the postwar period, toward more inclusive "rituals of return" that relate to spaces of the imagination.[50]

Furthermore, the great resonance of postcolonial discourse in various geographical and social contexts has also led to discussions about its applicability to Eastern Europe. Todd Kontje's *German Orientalisms* (2004) and Kristin Kopp's *Germany's Wild East* (2012) have been groundbreaking in this area, and they are evidence of the transnational reorientation of German studies through an interest in Germany's relationship with an Eastern Other. Among other things, both scholars examine how literary works both reflect and have contributed to a long-standing othering of the East; for example, through German stereotypes of Polish backwardness and mismanagement. Such stereotypes are still present, and they are part of the disrupted narratives that border poetics challenges, as my analysis will show. Scholarship that considers German-Polish relations within a postcolonial framework continues to grow, although some scholars, especially in Poland, are also wary of its political instrumentalization for nationalist and exclusionary narratives.[51] This book is enriched by postcolonial scholarship, and I refer to concepts that are central to postcolonial studies, such as marginalization, exclusion, home, belonging, contact zone, and hybridity, but my analysis is not situated within the stricter confines of that framework.

By drawing on the nation, Europe, and the world as three major frames of reference, this book seeks to intervene in several areas of study. First, and broadly speaking, its goal is to enrich existing scholarship on world literature by reflecting explicitly on border poetics as a world-making strategy. It treats the border not simply as a phenomenon that authors engage with thematically or as a threshold for literary works to cross in order to circulate globally. Instead, it emphasizes that borders are central to the very structures of thinking, observing, and writing. Second, this study contributes to the limited body of scholarship that explores the deep connection between borders and contemporary cosmopolitanism, adding a much-needed literary studies perspective.

50 Coleman, *The Right to Difference*, 125–35, here 133. Coleman also provides a concise overview of the ideologies and exclusionary effects of "Heimat" in Germany under National Socialism and after the Second World War, especially as it pertained to Eastern Europe. Both Eigler and Coleman read Sabrina Janesch's *Katzenberge*, discussed in chapter 3, within the context of changed understandings of "Heimat." See also Berger, *Heimat, Loss and Identity* for a nuanced analysis of "expulsion literature" since the 1950s, which shows that not all such literature was necessarily revisionist.

51 In a special issue of the journal *Teksty Drugie* in 2014, Dorota Kołodziejczyk argues that consideration of the distinct condition of Central-and-Eastern Europe can infuse postcolonial studies with a much-needed comparative perspective, but she also cautions that the postcolonial discourse all too often "helps intensify national historicism of a vividly conservative ideological program." Kołodziejczyk, "Post-Colonial Transfer," 139, 125. In the same issue, see also Fiut, "In the Shadow of Empires."

18 ◆ INTRODUCTION

Here too, the central question is not how cosmopolitanism happens despite or across borders, but how the border can be regarded as an important locus of the cosmopolitan imagination.[52] Thinking about borders and cosmopolitanism as linked concepts allows for a reassessment of conceptualizations of Europe and the construction of national spaces in contemporary literature while also shedding new light on the literary production of alternative spaces. Finally, and addressing the German-Polish context specifically, this book is the first extensive study of German and Polish border narratives through the double lens of cosmopolitanism and borders. Despite the prevalence of transnational approaches in the study of literatures and cultures, there are today few book-length studies of cosmopolitanism and either contemporary Polish *or* German literature, and to my knowledge there are none taking this approach to examine German-Polish literary relations. In the area of German studies, two monographs are notable exceptions to this paucity, and as will become clear throughout this book, they have influenced my conception of border poetics. They are B. Venkat Mani's *Cosmopolitical Claims* (2007), which focuses on German and Turkish narratives, and David Kim's *Cosmopolitan Parables* (2017), which applies a cosmopolitan lens to novels that address entangled histories of violence related to the Holocaust and colonialism. Elsewhere, Kim has emphasized that the very survival of German studies depends on the field's cosmopolitical engagement with the world, and this argument can be expanded to literary studies more broadly, which are still largely defined along national lines.[53] Borders, including their symbolic manifestations, are a frequent area of investigation, but they are not usually placed in dialogue with questions of cosmopolitanism or world literature.

Analytical Frameworks: Between Nation, Europe, and World

Literary and cultural studies scholars have been working for several decades toward more flexible and open understandings of the boundaries of nationally defined fields, and with this book, I also hope to advance these conversations.[54] As part of the work of expanding the scope of German studies,

---

52   Important reference points outside the field of literary studies include Rumford, *Cosmopolitan Borders*; and Agier, *Borderlands*.

53   Kim, "German Studies and Cosmopolitanism."

54   For example, German studies scholars have been expanding our understanding of "German" into more open and inclusive concepts. In the Anglophone world, the work of scholars such as Leslie Adelson, Hiltrud Arens, Anke Biendarra, Deniz Göktürk, B. Venkat Mani, Azade Seyhan, and Stuart Taberner are crucial for this expansion. Newer developments in this area are discussed, e.g., in Arslan et al., "Forum: Migration Studies"; Coleman, *The Right to Difference*; Johnson, *Germany from the Outside*; Taberner, *Transnationalism*; and Braun and Schofield, *Transnational German Studies*.

some scholars have also turned to the concept of world literature; for example, Thomas O. Beebee, B. Venkat Mani, and Sandra Richter. Within Polish literary studies, the first major applications of this concept were presented in the edited volumes *The Routledge World Companion to Polish Literature* (2021) and *Polish Literature as World Literature* (2022).[55] Despite these efforts, the nation remains a persuasive framework for interpreting and promoting literature. The 2018/19 Nobel Prize in Literature is a case in point. After the literary Nobel committee was engulfed in a scandal and no prize was awarded in 2018, two recipients were announced in 2019. Olga Tokarczuk was the 2018 winner, and Austrian author Peter Handke received the prize for 2019. The choice of Handke "dumbfounded" many, as a PEN America statement expressed poignantly.[56] Critics pointed to the author's denial of the 1990s Bosnian genocide and his controversial support of the former Yugoslav and Serbian president Slobodan Milošević. The controversy was also felt in German studies in the United States. While some referred to Handke's problematic political stance, others perceived him as a winner of which Germans should be proud, and whom students, instructors, and scholars of German should celebrate, presumably because of linguistic affinity and a perceived proximity of national identities between Austrians and Germans. In this controversy, Handke received the majority of the attention—both in a positive and in a negative sense. The significance of Tokarczuk's writing for Germans or German studies scholars was hardly recognized, even though much of her writing focuses on German-Polish borderlands, and several of her works had been available in German translation long before she was awarded the Nobel Prize.[57] Such omissions are both limiting and isolating, and this book seeks to advance the transnational

55   Beebee, *German Literature as World Literature*; Mani, *Recoding World Literature*; Richter, *Eine Weltgeschichte*; Bilczewski, Bill, and Popiel, *The Routledge World Companion*; and Florczyk and Wisniewski, *Polish Literature as World Literature*.

56   PEN America, "Statement."

57   The different views could be discerned from the social media discussions of the American Association of Teachers of German (AATG) and the German Studies Association (GSA), the two leading professional organizations for teachers and scholars of German in the United States. The AATG's initial Facebook announcement cited the Swedish academy's praise of Handke's achievements. Criticism of Handke was initially only articulated in the ensuing discussion, which pointed also to the failure to acknowledge Olga Tokarczuk's achievement. Meanwhile, the GSA announced the prize with a direct criticism: "This year's Nobel prize in literature goes to two people—one being an Austrian defender of Milosevic who denies that the Srebrenica massacre happened." In both cases, the initial focus was on Handke and not on Tokarczuk's work or her significance for German Studies. American Association of Teachers of German, "Post"; German Studies Association, "This Year's Nobel Prize"; and German Studies Association, "GSA Statement." For an analysis of these discussions and their broader meaning for German Studies in the United States, see Costabile-Heming, "Imagining German Studies," here 81–83.

20 ♦ INTRODUCTION

project not by dismissing the nation as an important reference point for literature but rather by not taking it to be "an a priori constituted unit nor the sole precondition for comparison," as Søren Frank urges. Instead, Frank continues, we need a comparative method that "starts off from a position of transculturality, emphasizes interconnectedness and cross-border transfers, and questions the primacy of national borders."[58] For this reason, Europe and the world—or European literature and world literature—serve as nodal points through which I link Polish and German literary spaces to each other as well as to the larger literary sphere.

The authors and works discussed here rarely allude to the notion of a European identity directly, let alone the European Union or its institutionalized framework, but underlying their narratives is a decidedly outward orientation and a cosmopolitan sensitivity. These authors and their characters are situated in Europe and in specific locales or nations. At the same time, they are thinking on larger scales and are critiquing these boundaries by moving between their temporal and spatial coordinates. The dynamism of this negotiation is important, and it reflects the fact that Europe is today widely regarded as an ongoing project and a dynamic constellation of variously defined affiliations and multidirectional processes—from the local through the transnational.[59] It is a project that we cannot even begin to discuss without considering the significance of cultural expressions. Never mind that Europe is notoriously hard to define and that finding a common cultural basis has been one of the greatest challenges of the European project since its inception.[60] Considering the many challenges Europe faces, it has by now become abundantly clear that Europe cannot function only as an economic and market-oriented project. Rather, as Delanty points out, there must be "stronger emphasis on Europe as a social and cultural project."[61]

Ulrich Beck and Edgar Grande argued two decades ago that Europe largely acts and thinks of itself in national terms and that it suffers from a "national self-misunderstanding" in which the nation-state and European integration are pitted against one another. Such binary thinking preempts the emergence of alternative models for Europe in which nationally inflected particulars might be reconciled with shared (European) universals. As a necessary alternative, Beck and Grande have proposed a "cosmopolitan Europe."[62] This cosmopolitan Europe, however, is faced with a "boundary dilemma" because "the national must be both overcome *and* preserved."[63] A definition of cosmopolitanism that Beck provides elsewhere reflects this challenge:

58   Frank, "Literary Studies," 379.
59   Halle, *The Europeanization of Cinema*, 4–5; Wetenkamp, *Europa erzählt*, 7–20.
60   Levy, Pensky, and Torpey, "Editors' Introduction," xxii.
61   Delanty, *The Cosmopolitan Imagination*, 202.
62   Beck and Grande, *Cosmopolitan Europe*, 2–5.
63   Beck and Grande, *Cosmopolitan Europe*, 261. Emphasis in the original.

"cosmopolitanism . . . is *an idea and a reality*—an idea and a reality of universalism that contains a particularistic dimension of meaning, an idea and a reality of globality that includes nationalism, and an idea and a reality of transnationalism that does not exclude a plurality of ethnicities and cultures."[64] As this quote aptly illustrates, the dynamic relationship between the particular and the universal is a central part of contemporary theorizations of cosmopolitanism. This focus also calls attention to the significance of the border concept for the cosmopolitan imagination, which must constantly negotiate borders. Because the particular cannot be erased or eliminated, this imagination must find ways to hold the universal and the particular in suspension. Some scholars have theorized the idea of temporarily suspending difference without dissolving it under the term "transdifference."[65] Border poetics, I argue, can be described as a strategy of working toward transdifference, of oscillating between the particular and the universal. Understood as critical spaces, world literature studies, critical European studies, and transnational studies are fundamentally about finding and analyzing instances of transdifference. This is the case even when the phenomenon itself is approached with other terms, such as "betweenness" or "transculturality."

Literature, and in my case European literature and world literature, are part of these cosmopolitan constellations. European literature, defined as literature set in Europe or addressing European themes and principles, plays a role in the imagination of a shared European culture and therefore in Europeanization.[66] Sibylle Baumbach points to the deep connections between world literature and European literature, but she also notes that there is a distinct yet open and flexible literary formation that can aid in "the promotion of a new European identity," and she refers to it as "new cosmopolitan European literature."[67] A critical cosmopolitanism is also present in what Lena Wetenkamp identifies as a "Poetik des Europäischen" (poetics of Europeanness). This poetics is defined by a thematic and formal orientation that addresses fluid geographies and identities, borders and exclusions, and memory and history. Through it, literature participates in the discursive construction of Europe.[68] Current conceptualizations of European literature and world literature share a concern for how works from various languages and (national) contexts circulate and communicate with each other. While European literature logically retains its focus on Europe, world literature is more global in scope. Without equating them, I

---

64 Beck, "European Crisis," 642. Emphasis in the original.
65 Breinig and Lösch, "Introduction: Difference and Transdifference."
66 See, for example, Domínguez, "Local Rooms with a Cosmopolitan View."
67 Baumbach, "Rooting 'New European Literature,'" 57–58.
68 Wetenkamp, *Europa erzählt, verortet, erinnert*, 339–44.

22 ♦ Introduction

am considering these two frameworks together here, as discursive formations that can enrich one another in their critique of borders.[69]

Current understandings of world literature represent a wide array of definitions, theories, and approaches, so I want to briefly clarify what world literature means, and does not mean, here. As one might guess, the label alone does not ensure a departure from a nation-focused understanding or a move toward transdifference. For example, some scholars in German-Polish studies have argued that since the end of the Cold War, Polish literature has become more "worldly" and "European" and therefore more accessible to Western European audiences, as Natasza Stelmaszyk explains. In this view, Polish literature produced after 1990 better expresses shared experiences, interests, and desires and addresses more universally human themes—something it presumably did not do before.[70] Some scholars contend that this alleged move away from specifically "Polish" themes has resulted in greater readability, and they frame this move as a shift from national literature to world literature (a shift that is also lauded for making this literature more marketable).[71] Readability and marketability also increased because this new Polish literature is said to be less steeped in the Polish literary tradition and more in dialogue with foreign literatures, which it owes to the fact that many of these works were written by Polish writers living abroad.[72] This kind of equation of *worlding* and *world literature* with marketability and readability; that is, the successful circumvention of any allegedly unreadable (national) specificity is problematic, and scholars of world literature are critical of such approaches. David Damrosch argues that such easy-to-read literature is "a notional 'global literature' that might be read solely in airline terminals, unaffected by any specific context whatever."[73] World literature, however, does not mean legibility unencumbered by difference.

The texts discussed in this study address universal themes, but this does not come at the cost of specificity. On the contrary, the narratives are tied to specific historical and geographical contexts, but rather than being replaced with universal concerns, specificity is made more legible through its connection with them. Furthermore, these works are not lacking in complexity

---

69   For example, Walter Cohen has argued that "European literature emerges from world literature and, in our own time, returns to it," and Karol Sauerland believes that in the twentieth century the notion of a "neuere" (newer) European literature was displaced by the idea of world literature. Cohen, "Introduction," 1; and Sauerland, "Europäische Literatur," 173.

70   Stelmaszyk, "Die neue Situation der polnischen Literatur," 157. On the idea of shared experiences in newer Polish literature, see also Krzoska, "Die polnische Literatur zu Beginn eines neuen Jahrhunderts," 1030.

71   Stelmaszyk, "Die neue Situation der polnischen Literatur," 155–62.

72   Jan Tomkowski, cited in Stelmaszyk, "Die neue Situation der polnischen Literatur," 155–56.

73   Damrosch, *What Is World Literature*, 25.

nor are they easily readable, as Stelmaszyk implies.[74] In my understanding, a more complex narrative provides more points of access to the reader—and these multiple access points are an essential part of border poetics and its "world-making" and "worlding" potential. Indeed, following Damrosch, "the variability of a work of world literature is one of its constitutive features."[75] In the context of border poetics, then, world literature is an opportunity to step outside binary constructions of difference and national frames of reference. National categories are not ignored, but they lose their interpretive stranglehold and become one of many access points to the world. The world literature framework allows for an exploration of differences and connections, intersections, and the mobility of texts and ideas. Narratives that apply border poetics create worlds that go beyond assumed borders and limitations, and I foreground this aspect by using world literature as an overarching framework. This book asks how authors address particular and universal themes in their writing and how these narratives reflect a new, more open understanding of borders. Arguably, good literature always refers to larger questions, so my concern is not whether but *how* authors negotiate particular and universal themes in their writing through an intensified engagement with and critique of borders.

World literature is a "mode of circulation and of reading" that places a work "beyond its linguistic and cultural point of origin," according to Damrosch.[76] Yet, the notion of origin may be unnecessarily limiting, as Walkowitz has pointed out, arguing that many works of world literature are "born translated" and "[begin] in several places and languages at once."[77] Similarly, Ellen Jones has criticized the monolingual assumption underlying Damrosch's definition.[78] Within this tension of existing boundaries and their constant multiplication and dislocation I want to think about the world-making capacities of literature, which presupposes that it constantly creates and re-creates its own origins as it moves through readers, times, and places. In tandem with my understanding of poetics as a process of making or creating, which I explain in chapter 2, I understand world literature as a mode of world-making that is produced through reading and writing. Here I refer to Pheng Cheah, who has described "world literature as world-making activity" and world-making

---

74   This suggestion alone triggers questions that are worth asking, even if they cannot be answered here: Does a lack of complexity make a text more readable? What role do translations play in normalizing a text? Does readability automatically assume a lack of literary quality? Although Stelmaszyk asks this last question, she does not explore it further. Stelmaszyk, "Die neue Situation der polnischen Literatur," 161.

75   Damrosch, *What Is World Literature*, 5.

76   Damrosch, *What Is World Literature*, 5–6.

77   Walkowitz, "Comparison Literature," 576. For a thorough exploration of these ideas, see Walkowitz, *Born Translated*, e.g., 1–10.

78   Jones, *Literature in Motion*, 7.

24 ♦ INTRODUCTION

as an important vehicle for the cosmopolitan imagination.[79] Because it is part of a cosmopolitan constellation, this kind of world-making can be neither self-serving nor disconnected from the real world. As Ganguly argues, the world-making of world literature is a "mode of value creation that is attuned to the actual work of language, narrative, form, and genre in generating literary worlds," in which world is always a "temporal and spatial collage."[80] One can see how world literature, understood in this way, would provide intriguing access points for examining border poetics and vice versa.

The notion of world-making connects to border poetics through the kind of critical cosmopolitanism I referred to earlier: border poetics is a practice; that is, a particular mode of producing narratives with and about borders that—through the temporary suspension of difference—makes them conceivable as "cosmopolitan borders" and "cosmopolitan workshops," to use sociologist Chris Rumford's terminology.[81] Whether this kind of transborder connectivity is articulated explicitly or implied through formal and structural choices, border poetics aims at creating worlds that offer a (critical) cosmopolitan outlook. This view can have a "worlding" effect on the reader or recipient of these transborder narratives. But the process is not necessarily unproblematic. When the aim of "worlding," in the sense of educating others about the world, is too explicit, it can come across with a certain heavy-handed didacticism or with paternalistic overtones. This orientation places such narratives in closer proximity to what Berthold Schoene has criticized as "cosmo-kitsch" in novels that fail to engage with difference productively.[82] Instead of cosmopolitan world-making, they fall into a trap of superficiality. In the early 1990s, journalist, historian, and political scientist Klaus Bachmann observed a similar shallowness in German-Polish relations, and he termed the inflationary use of reconciliation narratives "Versöhnungskitsch" (reconciliation kitsch).[83] Works that produce such kitsch may be described as border novels, but they are not successful implementations of border poetics.

A centering of borders in the analysis adds several new dimensions to world literary studies: first, border poetics derives from an entangled approach to world-making. And while the interplay between the local and the global is a focal point for cosmopolitan studies, this important nexus still needs to be emphasized more generally in literary studies. For example, close reading, which can pay attention to the specific and the local, "is often bracketed

---

79 Cheah, *What Is a World?*, 2–3. Cheah regards world literature as an important articulation of cosmopolitanism. For a detailed exploration of Cheah's position with regard to narratives of refuge and world literature as crisis mode of narration, see Stan, "Novels in the Translation Zone."

80 Ganguly, *This Thing Called the World*, 80, 85.

81 Rumford, *Cosmopolitan Borders*.

82 Schoene, "Cosmo-Kitsch vs. Cosmopoetics," 105–6.

83 Bachmann, "Die Versöhnung muss von Polen ausgehen."

off as a methodology incapable of grasping the 'world' in world literature."[84] Focusing on this deficiency, Frank poses a question that reads like a flash point for border poetics: "What if it turns out that the local is in fact the most worldly, that is, the place where the metahistorical components and ontological conditions of human existence unconceal themselves most clearly?"[85] The border may be the very space, site, or concept where this dynamic is produced most forcefully and can be revealed most clearly. Second, even though real and figurative borderlands are major sites of conflict, negotiation, and contact and therefore shape our experience of "world" in significant ways, the interplay between borderlands and the world literary space is rarely considered explicitly. Aamir Mufti has conceptualized world literature itself as a "border regime" that produces its own exclusions, mainly through the dominance of English and the cultural and social practices resulting from it.[86] Mufti's critical examination of world literature as a mechanism that reinforces borders is of crucial importance. In the German-Polish case, too, power dynamics, translation, and finding a shared language are a concern; but English does not typically enter into that equation. World literature provides a suitable framework because it allows for a careful and equal consideration of Polish and German entanglements, with borders serving as the points of contact at which ideas, conflicts, and shared imaginations crystallize. Finally, a view from the border enables us to assume a broader perspective, and such an expanded view will benefit our definitions and categorizations of literature generally, whether we use the qualifier trans-, European, or world.

Chapter Overview

This study seeks to understand, both in theory and in practice, how literary strategies help articulate the multiplying and intersecting belongings and affiliations that are both facilitated and disrupted by borders. In doing so, it aims to activate a new critical vocabulary and analytical framework for talking about these constellations, and it seeks to situate the theory of border poetics within discussions of world literature. The book's three main dimensions are, first, the historical, social, and cultural context within which the practice of border poetics emerges in the German-Polish case; second, the theoretical framing of such a poetics; and third, the analysis of select novels that pays attention to how border poetics is actually practiced. And while I examine instances of border poetics that are convincing articulations of a cosmopolitan imagination, I also point to some of the pitfalls and limitations of these border narratives. In accordance with these main dimensions, the book is structured in two parts, with two chapters in each. The first part, "Context and Theoretical

---

84 Ganguly, *This Thing Called the World*, 79.
85 Frank, "Place and Placelessness," 75.
86 Mufti, *Forget English*, 9, 12–13.

26 ♦ Introduction

Frameworks," sets up a double framework that on the one hand establishes the specific German-Polish context, and on the other hand formulates in more general terms the theoretical foundations of my understanding of border poetics. The second part, "Reading Border Poetics," offers analyses of select texts and explains the narrative strategies that transmit an acute sense of complex and fluid border constellations.

Chapter 1, "Entanglements in German and Polish History, Literature, and Culture," provides an overview of German-Polish relations. Taking a *longue durée* approach, the chapter highlights some of the divergences and convergences in the "thousand years" of shared history, and it brings into focus the broader historical and cultural contexts with which border poetics engages in the German-Polish case. After providing a general historical overview, the chapter considers the literary entanglements in particular, as embodied by the works of Stefan Chwin and Günter Grass, for example. The overarching argument is that literature dealing with the Polish-German border since 1945 has moved from writing about the border as a dividing line to writing in which borders figure as spaces of connectivity, and finally to the narrative practice of border poetics, in which real and figurative borders are multiply entwined. This chapter explains the gradual emergence of border poetics from and despite specific political and social constellations. These constellations are often contradictory, and they include German-Polish reconciliation as well as persistent mistrust, disagreement, and conflict; a rise of global culture and the simultaneous reorientations toward the local and the regional; and a concern for building a stronger European Union alongside persistent national interests and anxieties of its member states. Through this focus, I center border poetics as a narrative and cultural practice that articulates knotted histories and strives to make them productive for a cosmopolitan imagination. The chapter also notes the challenges that arise from writing an entangled literary history by discussing questions of terminology and the difficulty of translating concepts such as "Grenzland" or "kresy" (borderland) or "Heimat" (homeland), which have distinct histories and connotations and do not easily transfer into new contexts.

From the knots and entanglements between Germany and Poland that can be observed throughout history and in literary relations, I turn to theoretical entanglements. Chapter 2, "Border Poetics," zooms in on the theoretical foundations for my conception of border poetics as a narrative and cultural practice and as an idiom of the cosmopolitan imagination. This chapter discusses assumptions about the fluidity of borders; a view of contemporary cosmopolitanism as a critical stance toward the universal and the particular; and an approach to the imagination as a mode of world-making. The goal here is not to come away with a definitive theory of border poetics but rather to highlight or create points of connection—to tie knots, so to speak—between different concepts that are productive for border poetics. The chapter works through associations to create an open theoretical frame that links borders, cosmopolitanism, and the literary imagination, and to articulate questions and points of connection between diverse fields. Two main ideas guide the chapter. The first is the relationship between imagining and making that informs my conception of border poetics as a practice of world-making. Here I examine the possibility that borders can be spaces of engagement, sites of "transdifference," or "cosmopolitan workshops," which counters a view that they are sites of difference and division beyond repair.[87] I draw attention to the literary imagination and its potential to inspire new expressions of belonging, resistance, and social change. Second, the historical conditions of the German-Polish borderland have created a deeply felt sense of disruption that persists today in collective and individual memory. Border poetics works through such disruptions and fragmentations to develop new and less divisive narratives that promote thinking in terms of entanglements and more flexible understandings of belonging.

After the contextual and theoretical frameworks have been established in part I, part II asks how border poetics functions in literature. In two chapters, I illustrate, complicate, and expand the theoretical framework, and I explore some narrative strategies that produce border poetics. As an idiom of the cosmopolitan imagination, border poetics differs from other, more one-sided or even divisive ways of engaging with borders. Because border poetics can be evident on various levels and in many forms, I devote one chapter to the articulation of border poetics through "story" (*what* is narrated or the sequence of events) and one chapter to "discourse" (*how* the story is narrated or communicated). This organization follows literary theorist Gerard Genette's distinction between story and discourse and the premise that "every narrative . . . is a structure with a content plane (called 'story') and an expression plane (called 'discourse')."[88] The division between story and discourse is less strict than it might seem here—each text could just as well be considered within the framework of the respective other chapter. It is a matter of each chapter's focus rather than of the works themselves, each of which would merit a discussion of border poetics on multiple levels.

Chapter 3, "Disruption: Fictions of Memory by Inga Iwasiów, Sabrina Janesch, and Tanja Dückers," is devoted to story, and it focuses on narratives that interrogate the unstable border between historical fact and subjective remembering. Azade Seyhan has defined memory as "a phenomenon of conceptual border zones" that occupies a space "between the past and the present."[89] Based on this notion, I argue that "fictions of memory" and border poetics form a symbiosis that enables the simultaneous articulation of historically formed and particular borders as well as figurative boundaries (e.g.,

---

87   For a discussion of "transdifference," see, Breinig and Lösch, "Introduction." The notion of "cosmopolitan workshops" is discussed in Rumford, *Cosmopolitan Borders*.

88   Chatman, *Story and Discourse*, 146.

89   Seyhan, *Writing outside the Nation*, 31.

28 ◆ INTRODUCTION

questions of remembering and forgetting).[90] My discussion centers on three novels in which history, and especially the disruptions caused by the Second World War, plays a central role: Inga Iwasiów's *Bambino* (2008), Sabrina Janesch's *Katzenberge* (Cat Hills, 2010), and Tanja Dückers's *Himmelskörper* (Celestial Bodies, 2003). I examine how these novels articulate the ambiguity of memory both as an individual and as a collective phenomenon. These novels' characters, plotlines, and relationships frequently undermine stereotypical and one-sided representations (albeit to varying degrees of success) by offering unusual viewpoints and narrative perspectives that are variously interpolated and intertwined with more conventional ways of remembering the past.

As border poetics is concerned with decentering established narratives, the multiplication of perspectives and voices is a crucial narrative strategy, and chapter 4, "Belonging: Defocalized Narratives by Günter Grass, Sabrina Janesch, and Olga Tokarczuk," highlights some of the discursive practices that help create this effect. Examining writing that transcends the boundaries of a traditional realist framework, I explore the affinity between border poetics and nonrealist modes of narration. I argue that certain choices in narrative perspective, narrative voice, and focalization tied to magical realist or fantastic narratives foster border poetics because they draw attention to ambiguity, defocalization, and resistance to hegemonic discourses. Such choices can challenge the reader to think of alternative forms of belonging. By reading Günter Grass's *Die Blechtrommel* (1959; *The Tin Drum*, 1961 and 2009) as an early example of border poetics, this chapter contributes a new perspective to the extensive scholarship that exists on the author and his breakthrough novel. The other works considered in this chapter are Sabrina Janesch's *Ambra* (Amber, 2012) and Olga Tokarczuk's *Dom dzienny, dom nocny* (1998; *House of Day, House of Night*, 2002).

I have chosen and grouped my literary examples based on themes or narrative strategies they share rather than the "home" of their authors or the language in which they were first published. Thus, when speaking of German or Polish texts, I am referring mostly to the language in which they were first written. I examine texts in both languages alongside each other, and at times the discussion also draws on published translations—though in some cases, translations do not exist. In analyzing and considering German and Polish narratives together, I privilege an open and flexible comparative approach steeped in an awareness that any comparison requires constant critical reevaluation and is subject to change over time.[91] This flexibility is already written into the texts themselves. It applies not only to the objects we compare but also to the literal and the figurative ground from which we do so, and which itself also

---

90   On "fictions of memory," see Neumann, "Literary Representation of Memory."
91   Felski and Friedman, "Introduction."

changes.[92] This specific ground is the necessary foundation that influences our perspective, but it matters whether this ground is a rocky, inhospitable terrain or a grassy landscape in which the effects of a painful past have softened over time. It matters whether an observer is standing alert and ready to take flight, or whether someone lies in the newly grown grass, relaxed and enjoying the sky. Nobel laureate Wisława Szymborska conveys this sentiment in the last stanza of her poem "Koniec i początek" ("The End and the Beginning"): "In the grass that has overgrown / causes and effects, / someone must be stretched out / blade of grass in their mouth / gazing at the clouds."[93] Changes in the conditions under which we—as scholars, authors, or inhabitants of border-lands—are able to observe, think, and write necessarily have an impact on what and how we compare. In border poetics, both the objects and the grounds of comparison are fluid and flexible, and the following four chapters highlight different aspects or dimensions of this flexibility.

92   On the changing conditions for comparison, see, for example, Melas, *All the Difference*; and Cheah, "Grounds of Comparison," 3–6.
93   Szymborska, "Koniec i początek," 326–29, lines 43–47. Translation modified.

Part I

Context and Theoretical Frameworks

1: Entanglements in German and Polish History, Literature, and Culture

> *People are like knots: nobody knows what gets caught up in them and whether they can be untangled. Whoever thinks that this is material for myths or sagas is mistaken. Knots are knots. Nothing less, nothing more. Knots.*
>
> *Ludzie są jak węzełki: nie wiadomo, co się w nie zabierze i czy dadzą się rozplątać. Kto myśli ze można z tego zrobić mit lub sagę, jest w błędzie. Węzełki są węzełkami. Ni mniej, ni więcej. Węzełki.*
>
> —Inga Iwasiów, *Bambino*, 66

THE 2008 NOVEL *Bambino* by Polish author Inga Iwasiów follows the lives of five individuals whose fates become entwined when they meet after the Second World War in the now Polish city of Szczecin (formerly German Stettin). The protagonists had to cross various boundaries before arriving in the city, but they also *have been* crossed by the shifting national borders of the twentieth century. The novel delves into the multiple and overlapping senses of belonging that these protagonists carry within themselves. In the above epigraph, the narrator notes that this complexity is characteristic of people in general and that it is, in fact, entirely unremarkable. Variegated attachments, memories, or experiences lead to entanglements within and between individuals, and they wield their effects on all aspects of life. And even though these metaphorical knots may be too ordinary for sagas or myths, they deeply impact the social environment and all forms of human interaction and aesthetic expression. I discuss Iwasiów's novel in more detail in chapter 3, but I begin here with her idea of knots because it exemplifies a sense of entanglement that I try to follow throughout this book.

The idea of entanglement is also central to Rebecca Walkowitz's notion of a "cosmopolitan style" in her examination of modernist novels. This style entails "the literal knotting together of cultures and experiences that seem to be disparate," and it produces "the effect of ethical discomfort or embarrassment that is generated by incommensurate or unconventional associations."[1] By looking at borders through a critical lens, the authors I discuss in this study draw attention to all kinds of disruptions and challenges to belonging, and they thereby frequently highlight and bring together seemingly incommensurate

---

1 Walkowitz, *Cosmopolitan Style*, 20.

associations or disconnects. I draw on these entanglements, which are often uncomfortable or even painful, because the constant knitting and knotting together of histories and experiences (metaphorically and on a structural level) shapes the cosmopolitan imagination. The goal of this chapter is to examine the origins of some of these knots—at times zooming out to get a view of the larger historical and literary network of which they are part, and at other times zooming in to examine their particulars, such as problems of translation when it comes to borders and borderlands in the German-Polish context. The goal is not to untangle these knots but to get a better sense of what might be caught up in them and how they might animate the cosmopolitan imagination. By presenting the long and complex history of relations between Germany and Poland in such broad strokes, I want to both offer an overview of the history of Germany and Poland that contextualizes the later analyses and help explain the situation from which border poetics eventually emerges.

The political borders between Germany and Poland have moved significantly over the centuries: from the three partitions of Poland in the eighteenth century and the reemergence of the Polish state in 1918 to the shifting borders during, and then again as a result of, the Second World War. In these shifts, borders were moved violently over people and places, cutting through communities, families, and the lives of individuals. The people who were crossed in such multiple ways rarely chose their affiliations according to the current political boundaries. Rather, for many of them the idea of "their" nation-state and a lost or regained homeland remained powerfully present in their imagination and self-identification. At the same time, they also expressed attachments that would be more adequately described in subnational or transnational terms, such as strong local or regional identifications. Naturally, individuals feel tied to more than one group or cause, and they can have a variety of simultaneous attachments. On a large scale, such entangled relationships are, as Iwasiów notes, quite ordinary.

Literature has been an important arena for exploring these complex attachments and the effects of their changing constellations, and it is not surprising that literary texts and other narrative representations contribute to the increasing awareness of the inherent contradictions and dynamism of borders, border spaces, and border subjects. Looking at narratives of German-Polish contact in the twentieth and twenty-first centuries, one can make out a uneven shift of emphasis from literature about the border as a dividing line until 1989 (albeit with a significant break and change in perspective in 1945) to a new borderlands literature that emphasizes contact and exchange after 1989, and then to the gradual emergence of border poetics that goes beyond the notion of transnational contact. This simplified categorization can hardly capture the heterogeneous narratives produced in Poland and Germany over the past century, but its purpose here is to outline in broad strokes the different options for the narrative representation of borders—a model that can then be complicated, questioned, and destabilized by looking

ENTANGLEMENTS IN GERMAN AND POLISH HISTORY ♦ 35

at specific texts.[2] For now, this characterization can serve as a kind of background as I take a closer look at the historical context of my analysis. It serves as a starting point to explain how border poetics differs qualitatively and in thematic orientation from other engagements with borders.

One Thousand Years of History

Germany and Poland's shared history encompasses over one thousand years, even though one cannot speak of "Poland" or "Germany" in the modern sense for most of this period. Germanic and Slavic tribes came into contact in the early Middle Ages: Germanic settlers were present in what is today Poland, and Slavs, in turn, left their mark on territories that later became part of Germany. In the early modern period, too, relations between Germans and Poles were shaped not by national identity but rather by local alliances and the interests of the nobility. Throughout their prenational and national histories, Polish-German relations have gone through periods of peaceful coexistence that resulted in fruitful political, economic, and cultural exchange as well as periods of intense conflict over territory and influence that were motivated by racial and ethnic group thinking.

German historian Klaus Zernack, whose work is fundamental for the field of German-Polish history, identifies three major stages in the history of German-Polish relations: in his view, two periods of "normalcy," one between 1000 and 1701 and the other after 1989, were interrupted by a long phase of intense hostility against Poland between 1701 and 1989. And even though West German Chancellor Willy Brandt's politics of rapprochement with the East ("Ostpolitik") brought about a warming of relations in the 1970s, Zernack contends that it was not until 1989–91 that the three hundred years of negative German (or Prussian) politics toward Poland ended. Only the end of the Cold War and united Germany's official recognition of the post-1945 border between Germany and Poland as the final border made it possible for the two countries to come together in a shared interest in Europe.[3] To be sure, when Zernack speaks of "normal," he understands it as a relative term, meaning that the German-Polish relationship oscillated "normally" between periods of conflict and periods of agreement when compared with other European constellations at the time. In the seventeenth and eighteenth centuries, however, this relative "normalcy" was severely disrupted when systematic hostility against Poland set the relationship on a course that led toward catastrophe. Zernack regards this hostility as a "great exception in the history of relations among

---

2   See, for example, Holt, "Cold War Crossings," for works from the postwar period that might complicate such a categorization.

3   Zernack, "Deutsch-polnische Beziehungen," 90. Here Zernack also describes the period as the "*longue durée* von 'negativer Polenpolitik.'"

36 ◆ ENTANGLEMENTS IN GERMAN AND POLISH HISTORY

European nations."[4] Indeed, this history of German aggression and extreme violence against Poland have shaped and continue to impact German-Polish relations today. At the same time, the periods of "normalcy" have also allowed for positive transborder exchanges and interactions.

Today, the idea of Europe plays an important role in the more positive exchanges, even if not always in explicit ways. Europe (a term often used synonymously with the European Union) mostly fashions itself as a peaceful political unit in which national interests are secondary to broader continental concerns. In this still dominant reconciliatory EU-narrative, which was bolstered by the 2012 Nobel Peace Prize for the European Union, Poland and Germany figure as old neighbors whose relationship dates back over a millennium.[5] The year 1000 CE is typically named as the beginning of German-Polish diplomatic relations. It was the year in which Holy Roman Emperor Otto III set out on a pilgrimage to Gniezno, the "cradle" of Poland, to meet with Polish Duke Bolesław Chrobry (the Brave), who later became the first king of Poland. On this pilgrimage, the emperor recognized Poland as a Christian land and acknowledged the independence of its church, and he also declared the country an ally of the Holy Roman Empire.[6] Yet, this hopeful beginning was followed by centuries of forged and then broken alliances, threats from pagan tribes and the religious order of the Teutonic Knights, attacks by Mongolian and Ottoman forces, multiple territorial shifts, and various periods of internal instability and external dangers.

The crusading Teutonic Knights in particular would prove to have a lasting impact on Polish-German relations, and we will encounter them again in the novelistic landscape of Tokarczuk's *House of Day, House of Night* (see chapter 4, "Belonging: Defocalized Narratives by Günter Grass, Sabrina Janesch, and Olga Tokarczuk"). Invited initially in the early thirteenth century by Polish prince Konrad of Mazovia to help fight Prussian expansionism, by the end of the century, the Teutonic Knights had gained control over these and other lands, leading Poles to lose their influence in the region. The centuries-long conflict reached a climax in 1410, when Polish and Lithuanian forces

4   Zernack speaks of a "katastrophale Zuspitzung" (catastrophic aggravation) and of the German-Polish relationship as "[der] groß[e] Sonderfall in der Geschichte europäischer Nationalbeziehungen" (94). My translation.

5   There are frequent references to "1,000 years" of shared history, and the trope of the "neighbor" is commonly used. Both appear in titles of books, documentaries, and exhibitions; e.g., a 2011–12 exhibition in Berlin and Warsaw titled "Obok: Polska—Niemcy. 1000 lat historii w sztuce/Tür an Tür. Polen-Deutschland 1000 Jahre Kunst und Geschichte" (Next Door: Poland—Germany. 1000 Years of History in Art). In 2016, a three-part documentary series, titled "Die Deutschen und die Polen: Geschichte einer Nachbarschaft" (Germans and Poles: History of Two Neighbors), was completed as a collaborative production that aimed "to take a joint, fresh look at 1,000 years of neighborhood" (my translation).

6   Dabrowski, *Poland: The First Thousand Years*, 16–17.

ENTANGLEMENTS IN GERMAN AND POLISH HISTORY ◆ 37

fought and defeated the religious order in the Battle of Grunwald (German: "Schlacht bei Tannenberg").[7] This Polish victory lives on in the popular imagination today: it was memorialized in Nobel laureate Henryk Sienkiewicz's historical novel *Krzyżacy* (1900; *The Knights of the Cross*, 1900), which was written in a spirit of defiance and as an invocation of national unity at a time when Poland did not exist as an independent state, and it has gone through multiple adaptations since.[8] The Teutonic Knight thus continues to figure prominently to express anti-German sentiments; for example, when a battle of stereotypes ensued between German and Polish media during the Euro 2008 soccer championship. On one Polish tabloid's front page, a German soccer star, dressed as a Teutonic Knight, was about to be beheaded by the trainer of the Polish national team.[9] While its 1410 defeat did not result in the order's demise in Europe, and Polish territorial gains were minimal, it did bring Poles and Lithuanians closer together until they eventually formed the Polish-Lithuanian Commonwealth.[10] This federation existed formally from 1569 to 1795, and it experienced its "Golden Age" and greatest territorial expansion in the sixteenth and early seventeenth centuries. However, several Polish-Swedish-Russian wars weakened the powerful union, and its decline began in the mid-seventeenth century. A last major victory was won in 1683, when Polish forces of the Holy Alliance under King Jan III Sobieski defeated the Ottomans at the gates of Vienna. Many believed that King Sobieski had saved European Christendom, and the event came to play a key role in Polish national mythology and still reverberates in the present.[11] Despite this victory

7   For the history of the Teutonic Knights in Poland, see, Dabrowski, *Poland: The First Thousand Years*, 26–29; for the Battle of Grunwald, 62–68.

8   The novel is part of the Polish literary canon. It was adapted to the screen in 1960 and in 2011 as well as to videogames. Annual reenactments of the battle also help keep it alive in the popular imagination.

9   The daily tabloid *Fakt* showed Leo Beenhakkler, a Dutch trainer and at the time acting coach of the Polish national soccer team, as a sword-wielding knight in medieval armor, his large red shield with the white Polish eagle resting on the ground before him. Kneeling next to him is soccer star Michael Ballack from the German national team. He is donning a white cape with a large black cross, the symbol of the Order of the Teutonic Knights. Just to be sure the young man is identified as "German," he is also wearing a "Pickelhaube"—the iconic spiked Prussian helmet—and holding a soccer ball. The headline demands: "Leo powtórz Grunwald" (Leo, repeat Grunwald). For a copy of this and related images, see "Atak brukowców, spokój kibiców." The German media, in turn, used the stereotype of the car-stealing Pole. Ironically, many of the opposing actors involved in this media battle are part of the German media conglomerate Springer. Weiß, "Aufreger um Pinkelpause."

10   Dabrowski, *Poland: The First Thousand Years*, 62–68.

11   Dabrowski, *Poland: The First Thousand Years*, 223–27. The event's importance is, for example, evident in the long debate over the construction of a monument honoring King Sobieski on the site of the battle, the Kahlenberg near Vienna. Initial

against the Ottomans, precarious economic conditions and domestic conflicts led to the commonwealth's steady decline.[12]

It is at this historical juncture that Zernack sees the beginning of the turn away from "normalcy" and toward a systematic attempt to undermine Poland. When Frederick III of Brandenburg crowned himself as King Frederick I in Prussia in 1701, the event marked the beginning of the Kingdom of Prussia and its rise to a major European power.[13] By the middle of the eighteenth century, the Polish-Lithuanian Commonwealth had lost all its influence and was caught up in Russian, Austrian, and Prussian power politics that aimed to keep the Commonwealth as weak as possible.[14] Poland's elites fought against this fate, but after a major uprising against Russian oppression, the country was partitioned for the first time in 1772. The Commonwealth lost almost one-third of its territory to Prussia, Russia, and Austria. A Second Partition followed in 1793 when, inspired by the French Revolution, Poland sought to implement necessary state reforms, which—like previous attempts—were blocked from the outside. Following another uprising, the three powers responded with a Third Partition in 1795, which erased Poland from the world map for the next 123 years. Against all odds, the period of the three partitions, during which Polish elites fought desperately to win back their country's sovereignty, was also a period of important reforms in the political, financial, military, and educational sectors. For example, the Constitution of May 3, 1791, which established Poland as a constitutional monarchy with a parliament, became the first written constitution in Europe.[15]

While Prussia profited from the partitioning of Poland, many Germans sympathized with the Polish cause. In an essay on German-Polish literary relations, translator Karl Dedecius describes how the partitions and, ultimately, the loss of Polish sovereignty triggered protests and proclamations of solidarity among poets, philosophers, and other intellectuals throughout Prussia and the German states. Polish uprisings against the partition powers inspired German liberals, and their support of Polish independence was especially high after the November Uprising in 1830/31 in Warsaw. Poems, songs, and letters by prominent authors such as Graf von Platen, Ludwig Börne, Adalbert von Chamisso, Gustav Schwab, Christian Friedrich Hebbel, and Georg Büchner are testament to the sympathies for Polish self-determination. Polish refugees passing through Saxony, Franconia, Hesse, and the Palatinate were met with cheers and expressions of solidarity.[16] Berlin coffee houses and literary salons,

---

construction began in 2013 but was halted, and the monument was finally rejected in 2018. Science.ORF.at, "Streit."

12   Müller, "Polnische Geschichte," 26–27.

13   Zernack, "Deutsch-polnische Beziehungen," 94–95.

14   Müller, "Polnische Geschichte," 27–28.

15   Müller, "Polnische Geschichte," 28–32; and Dabrowski, *Poland: The First Thousand Years*, 269–70.

16   Dedecius, *Deutsche und Polen*, 21–31.

frequented by eminent literary figures such as E. T. A. Hoffmann, Christian Dietrich Grabbe, and Chamisso, cultivated a "Polenfreundschaft"—a friendship with Poland or the Poles.[17] About one thousand Poland songs also came out of this so-called "Polenschwärmerei" (infatuation with Poland). The enthusiasm for the Polish cause never translated into any political action on behalf of Poland among German liberals, however, and it came to an end in 1848.[18]

The 123-year absence from the map of Europe was a period in which "the history of Poland was a history of Poles in Europe," according to historian Manfred Alexander. This history varied according to the specific conditions and developments in each partition, and it also saw the rise of "Polonia" migrant communities all over the world.[19] Historian Włodzimierz Borodziej explains how, during the First World War, Poles fought against one another as members of the Prussian-German, Russian, or Austrian armies. It wasn't until the establishment of the Polish National Committee in Lausanne, Switzerland, in 1917 that an organization came about that could claim to represent the voice of the Polish people. This exile government moved to Paris soon after its formation and was officially recognized by the Allied Powers. When US president Woodrow Wilson presented the Fourteen Points that outlined the conditions for peace, the reestablishment of the Polish state was included as Point 13. As a result, after having been erased from the political map of Europe for over a century, Poland reemerged as an independent state in November 1918.[20]

The war on the Western Front ended in 1918, but for Poland the fighting continued in a series of wars and armed conflicts, especially in the east, until 1921. In the end, Poland's initial western border was largely determined by the Greater Poland Uprising of 1918 and 1919 (when Poland won back much of its core territory around Poznania from the tenth century) as well as the Treaty of Versailles (which granted Poland additional territories).[21] Historians have pointed out that in this new European order, Germany and Poland could only be enemies: Posen and large parts of West Prussia became part of Poland; East Prussia was cut off from Germany to grant Poland access to the Baltic Sea; parts of East Prussia and Upper Silesia held referenda to determine the course of the border; and Danzig became a free city under the protection of the League of Nations.[22] In essence, the state's new borders were still in flux, and territorial disputes continued with Germany, the Soviet Union, Lithuania, and the Czech Republic. From its very beginning, the young Polish Republic therefore suffered from external pressures and internal instability. Meanwhile,

17   Dedecius, *Deutsche und Polen*, 41.
18   Brudzyńska-Němec, "Polenbegeisterung."
19   Alexander, *Kleine Geschichte Polens*, 163. My translation.
20   Borodziej, *Geschichte Polens im 20. Jahrhundert*, 75–96, esp. 87, 89, and 93.
21   Borodziej, *Geschichte Polens im 20. Jahrhundert*, 97–124, esp. 101–3 and 109–10.
22   Borodziej, *Geschichte Polens im 20. Jahrhundert*, 97–110, esp. 109–10. See also Dabrowski, *Poland: The First Thousand Years*, 380–92.

40 ◆ Entanglements in German and Polish History

Germany's first parliamentary democracy, the Weimar Republic, was unable to stabilize politically because of strong opposition to the Treaty of Versailles and outrage over Germany's territorial losses among Germans of all political persuasions.[23] These border issues and the desire to regain lost territories helped bring the National Socialists to power in 1933 and set Germany on a path to the next war.

The Second World War began with Germany's invasion of Poland on September 1, 1939, with one of its immediate aims being to win back Danzig for Germany. By the end of the war on May 8, 1945, between five and six million Polish citizens had lost their lives, among them at least 3 million Jews. Germans established ghettos and concentration camps in occupied Poland, and they created death camps in which Jews from all over Europe were systematically exterminated. Gentile Poles also suffered greatly under German occupation and Nazi racial policies. The Polish intelligentsia was eliminated, and mass shootings, forced labor, deportations, and other forms of violence terrorized and instilled a continuous fear in the Polish population. On September 17, 1939, shortly after Germany's attack, the Soviet Army invaded Poland from the east, thereby putting the country under a double occupation. Here too, members of the intelligentsia and the military were murdered or deported to forced labor camps further east (e.g., Siberia), and Sovietization policies were pushed through with brutal measures.[24]

At the end of the war, the Allies redrew the borders of Germany and Poland. Poland's borders were shifted westward, which equated to a loss of about half of its previous state territory (approximately seventy thousand square miles) to the Soviet Union. As compensation, Poland received about forty thousand square miles of Germany's eastern territories.[25] These border shifts were accompanied by changes in geographic place names: Danzig became Gdańsk, Gotenhafen turned into Gdynia, Stettin was renamed Szczecin, and Breslau was henceforth Wrocław—to mention only those cities that play a role in the novels I discuss later. The border changes also went hand in hand with massive population shifts: Soviets expelled ethnic Poles from Poland's former eastern territories, and Germans were forced to leave the areas that had become part of Poland. These shifts added to the trauma and upheaval already caused by the war itself. The experience of war, the subsequent forced relocations, and the loss of the homeland became long-lasting issues in Polish and German politics, and, unsurprisingly, they have left their traces in postwar literature and culture, and they continue to be present in the literary imagination today.

After the war, Poland fell into the Soviet sphere of influence. The Soviets and the Polish Communist leadership believed that political stability

---

23   Winkler, "Im Schatten von Versailles," 65–67.

24   Borodziej, "Der Zweite Weltkrieg," 68–70, esp. 68; and Dabrowski, *Poland: The First Thousand Years*, 408–18, esp. 418.

25   Borodziej, "Der Zweite Weltkrieg," 68.

depended on a dual strategy of creating the illusion that Poland was an ethnically homogenous state and constructing a Polish tradition for the previously German areas. An effective way of doing so appeared to be erasure of the German past: street names were changed, inscriptions on buildings removed, German monuments dismantled, documents and books destroyed. Polish writer Stefan Chwin, born in 1949 in Gdańsk, explains that, considering the countless crimes and barbaric acts the Germans had committed against the Polish population, few objected to such measures.[26] Yet, while deep hatred of Prussia and Germany dominated in the postwar period, it was difficult to remove all traces of a German past.[27] Chwin and other writers have reflected on their personal experiences with this incomplete process.[28] The encounter with German traces is an important trope in more recent literary works as well, including in the novels I discuss later. For example, part of the plot of Sabrina Janesch's *Katzenberge* revolves around a former German castle in the Silesian countryside.[29] The topography of Olga Tokarczuk's *House of Day, House of Night* is filled with objects and documents left behind by its former German in habitants—items termed "poniemieckie" (post-German) in Polish.[30]

These physical traces highlight the continuity of the landscape while also shining a light on the disruptions experienced by the people who were forcefully resettled into these areas and had to cope with trauma while adjusting to a new reality. After the violence and upheaval of the Second World War and in light of the ideological divisions and political tensions of the Cold War, it was not easy to translate the shared German and Polish history of spaces, objects, and people into official relations and bilateral politics. In addition, Germany's postwar division means that Polish-German relations after the Second World War must be understood as separate sets of relations between Poland and West Germany (the Federal Republic of Germany, FRG) and between Poland and

26   Chwin, "Grenzlandliteratur," 8; and "Literatura pogranicza," 7.

27   Zernack refers to "Preußenhass" (hatred of Prussia or the Prussians) among Poles: "Deutsch-polnische Beziehungen," 97.

28   For examinations of how this reality impacted authors such as Stefan Chwin, Paweł Huelle, and others, see, for example, Schmidgall, "Die Macht des Genius loci," 98–99; Chwin, "Grenzlandliteratur," 7–8; and Wagner, "Literarische Grenzüberschreitungen." Journalist Adam Krzemiński (born in 1945) describes similar experiences in postwar Wrocław; see, e.g., *Deutsch-polnische Verspiegelung*, 16.

29   For an analysis of these traces in Janesch, see Wagner, "Literarische Grenzüberschreitungen," 123–27. A detailed analysis of the erasure and recovery of the former German traces, including how Janesch addresses the process, is offered in Palej, *Fließende Identitäten*, 190–203.

30   I discuss the idea of "poniemieckie" in the next chapter. The term is often translated as "post-German," but the preposition "po" (after) refers in this context to things "left behind by the Germans," rather than to a time or phase that begins after the Germans have left. Karolina Kuszyk examines these traces of Germanness in *Poniemieckie* (Post-German, 2019; translated as *In den Häusern der Anderen*, 2022).

42 ♦ ENTANGLEMENTS IN GERMAN AND POLISH HISTORY

East Germany (the German Democratic Republic, GDR). As Dieter Bingen explains, West German political discourse after 1945 was dominated by border-related issues, including the loss of former German territories to Poland and the expulsion of ethnic Germans from those regions. While the Polish People's Republic (Polska Rzeczpospolita Ludowa, PRL) and East Germany, although only under pressure from the Soviet Union, signed a treaty in 1950 that recognized the German-Polish border, West Germany long refused to do so. West German chancellor Konrad Adenauer, like much of his electorate at the time, did not accept Poland's western border, thereby keeping the border issue open. This stance played a major role in the lack of diplomatic relations between Poland and West Germany in the first two decades of the postwar period.[31] It also fed into a view advanced by Communist propaganda that West German politics was merely a continuation of Prussian interests.[32]

Two highly symbolic events stand for the reconciliation process between West Germany and Poland during the Cold War. Remarkably, a first major step came not from the German but from the Polish side. In 1956, Polish bishops sent a letter to their German colleagues with the words "Przebaczamy i prosimy o przebaczenie" (We forgive, and we ask for forgiveness). Polish Catholics were, however, irritated that the church had asked for forgiveness in their name, a feeling only amplified by the fact that the German Catholic Bishops Conference responded with a noncommittal letter that avoided any statement regarding the Polish-German border. The gesture was also a risky move for the Polish Catholic Church, which was already facing state oppression, and the letter only intensified the government's anticlerical campaign. The growing tensions between state and church in Poland were akin to a new "Kulturkampf" that aimed to minimize the influence of the Catholic Church, a battle that finally ran its course when Kraków's Archbishop Karol Wojtyła was elected Pope John Paul II in 1978.[33] Gradually, the gesture from the Polish side, changes in the Polish government in 1970/71 following demonstrations and strikes, and a reorientation in West German politics through Social Democratic chancellor Willy Brandt's "Ostpolitik" led to improved diplomatic relations between West Germany and Poland and a second symbol of reconciliation. During a historic visit to Warsaw on December 7, 1970, Chancellor Brandt paid his respects at the Tomb of the Unknown Soldier, followed by a visit to a monument dedicated to the 1943 Warsaw Ghetto Uprising. In an unscripted act, Brandt knelt down in front of the memorial. This event, known as the "Kniefall" (genuflection), is today seen as a powerful representation of the warming of West German–Polish relations, although scholarship shows that contemporaries in Germany and Poland had little appreciation

---

31   Bingen, "Deutschland und Polen," n.p.
32   Zernack, "Deutsch-polnische Beziehungen," 97–98.
33   Borodziej, *Geschichte Polens im 20. Jahrhundert*, 309–11; and Felsch and Latkowska, "Brief der (polnischen) Bischöfe," 396–405.

for Brandt's gesture.[34] On the same notable day of the "Kniefall," Brandt also signed the Treaty of Warsaw, in which West Germany officially recognized the finality of the German-Polish border, or Oder-Neisse border (named after the two border rivers, the Oder in the north and its tributary the Neisse in the south). The treaty, however, also stipulated that this was a contract between the Federal Republic of Germany and Poland; it did not pertain to a possibly unified Germany of the future.[35]

All these rapprochements took place on the stage of grand politics and within the constraints of Cold War power dynamics, as political scientist Andrea Genest compellingly demonstrates. When the Polish opposition, which had been growing over the previous decades, came together in the Solidarność (Solidarity) movement in 1980, West Germany's official stance remained cautious and even distanced. It seems that Solidarność, named after the first independent trade union in the Soviet bloc, should have enjoyed the unequivocal support of West German Social Democrats. Solidarność activities were, however, perceived as potentially destabilizing and did not square well with Brandt's "Ostpolitik." Its goal had been to work *with* the Communist regimes—especially the Soviet Union—to gradually instigate change from above. In this equation, political opposition was an incalculable risk in an already volatile situation, and the West German government was cautious not to antagonize the Soviets or endanger diplomatic relations with East Germany. Nonetheless, there was important extragovernmental support; for example, in the form of care packages sent by West German unions and individuals. This was especially the case between 1981 and 1983, when the Communist government sought to put down Solidarność by instating martial law.[36]

By comparison, the GDR and the PRL should have enjoyed better relations owing to their ostensibly shared political ideology. Historian Krzysztof Ruchniewicz, however, gives insights into a relationship that was strained until 1972, and in which contact was mostly limited to official exchanges and political maneuvering. While the GDR guaranteed the stability of the Oder-Neisse border—first, by officially recognizing the border in July 1950, and second, by providing a physical buffer between Poland and West Germany—this friendship was largely a propaganda tool over which the state had sole power: The GDR, which fashioned itself as a bulwark of antifascism and as a countermodel to West Germany, was always keen to show its loyalty to the Soviet Union. Dissent and protests, such as an uprising in 1953, made GDR officials anxious and reinforced the notion that the state's survival depended on strong ties with the Soviets. This meant that any liberalization attempts in the Eastern Bloc, including those in Poland in 1956 and 1980/81, were met with increased

34   Felsch and Latkowska, "Brief der (polnischen) Bischöfe," 405–6.
35   Borodziej, *Geschichte Polens im 20. Jahrhundert*, 316–17.
36   Genest, "Solidarność aus deutscher Perspektive." For a brief summary of Poland under martial law, see Dabrowski, *Poland: The First Thousand Years*, 445–47.

44 ◆ Entanglements in German and Polish History

surveillance and security measures that sought to bring down these movements and prevent them from spreading to the GDR.[37]

Relations between the GDR and Poland improved only slowly following the death of Joseph Stalin in 1953, and it took until 1972 for the border to be opened. The development was halted, however, by worsening economic conditions in both countries. Product shortages in the GDR were blamed on Polish shoppers crossing the border, and negative stereotypes were on the rise. When the Solidarność movement gained momentum in Poland, the GDR leadership became increasingly worried about its own fate. In 1980 the GDR therefore closed its borders again and aimed to create a negative image of Poland to prevent the spread of ideas of democracy and freedom.[38] Solidarność sympathizers were watched closely, and the stereotype of the "lazy Pole" was used to discredit striking workers.[39] Initially, however, the changes of the early 1970s had created the preconditions for a more direct exchange between citizens, including German expellees, who had settled in East Germany. Now they could travel to their former homelands for the first time since the end of the war and visit the graves of relatives, although many of the gravesites had been destroyed.[40] Despite these contacts, flight and expulsion remained taboo topics, at least in official GDR discourse. When Christa Wolf fictionalized these Poland visits and excavated this shared German-Polish history in her 1976 novel *Kindheitsmuster* (*Patterns of Childhood*, 1980), it was seen as an astonishing breach of this taboo.[41]

The year 1989 marks what Zernack has called an "Epochenwandel," an epochal change, for German-Polish relations.[42] This change, however, was accompanied by much unease and outright fear. While Germans celebrated the fall of the Berlin Wall on November 9, 1989, Poles were watching anxiously as the events unfolded. Memories of the Second World War still loomed large, and many Poles wondered how German unification might affect them and the rest of Europe.[43] Some progress had been made since 1945 in easing the tensions between the two German states and Poland, but it seemed largely unclear

37   Ruchniewicz, "Die DDR," 194–99.

38   Ruchniewicz, "Die DDR," 203.

39   Archiv Bürgerbewegung Leipzig e.V. The site also contains a collection of documents that illustrate these anti-Polish and anti-Solidarność sentiments by the GDR government.

40   Ruchniewicz, "Die DDR," 202; and Borodziej, *Geschichte Polens im 20. Jahrhundert*, 346.

41   Ther, *Deutsche und polnische Vertriebene*, 249.

42   Zernack, "Deutsch-polnische Beziehungen," 98.

43   For an insightful exploration of how fear of Germany and the Germans impacted Polish foreign policy and German-Polish relations after the Second World War, see Weber, "Angst in der polnischen Deutschlandpolitik nach 1945." For Polish fears of German unification and the gradual alleviation of these fears, see especially 144–45.

what the position of a *united* Germany would be. Fears of Germany's cultural and economic dominance were coupled with residual doubts about the stability of the German-Polish border—an issue that was formally put to rest with the Border Treaty of November 1990 in which united Germany once and for all recognized the current German-Polish border as the final border. In June 1991 German chancellor Helmut Kohl and Polish prime minister Jan Krzysztof Bielecki as well as the foreign ministers of both countries signed the Treaty on Good Neighborly Relations. Although the Border Treaty of 1990 did not come about without external pressure, especially from Poland, and only after it had become a precondition for German unification, it set a new tone in diplomatic relations between Germany and Poland.[44]

Official relations continued to improve, but contracts and proclamations could hardly eliminate all fears or stereotypes. When visa restrictions were lifted, Germans were anxious that Polish workers would enter the German labor market and take away jobs from Germans. Such anxieties reached another climax on December 21, 2007, when Poland, which had been a member of the European Union since 2004, joined the Schengen Zone. This meant that the policed borders between Germany and Poland would be removed, and other restrictions (such as those regarding work and residency) would be eased or lifted. Underestimating the significant changes and economic growth that Poland had undergone since the end of the Communist period, and equipped with a rich arsenal of stereotypes about "the East," German news reports of the time show how people braced themselves for an onslaught of cheap Polish labor and organized crime.[45] Similar fears of an "Eastern Flood" were articulated around 2011, the year when any remaining restrictions on living and working anywhere in the European Union were lifted for Polish citizens.[46]

Despite continued tensions and the persistence of stereotypes, the post–Cold War era was, until 2015, a period of steady improvement in Polish-German relations both on an official and on the interpersonal level, and this process is generally hailed as a success story in reconciliation. This optimism was expressed, for example, in 2011, when Germany and Poland celebrated the twentieth anniversary of the Treaty on Good Neighborly Relations. On the occasion of the anniversary, Minister of State Cornelia Pieper, at the time also the coordinator for German-Polish cooperation, emphasized in an interview how much closer Poland and Germany had become in the past twenty years. She underscored German chancellor Angela Merkel's and Polish prime minister Donald Tusk's assessments that Polish-German relations were "better than

---

44 Borodziej, *Geschichte Polens im 20. Jahrhundert*, 386–88; and Weber, "Angst in der polnischen Deutschlandpolitik nach 1945," esp. 134–35.

45 Such news reports include Volkmann-Schluck, "Im Osten"; Messmer, "Türen zu."

46 Eigler, "Introduction," 2. Here Eigler also points out that such fears "hark back to nineteenth-century Prussia and Germany" as examined by Kristin Kopp in *Germany's Wild East*, 67–68.

ever" and noted that it was now time to develop these good relations "in and for Europe" for the future. Significantly, she also saw evidence of the excellent status of the relationship in the Polish presidential elections in 2010. According to the minister, the election had shown that Polish voters from "the middle of society" could not be persuaded by anti-German views and that most of them valued Germany as a reliable neighbor.[47]

Only five years later, this optimism was already waning. By the treaty's twenty-fifth anniversary in 2016, the official German-Polish relationship had cooled considerably, and anti-German and xenophobic sentiments were increasing in Poland. Since the early 2010s, Europe has undergone a notable political shift to the right, and in Poland this trend became especially evident after the 2015 parliamentary elections, which brought the Law and Justice Party (Prawo i Sprawiedliwość, PiS) to power. Besides seriously limiting the independence of the judiciary and replacing important positions in politics, education, media, and cultural institutions with persons sympathetic to the government, Poland's national-conservative leadership was also critical of the European Union and of Germany.[48] The parliamentary elections of 2019 and the presidential elections of 2020 confirmed the country's political direction and its anti-German stance. While change is on the horizon after the election of a pro-European Union government in late 2023, the preceding eight years have had a significant impact on Polish-German relations. Nevertheless, local and regional friendships and initiatives continued to thrive during that period, and personal relations were generally described as good.[49] Collaborations also continued in scholarship or in the cultural sphere, but limitations in funding or thematic reorientations due to the government's cultural and educational politics also made them more challenging. Maintaining these positive connections remains an important task, and cultural and academic relationships play a vital role in continuing to build mutual respect and understanding that can withstand political fluctuations.

Literary Knots

The long history of German-Polish relations has also brought about entanglements in the literary landscape—and here literature has both reflected and complicated or even contradicted official narratives and political developments. After the Second World War, literature demonstrated the ability to "entgiften" (detoxify) the German-Polish relationship, according to Polonist Heinrich Olschowsky, although he also explains how the process was different for each of the two Germanies. West Germans became interested in Polish

---

47   Pieper, "Die deutsch-polnische Nachbarschaft." My translation.

48   On the year 2015 as a turning point in Polish-German relations, see Traba, "Gra w Niemca."

49   Łada, "Auf persönlicher Ebene sind die Beziehungen sehr gut."

literature and culture after 1956, when, inspired by changes in the Soviet Union, Poland relaxed its censorship laws and temporarily opened up to foreign audiences. West German readers were especially interested in Polish literature that was critical of the Communist system, and they appreciated drama of the avant-garde as well as works by authors who had emigrated. At the same time, literature written prior to the First World War received very little attention. The translator, author, and cultural ambassador ("Kulturvermittler") Karl Dedecius was a key figure in the promotion of Polish literature, and his translations of poetry contributed significantly to its overall increase in popularity.[50] In East Germany, by contrast, the availability of literature was controlled by official cultural politics. Works that conformed to socialist ideology were supported, but everything else was censored or banned. Nineteenth-century literature was deemed ideologically safe and therefore made available, but contemporary writers were blocked until the mid-1960s because the GDR leadership feared that criticism hailing from Poland might destabilize the GDR's political system. Interestingly, Polish literature actually benefited from Germany's Cold War division: the existence of two different markets meant that a greater variety of texts became available in German translation. Some works were also translated twice and therefore with more care. At the same time, the quality of East German translations could be questionable; that is, when censors made sure that a text fit the desired ideological stance with translations that distorted the original.[51]

The end of Communism impacted cultural relations on multiple levels. The East German market for publishing and translation essentially collapsed, but Polish authors of a younger generation were nonetheless regularly translated into German and positively received by German readers. In 2009, Germanist Natasza Stelmaszyk therefore deemed the story of Polish literature in German-speaking countries over the previous two decades one of success.[52] But as she also notes, not everyone shared this optimistic assessment. Germany's most illustrious and prominent literary critic, Marcel Reich-Ranicki, argued that Polish prose continued to be inaccessible in form and content, and others lamented the limited interest in Polish culture, which, if present at all, related to universal themes and not Poland per se.[53] It should

---

50 Olschowsky, "Polnische Literatur in Deutschland," 162, 159–67.

51 Olschowsky, "Polnische Literatur in Deutschland," 164–67.

52 Stelmaszyk, "Die neue Situation der polnischen Literatur," 153.

53 Stelmaszyk, "Die neue Situation der polnischen Literatur," 157–59. Reich-Ranicki (1920–2013) himself is an example of the complex navigations of German-Jewish-Polish identity, as his autobiography illustrates. He was born in Włocławek into a Jewish German-Polish family. The family later moved to Berlin but was deported to Warsaw in 1938. Ranicki and his wife survived the Holocaust in hiding, but his parents and brother were murdered. In 1958, Reich-Ranicki emigrated from Poland to West Germany. That same year, he met the young Günter Grass, who asked him *what* he was: German or Pole. Reich-Ranicki responded, "Ein halber Pole, ein halber Deutscher und

48 ♦ Entanglements in German and Polish History

also be noted that while Polish literature in Germany has enjoyed some success after 1989, popular reception has focused mainly on contemporary Polish authors, while canonical works from earlier periods were being read mostly by academics and specialists.[54]

A crucial event for the increased reception of Polish literature in Germany was the Frankfurt Book Fair in 2000, at which Poland was a guest of honor. This role was accompanied by a series of events and initiatives across Germany that included readings and other cultural events as well as long-term publishing and translation initiatives.[55] Still, taking into account the time period from 1989 to 2020, Renata Makarska's assessment of the market conditions, reception, and availability of literary translations shows a gradual decline in translations from Polish into German. And while young adult fiction and children's books have enjoyed great successes, a more deliberate effort to support and promote publishing and translation is again required. The full effects of Olga Tokarczuk's 2019 Nobel Prize in Literature are yet to be seen, but looking to a parallel example may give an indication of its limits: while it seems that Herta Müller's Nobel Prize in 2009 led to a greater reception of her work in Poland, it did not cause an increased interest in German literature more generally.[56]

As for the situation in Poland, here literature from the German-speaking lands has traditionally enjoyed only limited popularity. The issue, according to Tadeusz Namowicz, is that Poles have historically not thought of Germans as producers of great literary works. Their talents in other arts such as painting and music have been met with appreciation, but German literature was considered neither aesthetically interesting nor particularly important. Indeed, Poles never bought into Germany's self-image as the "country of poets and thinkers." By contrast, German philosophy was held in much higher esteem, especially during Poland's Enlightenment and Positivist periods, mostly because philosophy was considered a science and was judged by different standards. Despite this limited appreciation, German literature increased in popularity during certain historical periods. In the nineteenth century, for example, Polish national bard and Romantic poet Adam Mickiewicz expressed admiration for the writings of Johann Wolfgang von Goethe and Friedrich Schiller as

---

ein ganzer Jude" (Half a Pole, a half a German, and a full Jew). He admits to the reader that this response was hardly truthful: "Ich war nie ein halber Pole, nie ein halber Deutscher—und ich hatte keinen Zweifel, dass ich es nie werden würde. Ich war auch nie in meinem Leben ein ganzer Jude, ich bin es auch heute nicht" (I was never half Polish, never half German—and I had no doubt that I never would be. I was also never in my life a full Jew, and I am not one today either). Reich-Ranicki, *Mein Leben*, here 11–12. My translation.

54   Stelmaszyk, "Die neue Situation der polnischen Literatur," 163; and Krzoska, "Die polnische Literatur," 1028–30.

55   Stelmaszyk, "Die neue Situation der polnischen Literatur," 163–64; and Olschowsky, "Polnische Literatur in Deutschland," 168.

56   Makarska, "Übersetzen zwischen Deutschland und Polen," 6–7.

well as those of Johann Gottfried Herder and the Schlegel brothers. In the early twentieth century, too, interest in German literature increased, which included especially the writings of Thomas Mann, Rainer Maria Rilke, and Franz Kafka. Other canonical texts of German literature, however, have had only a very limited presence.[57]

After 1945, German literature in Polish translation was first represented by antifascist literature from the GDR as well as German classics. It wasn't until 1956, when Poland experienced a brief warming of the political climate, that post-1945 West German literature became available in Poland.[58] For example, Brian Porter-Szűcs explains how, following Stalin's death in 1953, strikes and demonstrations took place in many countries in the Eastern Bloc. In Poland, local protests against increased production quotas quickly turned into wider demonstrations against price hikes and low wages as well as anti-Communist protests. The demonstrations were violently put down, but they led to a brief period of greater freedom and openness to the West.[59] As a result, Polish readers discovered authors such as Heinrich Böll, Erich Kästner, and Egon Erwin Kisch, as well as Swiss writers Friedrich Dürrenmatt and Max Frisch and Austrian authors Franz Theodor Csokor, Robert Musil, and Joseph Roth.[60] Even though there was a relative increase in publications of German literature in Polish translation, German literature still lagged behind French and English literature during the entire period between 1945 and 1989. There was also no systematic translation program, which led to large gaps regarding the authors or the kinds of works that were being translated and published.[61] An important role in filling some of these gaps during the Cold War was played by the Polish underground press, the "drugi obieg" (literally, "second circulation," in German "zweiter Umlauf"). This was also the case with Günter Grass, and especially his novel *Die Blechtrommel* (*The Tin Drum*), which I discuss later as an important early example of border poetics. Grass's work has left a lasting impression on multiple generations of German and Polish writers and intellectuals, and its publication history merits a closer look here, as it also provides insights into the history of German-Polish literary relations as well as the ideological and political forces that usually ran counter to the interests of the general public. It also tells us something about the multiple scales of belonging and the uneven and surprising circulations of works of world literature.

57   Namowicz, "Deutsche Literatur in Polen," 170–81.

58   Namowicz, "Deutsche Literatur in Polen," 181; and Dedecius, *Deutsche und Polen* 55–56.

59   Porter-Szűcs, *Poland in the Modern World*, 233–45.

60   Dedecius, *Deutsche und Polen*, 55–56. Dedecius shows that this interest was not necessarily mutual, as demonstrated by the number of available translations: Between 1944 and 1961, only 282 Polish titles were translated into German, with demand increasing mostly after 1960. By contrast, between 1944 and 1963, 679 German-language works were translated into Polish (57–58).

61   Namowicz, "Deutsche Literatur in Polen," 182.

50 ♦ Entanglements in German and Polish History

When *The Tin Drum* was first published in West Germany in 1959, officials in both Germanies and in Poland had strong reactions, as journalist and cultural critic Adam Krzemiński summarizes: conservative politicians of the Christian Democratic Union (CDU/CSU) in West Germany rejected the novel because they regarded it as pornographic and anti-Christian; in the GDR the novel did not meet the expectations of socialist realism; meanwhile, in Poland it was criticized for the unfavorable depiction of Poles defending the Polish Post Office in Danzig (today Gdańsk) against a takeover by the invading National Socialists on September 1, 1939. Polish officials were also troubled by the characterization of Red Army soldiers as rapists and looters.[62] Such reactions help explain the turbulent history of censorship, publication, and reception of *The Tin Drum* that in itself is a history of many border crossings in German-Polish cultural history. As Krzemiński explains, this history begins with, or possibly even before, the novel's publication in West Germany, when an excerpt appeared in Polish translation in the weekly journal *Polityka*. Further chapter translations followed, but censorship barred the publication of the novel in its entirety. The Polish underground press circumvented this ban and published the book in 1979. Volker Schlöndorff's 1979 film adaptation was also banned, but much like the novel, it also made its way into the public and became an opportunity to practice opposition during the time of Solidarity. By 1981, one could thus view the film in student clubs, church gatherings, and at Warsaw University.[63] It took until 1992 for the film to be released in Polish cinemas.[64] The novel appeared first in 1983 in an official, albeit still censored, translation.[65] Even so, Poland was years ahead of East Germany, where the novel did not appear until 1987.[66] Over the following years, other works by Grass were published and became openly accessible to a Polish readership.[67]

After the end of the Cold War, Günter Grass became a popular and admired author in Poland, particularly in his hometown, Gdańsk. When scandal broke out in 2006 following Grass's late confession that he had joined the Waffen-SS at the age of seventeen, there was a major uproar in both Germany and Poland, due at least in part to the moral high ground Grass had claimed for most of his life (or which was at least ascribed to him). Yet, Krzemiński notes that the reaction in Poland was by no means uniform. While Polish national conservatives railed against Grass, many citizens of Gdańsk came together in his support. They defended him, even guarding the bronze statue that

62   Krzemiński, "1959: Die Blechtrommel."
63   Krzemiński, "Wie die Polen Günter Grass verteidigen."
64   Loew, *Danzig: Biographie einer Stadt*, 277.
65   The 1983 publication omitted about twelve pages from the original. The first uncensored edition did not appear until 1991. Surynt and Zielińska, "Der polnisch-polnische Krieg," 15n52.
66   Hage, "Kein Respekt."
67   Loew, *Danzig*, 277.

commemorates *The Tin Drum's* protagonist, drum-holding Oskar Matzerath. Gdańsk residents recognized

> dass er nicht nur sein Danzig, sondern auch ihr Gdańsk in die Weltliteratur eingeführt hatte und dass er als einer der ersten Deutschen offen für die Anerkennung der Oder-Neiße-Grenze durch die BRD ... eingetreten war. ... dass er auch auf ihre und nicht nur seine Stadt stolz war, auf ihren, der Polen Beitrag zur Öffnung der Berliner Mauer, kurzum, dass sie in Grass "ihren Deutschen" haben, der kaschubische Wurzeln hat und die polnische Komponente seiner Kindheit nicht verdrängte, sondern mit sich trug wie den Schlüssel zu einer anderen Welt.

> [that he not only introduced his Danzig but also their Gdańsk to world literature, and that he was one of the first Germans who stood openly for the recognition of the Oder-Neisse border by the FRG. ... that he was also proud of their and not only his city, of their, the Poles' contribution to the fall of the Berlin Wall, in short, that in Grass they had "their German," who has Kaschubian roots and who did not deny the Polish component of his childhood, but instead carried it with him like a key to a different world.][68]

In the same article, Krzemiński notes that Grass speaks the language of "deutsch-polnische Verknotung und Verrenkung" (German-Polish entanglement and contortion, with "Verknotung" referring literally to a process of "knotting" or a state of being "knotted" together). For Krzemiński, the Polish "Brocken" (chunks) in Grass's works are not mere exotic ornamentation but an integral part of this world and of the story world. This observation is key, for it is precisely the serious integration of Polish and German perspectives that is crucial for border poetics. It may well be that many narratives have this intention, but many also fall short in its implementation. They may at times use the "Polish element" decoratively and inadvertently slip into a kind of kitschiness, as I demonstrate later.

Scholars have emphasized the importance of Grass's work in weaving a German-Polish web in which Poles could also find themselves. Renowned literary scholar, critic, and public intellectual Maria Janion has often referred to Grass's Polish plot or a Polish knot ("Polski węzeł"), particularly in *The Tin Drum*.[69] Tomasz Lewandowski has drawn on another expression used by Janion, describing *The Tin Drum* as the "missing link" in Polish literature, which, fortunately, has been recovered.[70] Grass's impact was also felt after the

---

68   Krzemiński, "Wie die Polen Günter Grass verteidigen." My translation.

69   Janion, "Obraz poslkości u Grassa," 59.

70   Lewandowski, "Grass jako brakujące ogniwo," 240. Here, Lewandowski also argues that the novel can be read as "evidence of an experience that is inaccessible from the perspective of a specific national mentality, but which is somehow important to

52 ♦ Entanglements in German and Polish History

end of Communism, when he inspired authors who were in search of new narratives in post–Cold War Europe and who were interested in exploring the regional and local histories of their immediate surroundings. We learn from Peter Oliver Loew that many Poles discovered Gdańsk's past through Grass's works, and that writers and intellectuals took *The Tin Drum* as a motivation to dig deeper into the complex history of their city.[71] Here, authors like Stefan Chwin (born in 1949) and Paweł Huelle (born in 1957) are the most prominent representatives and, together with Grass, they form the "Prosa-Troika Grass-Huelle-Chwin."[72]

When the Cold War ended, writers were free to discover and write openly about previously silenced aspects of the past. But while the end of censorship meant intellectual freedom, the termination of GDR funding and subsidies for new publications posed significant challenges. As the book market became driven by profit, the presence of German literature on the Polish market decreased.[73] Considering literature an important gauge of one's neighbor's feelings, in 2000 Namowicz expressed concern about the negative impact of this development on German-Polish relations. He worried that only very few contemporary German authors were being translated and published in Poland and that Polish readers were more interested in transnational or broader European topics and discussions and less in German literature.[74] One can again question what "German" literature means in this context and why it would stand in opposition to literature with transnational or European concerns. The argument seems to echo Stelmaszyk's and other scholars' assessment that Germans began to be more interested in contemporary Polish literature because of its increased "worldliness."[75] In the introduction to this book, I took issue with the equation of world literature with easy readability as well as the related idea that some works may be "too local" to be considered world literature. Namowicz seems to suggest the reverse; namely, that some works are simply too "worldly" to also be part of a national literature. Yet, a work's "locality" and its "worldliness" are not mutually exclusive, and neither are world and national literature, as an entangled literary history can demonstrate.

Still, the reality is that German literature enjoys limited popularity in Poland. Its presence on the Polish market was briefly boosted in 2006 and again in 2017, when Germany was a special guest at the Warsaw Book Fair, but Makarska confirms the general decline in the sale of translation licenses

---

our culture" (my translation). This observation can be read within the framework of transdifference; i.e., it underlines that a temporary suspension of difference also allows a closer look at the self.

71   Loew, *Danzig*, 276–81.

72   Loew, *Danzig*, 288.

73   Namowicz, "Deutsche Literatur in Polen," 183.

74   Namowicz, "Deutsche Literatur in Polen," 185.

75   Stelmaszyk, "Die neue Situation der polnischen Literatur," 156. Citing Hedwig Nosbers, Stelmaszyk uses the term "Verweltlichung" (worlding) here.

of German books to Poland between 2009 and 2020—a trend that aligns with a general decline in translations on the Polish book market.[76] The political changes in Poland in 2015 are a contributing factor, but they are not the only reason for this development. Makarska speculates that the relatively stable interest in other countries' literatures between the end of the Communist period and at least 2015 could be attributed to more solid support structures for cultural collaboration during that period, rather than being directly related to political changes or the nature of the works themselves.[77] The 2023 literature festival Literacki Sopot in the city on the Polish Baltic coast indicates that funding and politics are in fact related, but it also points to the importance of nongovernmental support structures: after the Polish government declined financial support for the festival because Germany was the featured guest country, the needed funds were raised from other sources, including the European Commission and the Goethe Institut.[78] Thus, literary knots between Germany and Poland have always existed, but they also always depend on people's active engagement with each other's literatures and cannot be taken for granted.

Terms of Entanglement:
From Borders to Border Poetics

Another measure of entanglement between Polish and German literary histories lies in the mutual intelligibility of terms. Terminology is steeped in historical developments and political conditions, but transfers between languages, histories, and localities can also obscure their specific contexts. German "Grenze," "Grenzland," "Grenzliteratur," and "Grenzlandliteratur" and Polish "literatura kresowa," "kresy," "granica," "pogranicze" all address borders and literature about borders, but they also carry different (and often contested) meanings, depending on who uses them when and where. My use of the terms "border" and "borderlands" with regard to border poetics is in large part inspired by Gloria Anzaldúa's definition of the borderland, but it also contains the specifically Polish-German history and the divergent meanings that the English terminology conceals. Issues pertaining to translation and comparisons between original texts and their respective English, German, or Polish translations—or often the lack thereof—are addressed throughout this book, but even the terminology itself reveals these particularities and problems

76   Makarska, "Übersetzen zwischen Deutschland und Polen," 3, 5–7. Translations made up 19 percent of all new publications in 2020, down from 26 percent in the 1990s (2).

77   Makarska, "Übersetzen zwischen Deutschland und Polen," 2.

78   In an interview, the festival's director notes that Germany was chosen as the guest country because of the anti-German rhetoric and attacks on German-Polish relations by the governing party, PiS. This resulted in a decline of funding by the Polish Ministry of Culture. See Cichocka-Gula, "Literaturfestival," 00:00:32–00:01:30.

54 ♦ Entanglements in German and Polish History

of usage. A brief discussion of what could be termed "border literature" in Germany and Poland since 1945 will help explain how meanings have changed over time, and how these differences impact our conversations about German-Polish border narratives today. The following pages aim to highlight some of the complexity of these terms and show how translated, and thereby (successfully or unsuccessfully) transmitted, political histories and fluctuating meanings of border-related concepts inform the practice of border poetics. Since border poetics entails a critique of specific borders and borderlands, the border in border poetics carries within itself also this multiplicity of meanings.

In 1997, Stefan Chwin published an essay, simultaneously in Polish and in German translation, that provides an apt springboard for a discussion of some of these complexities. The essay, whose title can be translated into English as "Borderlands Literature and the Central European Dilemma," describes the development of Polish borderlands literature after the end of the Second World War and again after 1990. According to Chwin, Polish literature after 1945 initially served as a medium to deal with the aftermath of the war, expulsions and relocation, lost homes in the East, and new places in the formerly German territories. The texts produced at the time fit into the then current political narrative: omitting sensitive subject matter (e.g., the expulsion of Poles in the eastern territories by the Soviets) and underscoring the ethnic purity within— and hence the political stability of—the newly created Polish state. Dissenting narratives were silenced until the end of Communism. After 1989/90, political tensions between Germany and Poland and Polish concerns over the stability of the present political border initially heightened, but there was also an increased awareness of the long-suppressed transcultural and multiethnic histories of these border regions. For Chwin, this transformation went hand in hand with the emergence of a new "borderlands mentality" ("mentalność kresowa" or "Grenzlandmentalität") that included a softening of previously defensive attitudes.[79]

As a result of this softening, by the middle of the 1990s a literature gained prominence in Poland that Chwin terms "newest borderlands literature" ("najnowsza literatura pogranicza" or "neuste Grenzlandliteratur"). Works encompassed by this term were no longer just *about* the border in its divisive role, but they were now generated by the multiplicity of connecting experiences and exchanges that the same border also afforded. A new generation of authors began exploring the German-Polish past from a new perspective: They parted with stereotypical representations and a nostalgic view of a lost childhood in the east. Instead, they began to insist on mobile and "defocalized identities" ("nieostra tożsamość" or "unscharfe Identitäten"). Chwin considers those who inhabit the German-Polish borderland defocalized because their regional or

---

79 Chwin, "Grenzlandliteratur," 5–7. Page numbers refer to both the Polish original and the German translation of the essay. Where page numbers are not identical in each version, they are listed separately. All English translations are mine.

local affiliations did not align with the shifting borders of the nation. These inhabitants, he argues, came to understand the border space itself as dynamic and heterogeneous: it was German, Polish, regional, local, and global all at the same time. Chwin notes that after 1989, the term "borderlands" therefore did not just refer to the eastern and western borders of Poland but also became a "metaphor for the meeting of different cultures." A focus on the recovery of the hitherto silenced multicultural pasts of regions such as Pomerelia (Eastern Pomerania), Masuria, or Silesia was accompanied by a "general reflection on Europe's multicultural future."[80]

The essay further argues that Polish authors have not only "recovered" the formerly marginalized western borderlands as a central part of Polish self-understanding; they have also constructed and reconstructed them as a "general model" for European culture.[81] Chwin's choice of the word "recovered" ("odzyskane" or "wiedergewonnen") is telling here, as it plays on the term "ziemie odzyskane" used by Communist authorities after the Second World War. It refers to those territories that Poland "regained" or "recovered" from the Germans after the war, and it is controversial because it goes back to an idea of Poland as it existed in the Middle Ages. These territories, however, had never been "Polish" in the modern understanding of the term. Still, after the Second World War, the term was used to foster national unity and homogeneity by establishing a continuity with a long-bygone past and to emphasize Poland's rightful claims to these territories.[82] By using the term in this way, Chwin turns it on its head: instead of signifying national homogeneity, the term now means multicultural relations, contact, and exchange.

At times Chwin moves somewhat confusingly between Poland's eastern and western borderlands, but he establishes the "broadly understood 'western borderlands'" (i.e., referring to a ubiquitous nonterritorial border) as the "symbol of a postulated value system" and cultural model.[83] This conflation of different borders, and the broad brushstrokes with which he paints the borderland as a beacon for a Western-oriented and European "value system," are not without problems, but they fit the essay's programmatic tone and provide impulses for a critical reevaluation of various borderlands narratives. Also striking is the emphasis Chwin places on the diversity of the borderland while considering only *Polish* authors concerned with the *Polish* borderlands in his definition of "Grenzlandliteratur." Even though Chwin claims to look at the border as a "cultural model" for Europe, he does so from a single—a Polish—perspective. Consequently, he does not address the various and quite different connotations that the very term "borderlands literature" has in German and in

---

80   Chwin, "Grenzlandliteratur," 8–9.

81   Chwin, "Grenzlandliteratur," 6–7; "Literatura pogranicza," 5–7.

82   Porter-Szűcs, *Poland in the Modern World*, 201.

83   Chwin, "Grenzlandliteratur," 6; "Literatura pogranicza," 5–6.

56 ◆ Entanglements in German and Polish History

Polish. I want to take these additional steps here, as they are crucial for telling a story about borders as contact zones and about border poetics.

Throughout the original Polish essay, Chwin uses different terms for what appears in the German-language version only as "Grenzland" (borderland) and compounds thereof. The Polish terms range from "pogranicze" to "kresy" to "granica." The term "pogranicze," which also appears in the essay's title, means "borderland," and it is often used with the intention of sounding more neutral.[84] The other terms, "kresy" or "literatura kresowa," as well as their equivalents in the German translation, "Grenzland" or "Grenzlandliteratur," carry a range of different connotations.[85] The essay's translator is sensitive to the varying meanings and provides the corresponding original Polish expression in parentheses. Since Chwin does not elaborate on the differences in terminology, this fact goes unexplained and perhaps remains even unnoticed by the average German-language reader. Also problematic in German, the term "Grenzlandliteratur" has traditionally been used for nationalist and völkisch literature, especially of the 1920s and 1930s, yet this context is omitted entirely. Still, not everything is a question of translation: Because Chwin's main concern is with the period after 1989, he himself refers to what is traditionally understood as "literatura kresowa"—namely, literature about Poland's eastern borderlands—only briefly. Likewise, as his focus is solely on Polish literature, "Grenzlandliteratur" and its original meaning are not discussed. Nevertheless, there is a continuity, as well as a certain discontinuity, between "new borderlands literature" ("neue Grenzlandliteratur") and its various iterations and predecessors. In order to achieve transborder significance, let alone serve as a European "model of culture," the concept of a new borderlands literature should include a reflection on this multinational, multiregional, and multilingual genealogy. It is through the differences that the progression of borderlands literature from writing *about* the border (and treating it as a dividing line) to being generated by it (and acknowledging it as a multiply entwined contact zone) becomes visible.

A similar problem of loss in translation applies to "literatura kresowa." The related Polish terms, "kresy" or "kresy Wschodnie," refer mainly to the formerly Polish territories in the east that had been annexed by the Soviet Union following the Molotov-Ribbentrop Pact and the invasion of the eastern territories in 1939. Today these regions are part of Ukraine, Belarus, and Lithuania, and they include as their major cities Lviv (formerly Polish Lwów, German

---

84   Czaplejewicz, "Jakie Kresy," 4. See also Orłowski, "Grenzlandliteratur," 17. For an overview of the history of kresy literature and its main currents, see Czapliński, "Shifting Sands."

85   For Krzysztof Kwaśniewski, "pogranicze" is a symmetrical term because it places no emphasis on either side of the border. By contrast, "literatura kresowa" designates for him a Polish perspective. Cited in Czaplejewicz, "Jakie Kresy," 1.

Lemberg) and Vilnius (formerly Wilno, Wilna).[86] The Bug River, which today constitutes significant stretches of the Polish-Belarusian and Polish-Ukrainian borders, occupies a central place in kresy mythology, and it plays an important role in the literature about this region. Expressions such as "zza Buga" (from behind the Bug) in reference to the kresy region or the Poles who have come from there also illustrate the river's role in mapping the region's mental geography. This function is also evident in some of the works I discuss later, where the Bug River represents an important boundary. In Sabrina Janesch's *Katzenberge*, the main protagonist crosses the national border at the Bug into a dark and unknown territory to backtrack her grandfather's escape west some sixty years earlier. In Inga Iwasiów's *Bambino*, "behind the Bug" is the homeland of one of the protagonists, who is forced to contend with stereotypes of backwardness that are associated with the region. Many literary works also deal with how Poles who were expelled from the eastern territories during and after the Second World War often ended up settling in the newly Polish western areas that had previously been inhabited by Germans.[87] Despite its originally very specific history, Chwin uses the term "kresy" mostly to mean borderlands generally, which reflects a newer and more universal application of the term in some scholarship.[88] But even if the term's geographic and historical specificity may gradually recede into the background, it remains an important context to consider when identifying a new, transnational borderlands literature.

There may also be limits to using the term "Grenzlandliteratur," and German literary production cannot be easily integrated into the concept of a "new borderlands literature" without a critical examination of the term. Germanist Hubert Orłowski explains that the term "Grenzlandliteratur" was established by National Socialist literary scholars to refer to a literary genre that staged the defense of Germany's borders, particularly against a feared Slavic expansion from the east.[89] Scholars, however, have also complicated various assumptions about the genre. Using the German-Czech case, Karsten Rinas shows that "Grenzlandliteratur," with its aggressive nationalist and propagandistic tone, was not a specifically German phenomenon but had variants on both sides of the border. He therefore argues for broadening the concept to include other nationalist literatures and to also take earlier works into account.[90] Jürgen Joachimsthaler takes such a more entangled approach when he examines the ways in which German literature has engaged and contended with central Europe's cultural diversity from the eighteenth century to

86   For more on the term "kresy" and its distinction from "Galizien" (Galicia), see, for example, Schimsheimer, "Galizien und die Kresy."
87   For a historical view, see, for example, Halicka, *Polens Wilder Westen*; and Ther, *Deutsche und polnische Vertriebene*. Polish writers who address the topic of "kresy" are, for example, Czesław Miłosz, Tomasz Różycki, Andrzej Stasiuk, and Adam Zagajewski.
88   Handke, "Przedmowa," 7.
89   Orłowski, "Grenzlandliteratur," 10–11.
90   Rinas, 118, 147–49, 155.

58   ♦   ENTANGLEMENTS IN GERMAN AND POLISH HISTORY

the present. His extensive analysis also includes German "Ostmarkenliteratur" (East Prussian literature, a variation of "Grenzlandliteratur"). This type of literature pursued an ideological agenda that set up Poland and the Poles as negative Other to the Germans. The structures and inventory of stereotypes of Ostmarkenliteratur persisted after 1945, but Joachimsthaler also discusses authors who have attempted to complicate these narratives, including Sabrina Janesch and Tanja Dückers. The negative treatment and representation of Poland also elicited responses by Polish writers, and Joachimstaler refers to works by Bolesław Prus (1847–1912) as paradigmatic examples for the "Rückseite" (flipside) of "Ostmarkentextur."[91] By taking a more expansive and transborder view on established concepts, Rinas and Joachimsthaler thus offer new insights into national literatures.

The second objection to narrow understandings of "Grenzlandliteratur" is a temporal one: in particular, the notion in older German literary scholarship that "Grenzlandliteratur" ended or lost its significance by 1945.[92] More recently, scholars have pointed to the continuity of this type of literature after 1945, albeit with a different focus and under changed conditions.[93] Works included under the label of "Grenzlanditeratur" are diverse and range from dehistoricized and nostalgic views of the former homeland to its distanced and critical evaluation. With regard to the latter, Zbigniew Światłowski discusses a "neue Ostlandliteratur" (new East Prussian literature) or "neue 'Heimatliteratur'" that emerges in the postwar period and works against the romanticization of the lost homeland, and Tadeusz Namowicz examines a "Postheimatliteratur" that begins to take shape in the 1970s in West Germany.[94] Underlining the phenomenon's continuity, Orłowski also argues for the emergence of a "neue Grenzlandliteratur" after 1945. Based on an entirely new set of premises, this type of literature developed not only in the two German states but also in other East Central European national contexts; although it was especially pronounced in Germany and Poland.[95] Thus, in contrast to Chwin, Orłowski places the beginning of a "neue Grenzlandliteratur" before 1989, and, like Rinas, he also understands it in geographically more expansive terms.

Bożena Chołuj, a scholar of Polish-German literary and cultural relations, raises another important point that feeds into my later argument of the potential of border poetics as expression of subversion and resistance. Chołuj argues that "Grenzliteraturen" (border literatures)—that is, texts that could be

91   Joachimsthaler's study, *Text-Ränder*, consists of three volumes. For a discussion of the "flipside" of East Prussian literature, see 2:147–262. For a discussion of Prus, see 2:198–207. For Janesch and Dückers, see 2:260–62.

92   Namowicz, 77–78. He disagrees with the argument that East Prussian literature ended in 1945.

93   Orłowski, "Grenzlandliteratur," 15.

94   Światłowski, "Die neue 'Ostlandliteratur,'" 96; and Namowicz, "Zwischen Historizität und rückwärtsgewandter Utopie," 78, 86–88.

95   Orłowski, "Grenzlandliteratur," 15.

subsumed under the categories of new and newest borderlands literature—seek active engagement with the in-betweenness of the borderland, and they also have "subversive Effekte" (subversive effects). In this view, borderlands produce a particular literary constellation, and the border needs to be considered in its divisive but also in its connective qualities. Border literatures themselves are "Kulturräume" (cultural spheres) that only partially align with political borders and that represent and produce "Mischkulturen" (mixed cultures). Furthermore, border literatures are about borders while at the same time producing them performatively.[96] In these border narratives, border zones are marked by multiplicity and dynamism and variously entangled border experiences. Chołuj does not speak of these cultural spheres in terms of border poetics, but it is precisely these ambiguous in-between spaces that motivate border poetics. Rethinking these spaces does not homogenize their historical and social diversity, nor does it mean that in-between equals emptiness or a sense of being "torn" between two sides. Rather, and as I discuss in more detail in the next chapter, spaces and moments of transdifference emerge—this means that differences, including the conflicts resulting from them, are brought into contact with one another and are temporarily suspended to imagine new ways of being in the world.

In sum, today some scholars use the notion "Grenzlandliteratur" to reflect but also to go beyond the term's nationalist and völkisch associations, others employ alternative formulations such as "Literatur der Grenze" (Lamping) or "Grenzliteratur" (as Chołuj does, and which can also refer to literature about divided Germany), and still others use the term "Grenzlandliteratur" simply to refer to contemporary phenomena, without reflecting on the term's nationalist and racist history.[97] "Literatura kresowa" has undergone its own transformations and has been updated to be broader and more inclusive. Within the context of this study, the terms "border" and "borderland" most certainly carry the weight of their historical contexts and developments. At the same time, they also stand for something new that allows for a refocusing of the discussion toward contemporary borderlands literature as a transborder phenomenon with the kind of subversive potential that Chołuj describes. The question of when exactly this kind of "new" borderlands literature begins, and in what ways 1945 and 1989 mark different breaks in its development, requires a more thorough study of texts written in German or Polish and from different time periods and geographic regions. Suffice it here to say that border narratives are always updated in light of the changed political and social conditions under which they were written and to which they respond. The borderland therefore holds a continuing relevance as a topic, motif, and structural element of narratives. We should consider it not only within one historical context but also across borders, and across not only territorial or political borders but other

96   Chołuj, "Grenzliteraturen und ihre subversiven Effekte," 84.
97   See, for example, Peter, "Grenzlandliteratur."

60 ♦ Entanglements in German and Polish History

kinds of boundaries as well. In this sense, border literature or borderlands literature, as I understand it here, is a set of narrative engagements with border spaces across different types of borders, spaces, and time periods.

The reassessment of terminology, as I have discussed it here, as well as a consideration of larger conceptual frameworks and contexts became both possible and prominent when Polish and German scholars and cultural actors began to view their respective national and local histories within more broadly European structures following the political and social changes of the 1990s.[98] These transformations in scholarship paved the way for an entangled literary history, and, needless to say, they happened in tandem with changes in the literary landscape and the texts themselves. In German literature, these transformations must be understood within the context of broader historical, political, and social changes since the 1990s that have affected the way in which Germans remember and interpret East and West German history. At the same time, the "Wende" (turnaround) of 1989/90 has also triggered a "Wende des Erinnerns," a turn in how Germans remember their country's National Socialist past. In literary works, this paradigmatic change is evident in a shift in focus to bystanders and perpetrators as a critical and often irritating probe into German history.[99] Furthermore, interest in topics of flight and expulsion have instigated new debates on the question of German victimhood, but they have also produced a more differentiated view of collective and individual memory.[100] For Polish literature, Chwin describes the emergence of a "newest borderlands literature" since the 1990s, and he refers to a type of literature that is more cognizant of Poland's multiethnic past. Likewise, Przemysław Czapliński speaks of "shifting sands" and explains Polish literature's increasing interest in uncovering the traces of this past in the present.[101] Clearly, a reorientation in writing about the past has taken place, and it has impacted both German and Polish literature. It has also affected the way in which Polish-German topics have been discussed in the decades following the end of the Cold War.

Referring mostly, but not exclusively, to contemporary German literature, Petra Fachinger and Werner Nell note in a 2009 special issue of *seminar* that a new generation of writers has emerged in both countries who deal in a more conciliatory tone with the complicated German-Polish past than their predecessors. They describe the texts discussed as sharing a desire to overcome the traumatic past that has so long stood between Poland and Germany. Even

98 Eigler, "Introduction," 3–4.

99 Beßlich, Grätz, and Hildebrand, *Wende des Erinnerns*, 7–8. For an insightful analysis of transformations in Holocaust memory, see also Kim, *Cosmopolitan Parables*, esp. 62–78.

100 Beßlich, Grätz, and Hildebrand, *Wende des Erinnerns*, 12–13.

101 Czapliński identifies four main types of shifts within the history of Polish prose. Those concern geography, class, ideology, and ethnicity. For more on the shift "from geopolitics to geopoetics," see Czapliński, "Shifting Sands," 373–80.

if they do not always succeed, the authors of these works try to break with stereotypical representations and, rather than showcasing German, Polish, or Jewish identities, seek to present a variability of experiences and actions. German authors no longer seek to "legitimize political or even racist claims," and they explore German-Polish history through the lens of the individual or the family. It has also become more common to explore the issue of "suffering on both sides" without questioning German guilt and responsibility. For this generation of writers, the transformation in collective memory is evident in the desire "to escape the traumatic legacy of the past, as seen through the specifically German, Polish, or Jewish lens, by attempting to offer a new set of individual experiences and ways of dealing with them. The texts that are influenced by current theories of memory . . . especially express discomfort with the old stereotypes and the narratives to which they gave rise." Even though these texts aim to deconstruct old narratives, however, "they sometimes seem also to express a certain fascination for the alleged 'otherness' of Poland and the Poles."[102] The generation of writers fostering the kinds of changes that Fachinger and Nell describe is often referred to as the "Enkelgeneration" (generation of grandchildren) of postwar literature. Its arrival to German literature was announced in 1999 by journalist and literary critic Volker Hage who argued that these authors were less burdened with the past than the generation that preceded them.[103] Subsuming these authors under one category regardless of their very different experiences, attitudes, and writing styles also has its limitations, however. The concept does not apply to Polish literature and is therefore less useful when attempting a more entangled perspective that aims to focus on connections.

Despite persistent divisions present in many border novels, for example, in the form of stereotypes, omissions or gaps, we can also sense an increasing acknowledgment of German-Polish connections, both within and outside the boundaries of the text. Such works and authors push against divisions, and they continuously work toward unsettling the traditional boundaries of "Grenzland" or "kresy" literature. This rethinking or reimagining of the borderlands results in more entangled narratives, and those call for a more entangled literary history. To fully appreciate these transformations in German and Polish border(lands) literature and to better understand what is at stake in them, there is much to gain from considering them within the broader context of a revival of cosmopolitanism, to which I refer in the introduction. Border poetics and my conceptual framing of it is an invitation to examine literary texts from a cosmopolitan and transborder perspective and within an open comparative framework. This expanded view decenters questions of national spaces and identities, as well as ideas of generational cohesion. Even though the notion of new or newest borderlands literature as outlined above can be

---

102 Fachinger and Nell, "Introduction," 192.
103 Hage, "Die Enkel kommen," 245.

regarded as a "transborder" literature, and even though it marks a kind of generational shift that corresponds to a more transnational or global mindset, those frameworks have so far still done only scant justice to narratives that complicate spatial and geopolitical relations through other, more figurative kinds of border crossings that push against ontic and epistemic boundaries. Border poetics emerges from the rich historical and cultural context as well as terminological and linguistic complications that I have outlined. It originates from the transcultural impulse of the newest borderlands literature, but it takes the proliferation of borders further. As narrative and cultural practice, border poetics is centrally determined by a particular situation, location, and context, but it also transcends these affiliations in complicated ways. Most importantly, it denotes not just a thematic orientation but rather a way of viewing, understanding, and making the world.

2: Border Poetics

> *. . . all stories require borders and border crossings . . .*
> —Susan Stanford Friedman, "Spatial Poetics," 196

> *The objective space of a house—its corners, corridors, cellar, rooms—*
> *is far less important than what poetically it is endowed with, which*
> *is usually a quality with an imaginative or figurative value we*
> *can name and feel; thus a house may be haunted or homelike, or*
> *prisonlike or magical. So space acquires emotional and even rational*
> *sense by a kind of poetic process, whereby the vacant or anonymous*
> *reaches of distance are converted into meaning for us here.*
> —Edward Said, *Orientalism*, 55

> *In today's world, to be an inhabitant of a particular place means to*
> *become conscious that we exist on the pages of a palimpsest.*
> —Przemysław Czapliński, "The 'Mythic Homeland,'" 364

WHAT DOES IT MEAN to "exist on the pages of a palimpsest"? Can we see the world as a manuscript whose pages are constantly being rewritten, but which still bear the traces of all inscriptions that came before? Do these traces contain new opportunities to belong, and how do we—as those who exist on those pages—connect ourselves to them? Both Edward Said and Susan Stanford Friedman offer possible answers to these questions: one, we endow that which is distant and unfamiliar with meaning; and two, we cross the border into the pages of the palimpsest and tell stories. Inspired by French philosopher Gaston Bachelard's metaphorical use of a house to explain the "poetics of space," Said highlights objective and subjective notions of space. He describes how objective reality is made subjective through a poetic process that is both rational (reflected in the ability to name an object's "value") and emotional (through the creation of emotional ties with this objective reality). Going beyond the spatial, Said also applies this same poetic, "imaginative, quasi-fictional" quality to time, asserting that "imaginative geography and history help the mind to intensify its own sense of itself by dramatizing the distance and difference between what is close to it and what is far away."[1] Przemysław Czapliński articulates this sentiment with reference to narratives and stories when he says that "a place can be a homeland only on the

---

1   Said, *Orientalism*, 55.

64   ◆   BORDER POETICS

condition that it can tell us a story; and it can speak only as text, plot, narration." This kind of "narrative work" also includes the willingness and ability to read palimpsests.[2] I draw from these ideas that a sense of belonging arises from a dynamic narrative process that creates opportunities to connect with those within and beyond our temporal and spatial horizons. Through narratives we not only imagine but also create and shape global, national, regional, local, and personal connections. Literature is part of the narrative constitution of the world, and, because of its ambiguous relationship to reality, it provides unique opportunities to establish connections outside conventional or stereotypical patterns. Literary narratives are therefore not detachments from reality but rather attempts to create attachments and reconnect with the world. They thus have the potential to be tools for cosmopolitan world-making.

In the field of world literature, scholars have been working through various inflections of the idea of world or world-making, and notions of "world" or "cosmos" are also at the heart of cosmopolitan thinking. It is therefore necessary to address these concepts here briefly, but I recognize that others have done so in much greater depth and in dialogue with the long philosophical and literary tradition of the meaning of "world."[3] What is most pertinent here is that the very idea of "world" presents a major challenge to the imagination. It is an abstract concept that lies outside any one individual's experience, and its spatial and temporal dimensions cannot be accessed directly. Bachelard and Said get to the heart of this problem with the metaphor of the house—a space that stands for a portion of the world and that is made hospitable through processes of imagination and narrative work. In other words, to acquire rational and emotional significance, "world" must be made conceivable by establishing connections with multiple smaller (e.g., national, regional, local) and therefore more (or less) familiar realms or "worlds" that an individual inhabits and has already endowed with various degrees and layers of particular meaning.

Making the unfamiliar meaningful and giving it a narrative requires imaginative labor, but this process does not eliminate disturbances, gaps, and disorientations. As the imagination strives to relate the often fractured particular experiences to a sense of something whole or universal, it must also devise strategies for dealing with these disruptions. Said expresses this ambiguity when he describes the spaces of a house as simultaneously "homelike" or "magical" and "haunted" or "prisonlike." The borderland is especially potent with such disturbances. These unresolved tensions motivate border poetics, where the subjective perception of local spaces serves as a starting point for entwining the particular—that which is grounded in individual experiences— with the universal: that which depends on abstraction and intensified imaginative labor to acquire meaning. Border poetics constructs "world" from the

2   Czapliński, "The 'Mythic Homeland,'" 364–65.
3   For example, Cheah, *What Is a World?*; Ganguly, *This Thing Called the World*; Hayot, *On Literary Worlds*; and Puchner, "Teaching Worldly Literature."

perspective of various intersections and makes it visible as a network of flexible and highly mobile constellations of belonging. I argue later that this kind of world-making and endowing a place with meaning can also be viewed as cosmopolitan "claim-making," but let me first clarify what I mean by poetics.

"Being imagined is the first stage of existence," and borders are "first and foremost ideational before they are material."[4] Encapsulated in these two statements is the fundamental relationship between "imagining" and "making" that is the very basis of poetics as I am using it in this study. This understanding builds on the meaning of Greek *poiesis*, which translates as "to make" or "to create."[5] According to philosopher Richard Kearney, it refers to the creation of new worlds in which reality and imagination are interdependent.[6] Imagining is understood as an individual act, but it is also defined by, and in turn defines, the larger social context and an individual's place in society. Kearney draws on the deep connection between imagination and world-making when he describes the faculty of the imagination as "the human power to convert absence into presence, actuality into possibility, what-is into something-other-than-it-is." Imagination, he continues, refers to the "ability to transform the time and space of our world into a specifically human mode of existence (*Dasein*)."[7] In this book, I therefore refer to poetics as a form of the social imagination, as put forth by Arjun Appadurai in his study *Modernity at Large* (2003). This means that poetics entails the production of meaning, and it constitutes a kind of world-making activity. Border poetics models a distinct— a cosmopolitan—kind of world-making that expresses an ethical stance and asks us to consider border spaces and border experiences in more interconnected and entangled ways.

Border poetics, as a narrative practice, follows a multidimensional approach to borders: It examines possible or impossible border crossings, engages with their mechanisms of inclusion and exclusion, and interrogates their conditions of establishment, existence, and maintenance. This chapter, however, does not aim to produce a definite theory of border poetics. The goal is rather to work through some themes addressed in the border novels I discuss in part II of this book and to create nodal points between different concepts and theories that I regard as central to understanding border poetics on a conceptual level. The result should be an open associative framework that links borders, cosmopolitanism, and the literary imagination.

---

4   Tokarczuk, "Nobel Lecture," 23. The original reads, "to, co wyobrażone, jest pierwszym stadium istnienia"; "Przemowa noblowska," 23. Halle, "Views from the German-Polish Border," 77.
5   Oxford English Dictionary Online, "poiesis, n." OED Online. March 2023. Oxford University Press, www.oed.com. See also Gourgouris, "Poiesis."
6   Kearney, *Poetics of Imagining*, 97.
7   Kearney, *Poetics of Imagining*, 4.

66 ◆ BORDER POETICS

Cosmopolitan Imagination, Cosmopolitan Style

Narrators play a crucial role in determining whether and how a work of fiction mediates a cosmopolitan outlook. Rebecca Walkowitz, for example, has pointed out that "decentering the first-person point of view" is one of "the principal hallmarks of modernist fiction" and part of a "cosmopolitan style."[8] Destabilizing or unsettling the narrator is thus not a new strategy, but it is a particularly prominent one in border poetics, and one to which I return in the fourth chapter. Olga Tokarczuk underscores the importance of the narrator for a more ethical narrative mode in her 2019 Nobel lecture. In it, she criticizes the current predominance of the self-centered first-person narrator and articulates the need for more entangled ways of thinking. Arguing that we need new narrative approaches to counter the individual's experiences of atomization and fragmentation, Tokarczuk calls for a "new kind of narrator—a 'fourth person' one, . . . who manages to encompass the perspective of each of the characters, as well as having the capacity to step beyond the horizon of each of them, who sees more and has a wider view, and who is able to ignore time."[9] This sensitive and feeling or "tender narrator" ("czuły narrator") should provide a comprehensive narrative perspective.[10] It should offer a view of the world that acknowledges the interconnectedness of all things, even if the connections are not immediately apparent. It is based on Tokarczuk's conviction "that every gesture 'here' is connected to a gesture 'there,' that a decision taken in one part of the world will have an effect in another part of it, and that differentiating between 'mine' and 'yours' starts to be debatable."[11]

Some scholars and critics have wondered how the tender narrator differs from the omniscient narrator or why a new narrative category is needed in the first place, and they have suggested that this narrator is a purely utopian construct.[12] Tokarczuk does not provide clear answers to these questions, but

---

8   Walkowitz, *Cosmopolitan Style*, 80.

9   Tokarczuk, "Nobel Lecture," 21. The original reads, "Marzy mi się także nowy rodzaj narratora—'czwartoosobowego,' który . . . potrafi zawrzeć w sobie zarówno perspektywę każdej z postaci, jak i umiejętność wykraczania poza horyzont każdej z nich, który widzi więcej i szerzej, który jest w stanie zignorować czas"; "Przemowa noblowska," 21.

10   Translators Jennifer Croft and Antonia Lloyd Jones opted to translate "czuły narrator" as "tender narrator." The Polish adjective "czuły" or the noun "czułość" also encompass sensitivity and the idea of feeling for others.

11   Tokarczuk, "Nobel Lecture," 21. The original reads, "staje się oczywiste, że każdy gest 'tu' jest powiązany z gestem 'tam,' że decyzja podjęta w jednej części świata poskutkuje efektem w innej jego części, że rozróżnienie na 'moje' i 'twoje' zaczyna być dyskusyjne"; "Przemowa noblowska," 21.

12   These questions are discussed by Katarzyna Kantner and Krzysztof Koehler in a podcast by the National Centre for Culture Poland; Oklińska, "Czy czuły narrator

she emphasizes that the tender narrator is not a grammatical issue. Rather, it is a matter of *how* a story is structured or written—a new, more deeply connected mode of storytelling. My later discussions of novels by Günter Grass, Inga Iwasiów, and Sabrina Janesch demonstrate that the phenomenon of (or at least the aspiration toward) this type of narrator precedes its articulation by Tokarczuk and that it is a key strategy of border poetics. Still, Tokarczuk's term is helpful as it encapsulates a particular narrative stance that manifests a "cosmopolitan style"; that is, the politically charged narrative strategy that Walkowitz has identified in "novels that develop and examine new attitudes of cosmopolitanism and do so in the service of a kind of critique."[13] I argue that the tender narrator's distinguishing characteristics vis-á-vis the omniscient narrator are its decidedly ethical stance and cosmopolitan sensitivity, which are independent of narrative perspective or voice.[14]

I see strong correspondences here between Tokarczuk's narrative vision and David Kim's call for a more entangled understanding of global histories of violence, a view that is reflected in his definition of cosmopolitanism as a "self-critical and melancholy exercise in sharing whereby traumatic experiences are related across cultural, national, and historical boundaries."[15] It is noteworthy that Tokarczuk and Kim both center melancholy and sharing as important aspects of an entangled understanding of the world, albeit from different perspectives. Tokarczuk does not use the term "cosmopolitanism," but the sentiment is clear when she explains that the narrator's tenderness "is spontaneous and disinterested; it goes far beyond empathetic fellow feeling. Instead, it is the conscious, though perhaps slightly melancholy, common sharing of fate."[16] In contrast to Kim, Tokarczuk is less explicit in her lecture about trauma and violence, but she addresses these issues powerfully throughout her oeuvre. With the "tender narrator," Tokarczuk asks for stories that both produce and are products of a cosmopolitan imagination: stories that reflect an acute sense of entanglement between an individual's emotions, experiences, and values,

---

istnieje." Tokarczuk provides no conclusive definition, but the genealogy of her thinking about the "tender narrator" and the process of writing through this kind of narrative lens becomes clearer in a collection of lectures and essays, published as *Czuły narrator*, the title of her Nobel lecture. For the book's German translation, see Tokarczuk, *Übungen im Fremdsein*. The Nobel lecture is included with its German title "Der liebevolle Erzähler" (269–97).

13 Walkowitz, *Cosmopolitan Style*, 4.

14 This point will become clearer in my discussion of narrative voice and narrative perspective in chapter 4, "Belonging: Defocalized Narratives by Günter Grass, Sabrina Janesch, and Olga Tokarczuk." Suffice it here to say that the tender narrator is a way of seeing, an attitude toward the story world, and as Tokarczuk stresses, not necessarily a way of speaking in a grammatical sense, although it can be expressed through grammar.

15 Kim, *Cosmopolitan Parables*, 10.

16 Tokarczuk, "Nobel Lecture," 24. The original reads, "Jest raczej świadomym, choć może trochę melancholijnym, współdzieleniem losu"; "Przemowa noblowska," 24.

68   ◆   Border Poetics

and things that are universal and shared across times and places. These stories must convey the awareness "that everyone and everything is steeped in one common notion, which we constantly produce in our minds with every turn of the planet."[17] This all-embracing stance is at the core of border poetics.

Scholars have described storytelling itself as a border-crossing practice because it requires both a border and the transgression of that border.[18] Phrased differently, narratives are fundamentally about acknowledging a disruption or border and establishing transborder connections—as tenuous or fleeting as those might be. This double process is intensified in border poetics where the border-crossing practice of storytelling is placed within an actual border space and is further amplified by real and figurative border-crossing experiences. These border crossings are rarely smooth and harmonious, and often violent and painful. And even though the novels presented here can be flawed and at times inadvertently set up new boundaries, they display a high level of reflection on gaps, breaks, and discontinuities along with an eagerness to work through them. These narratives negotiate meaning by assembling or reassembling fragments, filling in empty spaces, and devising alternative ways of creating meaning in a world that has been experienced as disjointed since modernity. They create webs, knots, and nodes of connection, and I therefore regard them as evidence of a "cosmopolitan imagination." From the perspective of critical social theory, Gerard Delanty has described this imagination as a response to the "overwhelming interconnectivity of the world."[19] It derives from a "critical cosmopolitanism" that entails the "capacity for self-problematization and new ways of seeing the world that result when diverse peoples experience common problems."[20] The daunting conditions of the present—an ever-accelerating globalization, inequalities, conflicts, and divisions—underscore the urgent need to foster and train such an imagination for the future. Border poetics is an essential element in this process.

So far, I have highlighted some aspects of the relationship between border poetics, the imagination, and cosmopolitanism, and I have pointed to storytelling as an exercise in entangled thinking. To crystallize these points, I want to return to my argument that border poetics is an idiom of the cosmopolitan imagination because it rests on the same productive tension between the particular and the universal that also drives contemporary notions of cosmopolitanism. As discussed in more detail in the introduction, I am inspired by earlier theorizations of border poetics, especially the work of Johan Schimanski

17   Tokarczuk, "Nobel Lecture," 22. The original reads, "iż wszyscy i wszystko zanurzone jest w jednym wspólnym wyobrażeniu, które za każdym obrotem planety pieczołowicie produkujemy w naszych umysłach"; "Przemowa noblowska," 21–22.

18   Friedman, "Spatial Poetics," 196. Friedman draws here especially on the work of Michel de Certeau and Franco Moretti. On narrative as border crossing, see also Schimanski, *Grenzungen*, 33–34.

19   Delanty, *The Cosmopolitan Imagination*, 1.

20   Delanty, *The Cosmopolitan Imagination*, ix.

and Stephen Wolfe. For them, border poetics is primarily a tool of analysis that scholars apply to the examination of multiple and overlapping real and figurative borders in literary and cultural works; that is, border aesthetics.[21] By shifting the focus toward border poetics as a narrative and cultural *practice* that significantly shapes the perception of borders and the construction of story worlds, I ask how narratives themselves examine and critique borders, and how writers translate their critique into aesthetic form. This change in perspective centers border poetics as a strategy of world-making. Two ideas about the imagination are essential to this understanding; namely, that the imagination is a key component of cosmopolitan thinking, as embodied by Tokarczuk's "tender narrator," and a view of the imagination as a social practice, as articulated by Arjun Appadurai in his influential study *Modernity at Large*. For Appadurai, the imagination is "an organized field of social practices, a form of work (in the sense of both labor and culturally organized practice), and a form of negotiation between sites of agency (individuals) and globally defined fields of possibility." As an important political and social force and a motor of change, it depends on material, physical, or psychological realities, but it also pushes against and reshapes these realities. Appadurai argues that "the imagination is now central to all forms of agency, is itself a social fact, and is the key component of the new global order."[22] A major challenge to the cosmopolitan imagination is how to conceptualize the notion of "world," and how to accommodate difference within that world.

Critical Cosmopolitanism and Transdifference

There is extant scholarship on the long and complex history of cosmopolitanism and its contemporary refigurations, and I focus here only on a few select aspects.[23] At its core, cosmopolitanism could be described as an ideal of a universal community of world citizens in which every person is considered an equal member. It relies on an understanding of the world as a totality that is bound together by certain shared ideas, values, and responsibilities. In a more traditional understanding, cosmopolitans do not have their home in a particular nation or state but have overcome such local attachments and parochialism and perceive themselves as citizens of the world. Contemporary

---

21   Schimanski and Wolfe, *Border Poetics De-Limited*, 10.

22   Appadurai, *Modernity at Large*, 31.

23   For critical discussions of cosmopolitanism, see, for example, Appiah, *Cosmopolitanism*; Brennan, *At Home in the World*; Cheah and Robbins, *Cosmopolitics*; Kleingeld and Brown, "Cosmopolitanism"; and Nussbaum, "Patriotism and Cosmopolitanism." The negative aspects of cosmopolitanism, especially its use as antisemitic epithet, is explored, for example, in Gelbin and Gilman, *Cosmopolitanisms and the Jews*. For how the concept is entwined with globalization and imperialism, see Kent and Tomsky, *Negative Cosmopolitanism*.

cosmopolitanism, by contrast, is based on an understanding of world as multiplicity, and it asks how different worlds can be reconciled. It is the very composition of these worlds and the relations between them that occupies the tender narrator and drives border poetics: How is it possible to reconcile the multiple distinct, familiar spheres and the notion of world as an all-encompassing totality? As I discuss below, scholars have approached this conceptual gap in at least two ways. First, the idea of universalism as relating to a harmonious and unified whole has become a matter of debate and is being reexamined in light of the ideologies in which it has also been implicated. Second, there is an emphasis on cosmopolitanism's dependence on the simultaneity of rootedness and belonging to a specific local, regional, or national setting, on the one hand, and the transcendence of that setting and the participation in a universally conceived community, on the other hand. Border poetics, then, reflects a way of thinking about the world that is informed by a more plural and critical understanding of both cosmopolitanism and universalism.

While the orientation toward the universal is one of the underlying principles of the cosmopolitan idea, this very connection has also been the basis for staunch criticism. In such critiques, universalism is often faulted for violently imposing a Westerncentric normativity and promoting homogenization by dismissing the particular. Scholars from various fields have engaged with such critiques. For example, Daniel Chernilo examines the philosophical tradition of universalism as the basis of cosmopolitanism, and he makes three points that are especially relevant here. First, he shows that cosmopolitanism and universalism are not exclusive to "Western" thought and that they also predate the emergence of what we today consider "the West." Second, cosmopolitanism's universalism derives from an awareness of disintegration and crisis (initially of the Greek polis) and the concurrent desire to overcome the disintegration. It is therefore "a way of imagining a strong sense of unity *because current situations precisely emphasise difference, conflict, and change.*"[24] It bears repeating that the current revival of interest in cosmopolitanism began with the fundamental restructuring of the political and social world order after the end of the Cold War and the concomitant disarray and violence that spread across Europe and globally.[25] Chernilo underscores universalism's imaginative capacity and its foundation on the idea of unity through diversity. From this point he derives a third, which is that universalism does not occlude a view of the particular but rather "creates the very framework that makes such recognition and acceptance possible."[26]

In unpacking the idea of the universal, Chernilo is in conversation with scholarship that emphasizes cosmopolitanism's inherent plurality. Similarly,

24   Chernilo, "Cosmopolitanism and the Question of Universalism," 49–51, here 51; emphasis in original.
25   Kim, *Cosmopolitan Parables*, esp. 6–10.
26   Chernilo, "Cosmopolitanism and the Question of Universalism," 57.

Delanty focuses on diversity and proposes the notion of a "critical cosmopolitanism" as one that "is critical and dialogic, seeing as the goal alternative readings of history and the recognition of plurality."[27] While Delanty makes a semantic shift and argues that critical cosmopolitanism is actually "post-universal" because it "stands for a universalism that does not demand universal assent or that everyone identify with a single interpretation," his focus on openness and a drive toward self-examination are significant here.[28] Critical cosmopolitanism, he argues, is "an open process by which the social world is made intelligible; it should be seen as the expression of new ideas, the opening spaces of discourse, identifying possibilities for translation and the construction of the social world."[29] Border poetics follows the same principle when more-universally conceived borders or border-crossing experiences aid in understanding specific situations and conditions.

In the contemporary understanding, cosmopolitanism not only deconstructs or decenters the "universal" but also acknowledges its dynamic relationship with various forms of the particular, including regionalism, patriotism, or nationalism.[30] Scholarship today focuses on integrating long-presumed contradictions within the notion of cosmopolitanism; for example, through ideas of a "rooted cosmopolitanism," "regional cosmopolitanism," or a "situated" or "locally inflected" cosmopolitanism.[31] In these studies, cosmopolitanism does not represent an ahistorical ideal of a harmonious and detached humanity. Rather, this critical cosmopolitanism derives from a conviction that being a citizen of the world and a citizen of one's locality not only mutually reinforce one another but that these attachments are built through complex entanglements and negotiations between varied forms and levels of belonging that are situational and changeable. Within the German-Polish context, this sentiment is expressed in the notion of "open regionalism" ("otwarty regionalizm"). The concept was first proposed by Polish historian Robert Traba, and it essentially builds on the idea of a cosmopolitan constellation that begins from the local and opens up to a wider network. Open regionalism takes a decidedly practical stance and follows the motto "Think universally, act locally!" Its underlying belief is that the active engagement with local conditions and histories leads to a better understanding of oneself, one's neighbor, and Europe—and even "universal reality." Or, put differently, knowledge about the universal can only be gained through a critical examination of the particular, including its negative

---

27   Delanty, *The Cosmopolitan Imagination*, 35.

28   Delanty, "The Idea of Critical Cosmopolitanism," 42.

29   Delanty, *The Cosmopolitan Imagination*, 78.

30   See, for example, Brennan, *At Home in the World*; Clifford, *Routes*; and Nussbaum, "Patriotism and Cosmopolitanism."

31   Appiah, "Rooted Cosmopolitanism"; Robbins, "Introduction Part I"; and Berman, "Regional Cosmopolitanism."

72 ♦ Border Poetics

aspects, and those particulars must be evaluated within broader frameworks, such as national and transnational (especially European) contexts.[32]

As the cosmopolitan imagination strives to find a balance between the local and the global, between the particular and the universal, it must deal with the awareness of difference. In trying to comprehend this challenge while at the same time letting go of the idea that it is somehow a problem that needs to be solved, I find the idea of "transdifference" to be particularly enriching. The concept was developed by Helmbrecht Breinig and Klaus Lösch, and it describes the instantaneous process whereby difference is at once maintained and temporarily suspended. This nonlinear and nonbinary concept "refers to whatever runs 'through' the line of demarcation drawn by binary difference. It does not do away with the originary binary inscription of difference, but rather causes it to oscillate. The concept of transdifference interrogates the validity of binary constructions of difference without completely deconstructing them."[33] The notion of transdifference is illuminating with regard to border poetics, because it, too, does not aim to dissolve borders but seeks to critique them and bring them into oscillation. The particular and the universal, the familiar and the unfamiliar, can only be connected in this moment of openness and flexibility that is created by transdifference. I would even argue that it is *only* in these moments of oscillation that we can understand borders as what Chris Rumford calls "cosmopolitan workshops"; that is, as places where breaks, disruptions, and absences can be integrated into a radically expanded understanding of world without permanently defined boundaries.[34] This nonpermanence echoes an understanding of cosmopolitanism as a nonexistent but aspirational state of peaceful coexistence and equality, and it points to the futurity and utopian potential of border poetics.

Borders and Cosmopolitanism

Border poetics is at its core an optimistic, future-oriented practice, and it is so despite the divisiveness and violence of borders. In fact, it is precisely because borders mark a disruption and division that they inspire, or rather *demand*, a cosmopolitan imagination to devise alternatives to the existing reality. Much scholarship has framed cosmopolitanism as overcoming borders or as something that happens despite borders. Some scholars, however, have put borders themselves (including their invisible or symbolic iterations) at the center of their thinking about cosmopolitanism. Often this entails references to Étienne Balibar's much-cited ideas that "borders are vacillating," that they have dispersed throughout society and signify much more than a state's territorial

---

32 Traba and Loew, "Die Identität des Ortes," 100. My translation.
33 Breinig and Lösch, "Introduction," 23. For more on the concept, see also Lösch, "Begriff und Phänomen der Transdifferenz."
34 Rumford, *Cosmopolitan Borders*, 3.

boundaries, and that Europe itself must be considered a borderland.[35] The proliferation and dispersal of borders has obvious negative consequences as it turns borders into "Sortiermaschinen" ("sorting machines") that operate based on "desirable" and "undesirable" mobility.[36] At the same time, a multiplication of borders beyond a geopolitical demarcation of territory can trigger a corrosion of existing boundaries and a multiplication of possible contact zones between people and places, which can foster varying and changing affiliations and belongings. Gerard Delanty, for example, has argued that "European identity" is today "more diluted but also open to more interpretations."[37] When Rumford speaks of "cosmopolitan borders," he refers to the border-mobility of individuals, which is predicated not on "borderlessness but a proliferation of borders."[38] For Rumford, borders have become "engines of connectivity" that create "cosmopolitan opportunities through the possibility of cultural encounters and negotiation of difference." This feature is attributed to the fact that borders are no longer solely constructed and maintained by the nation-state but by "ordinary people" who are "making, shifting and removing borders."[39] Still, there is nothing ordinary or easy about cosmopolitanism, and Rumford views it as an "intervention" that requires an extraordinary amount of labor.[40] With Michel Agier, we can add that "ordinary cosmopolitanism"—that is, the border crossings and negotiations of border situations by nonstate actors—is not only an effort; it often occurs out of necessity for forced migrants who remain in border situations indefinitely and must adapt to new languages, rules, and customs.[41]

My objective here is not to view, in the highly securitized border regimes of today, opportunities for a cosmopolitan reality. First, I am not suggesting that violent borders are a precondition for cosmopolitanism, nor do I romanticize the dispersal and proliferation of bordering practices. Rather, I examine narratives that challenge divisive border regimes by thinking from the perspective of a border and by exposing their practices of violence and exclusion. Using various strategies of border poetics, writers transform borderlands into spaces of experimentation that foster a cosmopolitan imagination as an act of resistance against the status quo. Second, cosmopolitanism, like world literature, is a utopian project: always in the making; becoming rather than being.[42] According to Rumford,

35   Balibar, "The Borders of Europe," 219–20. See also Balibar, "Europe as Borderland."

36   Mau, *Sortiermaschinen.*

37   Delanty, *The Cosmopolitan Imagination*, 226.

38   Rumford, "Does Europe Have Cosmopolitan Borders," 328.

39   Rumford, *Cosmopolitan Borders*, 3.

40   Rumford, *Cosmopolitan Borders*, 10.

41   Agier, *Borderlands*, viii.

42   Johann Wolfgang von Goethe framed world literature as something that was "at hand," rather than a reality. Others have continued this line of thinking in their

74 ◆ BORDER POETICS

> Cosmopolitanism cannot be a new reality because it is evidence of incompleteness; its very existence is indicative that societies are characterized by fragmentation, transformation and multiplicity. Cosmopolitanism is likely to appear only under conditions in which identities are partially fixed and there is no firm barrier between, for example, inside/outside, self/other, individual/group. Moreover, there is no perspective from which we can view "cosmopolitan reality": the multiperspectival foundations of cosmopolitanism make it impossible to posit anything like a manifestation of cosmopolitan reality. In sum, cosmopolitanism is best thought of as an escape from permanence and solidity. A "cosmopolitan moment" would be fatally undermined by an attempt to make it more permanent and durable.[43]

Speaking perhaps more affirmatively, and applying this line of thinking to border poetics, I regard cosmopolitanism less as an escape from and more as an act of resistance against permanence and solidity, an act of imagining anew the structures of reality and making room for new ideas. This act is future-oriented, but it necessitates a critical engagement with the past and its political, cultural, and ethical implications—a process that Amir Eshel has described as "futurity" in connection with contemporary world literature.[44] Futurity refers to literature's ability to acknowledge "the pain of the past" and derive from it new possibilities. Although such literature deals with traumatic experiences, it also "presents us with an opportunity to imagine a better future."[45] The negotiation of the past and the future—with its openness to multiple perspectives and done in the spirit of a cautious optimism—also drives border poetics. I discuss Sabrina Janesch's *Katzenberge* in chapter 3, but it can serve here as an example of this negotiation. The novel tells the story of a young woman who travels east into present-day Ukraine to uncover a family secret. She thereby reverses a path that her grandfather was forced to take in 1943/44, when he had to flee from his home in Galicia. The narrator conveys the grandfather's traumatic experiences, but she also counters them with an optimistic and conciliatory perspective.

Both as a thematic focus in literature and as a theoretical concept that helps us think through the challenges of the present moment, the border's arbitrariness and fluidity can serve as a touchpoint for difficult explorations of the past and experimental thinking of alternatives. I am inspired by Rumford's insistence on the "centrality of borders to cosmopolitan thinking" and his view

---

conceptions of world literature, including Karl Marx and Friedrich Engels. Puchner, "Teaching Worldly Literature," 256.

43   Rumford, *Cosmopolitan Borders*, 10.

44   Eshel, *Futurity*, e.g., 4–5. I return to this concept in chapter 3, "Disruption: Fictions of Memory by Inga Iwasiów, Sabrina Janesch, and Tanja Dückers."

45   Eshel, *Poetic Thinking Today*, xii.

of borders as "cosmopolitan workshops."[46] Still, there is a lacuna in examining how literary and cultural production reflect on and at the same time contribute to the intricate connection between borders and cosmopolitanism, or, put differently, how the representation of borders in literature or other cultural expressions helps shape how humans imagine and negotiate (or "workshop") social practices that foster a vision of a shared humanity. Border poetics draws on the potential of borders to be sites of a cosmopolitan imagination, and it thereby promotes a multifaceted "seeing like a border" or reading as an act of multiple border crossings.[47] It challenges us as recipients of such works to consider how the actual physical spaces of the borderland and the borderlands of the imagination relate to one another, and it helps us better understand the interplay between the historical and political borders that regulate human movement, on the one hand, and the figurative boundaries that structure human perception and thinking, on the other hand. The cosmopolitan border novels that I discuss in part II of this book make visible where and how borders collide, intersect, entangle, or merge. By constructing narratives in this way, writers activate the border for their cosmopolitan world-making. These world-making strategies include a multiplication of perspectives and exchanges of people tied to different local contexts and a building of networks from these contacts. Even more, in literature these dynamic processes are often unconstrained: they can happen across vast spans of time, across faraway geographical regions, and even across languages. Such works destabilize established categories of difference and allow for the emergence of transdifference in its stead.

I stated earlier that the borderlands created by border poetics are spaces of transdifference; that is, spaces where difference is temporarily suspended. Balibar's description of borders as "vacillating" echoes in the idea that transdifference causes "binary inscription[s] of difference" to "oscillate."[48] This means that the borderland is, on the one hand, a deeply disjointed space in which reality is experienced as fractured and contradictory. On the other hand, borderlands invite alternate perspectives: splinters and fragments can be brought closer, stitched together, even if the bonds are fragile and may dissolve again at any moment. These tenuous entanglements are, for example, at the heart of Inga Iwasiów's novel *Bambino*, which I mentioned in the previous chapter and to which I return in the analysis. *Bambino* is set in a German-Polish borderland par excellence; namely, the now Polish city of Szczecin. The novel explores the messy affiliations and feelings of belonging, voluntary and forced, that are caused by geopolitical border changes as well as by the social norms and cultural boundaries that the protagonists have internalized. They come to the city after the Second World War with the hope for a new beginning. They

46 Rumford, *Cosmopolitan Borders*, 3.
47 Rumford, *Cosmopolitan Borders*, 18–19, 39–54; and Schimanski, "Reading Borders."
48 Breinig and Lösch, "Introduction," 23.

all find moments and spaces of transdifference here, but at the same time, their personal pasts as well as the historical legacies they carry impede their ability to form new lasting connections. Here and in the other examples I discuss, border poetics entails a working through a fluctuating network of disjointed histories and unstable senses of belonging. Nevertheless, it is made clear that a perpetual difference remains integral to the borderland. Border poetics approaches this difference without seeking to dissolve it, simply because it would be impossible to do so. But if difference cannot be dissolved, then it must be temporarily suspended to make space for new kinds of narratives, including better futures—even if those emerge only in the mind of the reader, and not for the protagonists. Border poetics does not aim to create a post-difference world in which all disruptions have been magically taken care of. Rather, it acknowledges the existence of borders and the violence that helped create them, but it also demands their simultaneous suspension and transcendence.

Transdifference also relates to questions of belonging and claim-making, and a helpful way to clarify this connection is via the notion of betweenness. I therefore end this section by creating another knot that brings these concepts closer together before turning more specifically to questions of memory and cosmopolitan claim-making in the next section. First, borderlands are frequently described as in-between spaces. In this view, borderlands are extended spaces of negotiation that result from the porousness of borders, their ambiguity, and the multiple contentious and peaceful contacts they facilitate. Still, some qualifications are required. "In-betweenness" does not need to signify a static and empty "no man's land," nor does it need to be read as just one more essentializing category, as Leslie Adelson has rightly criticized the proliferation of the "trope of 'betweenness.'"[49] Randall Halle has addressed this issue in his conceptualization of the "interzone," which he defines as an "ideational space, a sense of being somewhere that unites two places, if even only transitionally or temporarily."[50] Halle argues that betweenness can also be a productive notion and that these spaces are by no means empty. Rather, in the cinematic works he examines, "the 'neither, nor, and both' of the traveler is presented as a privilege," and it is a "cultural space of 'more than.'"[51] His description of the "interzone" as a "connecting zone" with its own "geopolitical relations" resonates with the borderlands constructed through border poetics.[52]

---

49   Adelson, "Against Between," 245. This negotiation of the in-between connects in particular to my analyses in chapter 4, where I discuss border narratives that articulate border crossings in the narrative mode of the fantastic. These texts represent different ways of coping with the disruptions caused by border transgressions. Moreover, the fantastic mode holds in balance the real and the supernatural—it creates an indeterminate and fluctuating in-between space that echoes the simultaneous suspension and maintenance of difference that is conceptualized in the notion of transdifference.

50   Halle, *The Europeanization of Cinema*, 4–5.

51   Halle, *The Europeanization of Cinema*, 167.

52   Halle, *The Europeanization of Cinema*, 4.

Susan Friedman likewise regards betweenness as productive, and she has criticized "the fixation on 'difference' . . . as a foundational principle in theorizing identity." She argues that this focus "tends to obscure the liminal space in between difference, the border space of encounter, interaction, and exchange, the space of relation and the narratives of identity such relations engender."[53] Friedman's and Halle's definitions of "between" are helpful for a better understanding of border poetics because they do not imply a space between two separate units (i.e., nations or cultures). Instead, this in-betweenness is a productive space of "transdifference," a space of constant movement and negotiation of various constellations of belonging. This indeterminacy can unsettle seemingly immutable paradigms (such as center/periphery) and reveal that these constellations are always subject to reimagination and change. Moreover, they "specify the liminal space in between, the interstitial site of interaction, interconnection, and exchange."[54] To the extent possible, I try not to rely too much on the term "identity" in this book. My focus, rather, is on belonging and affiliation, and thus on the deliberate practice of shaping narratives that push against the limitations that are often inscribed into notions of identity based on difference. It signals a shift in attention to the self as it is continuously involved in creating new constellations of belonging that enable cosmopolitan exchanges. Borderlands encompass many in-between spaces, and those offer a broad range of affiliations and constellations that can be claimed.

Memory, Storytelling, and Cosmopolitical Claim-Making

In thinking through borders as "cosmopolitan workshops," Rumford argues for an alliance-based understanding of bordering that relies on the agency of those engaging with borders. Such alliances emerge through "borderwork [that] can also be associated with a range of claims-making activity, not only claims to national belonging or citizenship, but also demands for transnational mobility, assertions of human rights, and demonstrations of political actorhood, all of which can comprise acts of citizenship." Borders thereby provide "opportunities for humanitarian assistance targeted at those (refugees, migrants) who may coalesce at the borders."[55] On the one hand, I find it difficult to fully appreciate situations that arise from highly securitized borders and that depend on the desperate needs of people seeking refuge as opportunities. On the other hand, I am interested in the claims-making opportunities that are built into the very structure of the borderland, and in particular the claim-making afforded by narratives wherein the border serves as a structural element of storytelling and world-making. The German-Polish borderland is a space organized by a

53   Friedman, "'Border Talk,'" n.p.
54   Friedman, *Mappings*, 3.
55   Johnson et al., "Interventions on Rethinking 'the Border,'" 68.

multitude of visible and invisible boundaries. In this context, claim-making is an attempt to establish locally and regionally specific continuities by inventing or re-creating narratives and by positioning oneself within those narratives. Memory is an essential element in this "symbolic act" of storytelling, which also aims to create connections beyond the local and the regional.[56] In this section, I explore how we might think about border poetics and its cosmo-political claim-making as an attempt to establish continuity by situating (disrupted) particular memories within more expansive, even global, contexts.

At its core, cosmopolitanism is concerned with overcoming fragmentation and disruption. In the Polish and German case, disruption is exemplified by historic border disputes and border shifts, and especially the traumatic experiences of the Second World War that are still deeply embedded in collective memory. The war and its aftermath—the expulsions, resettlements, and migration movements—upended lives and disturbed society at every level. People were forced to abandon their familiar surroundings and leave behind families and friends, houses, land, and personal belongings. This experience of a complete break only added to the trauma already produced by the war itself. For expellees and refugees, the new surroundings often appeared alien and even hostile because they were inhabited by someone else's history and memory. A perpetual sense of strangeness prevailed among the new inhabitants for many decades, and it was accompanied by feelings of insecurity caused by the lingering awareness that these regions were not as Polish as the Communist-led state insisted. German expellee organizations long held revisionist positions and refused to recognize the finality of the Polish-German border, which only intensified such anxieties. Under these conditions, how could the border be seen as anything but a dividing line?

Notwithstanding some notable literary exceptions, such as Christa Wolf in the GDR or Günter Grass in the FRG, the multiple layers of meaning beneath the patina of homogeneity—that is, the multiethnic reality and complex history of these places—was not publicly addressed until after the end of the Cold War. Only then could the borderland inhabitants, as well as scholars, activists, and other civil society actors, begin to openly examine the entangled narratives embedded in these regions.[57] For over three decades, artists and writers have played an important role in this process, and the sense of alienation among new arrivals continues to be a recurring theme in their work. Their reflections have helped remap the complex and fluid border landscapes by imagining new connections between people across different times and places. At times, a sense of entanglement could also be achieved by directly connecting the literary imagination with actual people and places. Here I return once

---

56 Seyhan, *Writing outside the Nation*, 4.

57 In the late 1980s and early 1990s the works of Stefan Chwin and Paweł Huelle were the most prominent examples of this trend in Poland. See also Iwasiów, "Die Ungeliebten."

more to Olga Tokarczuk, because her writing and involvement in these border-land communities has contributed to the critical and self-critical reevaluation of the borderlands and their role in Polish—and to some extent also German—collective memory.

In a 2001 essay about a gathering of former German and current Polish inhabitants in her hometown, Tokarczuk comments on the bifurcation of memory in the immediate aftermath of the Second World War and the per-manent mark left by traumatic experiences, disruption, and resettlement: "our predecessors have taken their memory with them, and we were thrown into a world without memory, and thus into a world that is incomprehensible, that resists appropriation, composed of fragments that the new inhabitants have brought here from many places."[58] She also insists that this split memory can and must be ameliorated. In a later essay, Tokarczuk named the psychological condition that afflicts the German-Polish borderland populations as result of this experience "Snow White syndrome" ("syndrom Królewny Śnieżki"). This condition is triggered at the moment of encounter with an unfamiliar space. As the first phase of expulsions was often implemented in haste, new occu-pants at times entered houses that were still warm from the previous owners or in which meals had been left out on the table. Even under the best of circum-stances, expellees had to leave most of their personal belongings behind.[59] "Snow White syndrome," Tokarczuk explains,

is based on the strange and somewhat unpleasant awareness that one has just stepped into someone else's intimate space. Just like the prin-cess, fleeing from her evil stepmother queen, who found herself in the dwarves' home while they were away. She saw the set tables, the made beds—everything was prepared for the owners' return and not for some foreign princess, an intruder. When she tried to rest on the bed, it turned out to be too short for her. When she tried to eat something from their plates, she found them quite small. Everything appeared fine, but noth-ing fit, things seemed foreign and strange, as if from a different dimen-sion. In the version of the fairy tale in which we participate after the war, the dwarves left and did not return. They left us with their rooms and

---

58   Tokarczuk, "Palec Stalina," 49. My translation. The original Polish reads, "nasi poprzednicy zabrali swoją pamięć ze sobą, a myśmy zostali wrzuceni w świat bez pamięci, a więc przez to w świat niezrozumiały, nie poddający się przyswojeniu, złożony z kawałków, jakie z wielu stron przynieśli ze sobą tutaj nowi mieszkańcy." The journal in which the essay was published is in itself a fascinating example of working across borders. *Kafka* was a multilingual literary and cultural quarterly that existed from 2001 to 2005. It was published by the Goethe Institut Inter Nationes e.V. The journal was devoted to Central European literature and culture, and each issue was published in four languages simultaneously (German, Polish, Hungarian, and Czech/Slovak).

59   For the particular memory of still-hot coals and warm soup on the table, see Tokarczuk, "Palec Stalina," 48.

80 ♦ BORDER POETICS

appliances, houses and streets, hills and trails, and we must now make them our own.[60]

The new inhabitants thus experienced a double sense of disruption: Not only had they been uprooted from their own places of belonging; they now also found themselves entering the personal spaces of not only strangers but enemies.

Just like in the Grimm brothers' version of the fairy tale, Snow White is out of place. She exemplifies otherness and is at the same time confronted with it: she is an intruder and a stranger to the dwarves, but she also perceives them as Other. Even before this encounter, she is already an outsider in her own family. To escape from her stepmother's murderous jealousy, she transgresses physical borders by fleeing into the woods beyond the mountains, where she stumbles upon the seven dwarves' secluded home.[61] When they return from work, they find Snow White sleeping in one of their beds and invite her to stay. As Tokarczuk notes, the "dwarves" in the German-Polish story did not return, but they did leave behind many traces and objects that the new inhabitants had to make their own. This necessary appropriation, however, was hindered by a long-lasting and persistent fear that Germans would soon recover from the lost war and come back to reclaim what they had left behind.[62] Encounters with the previous owners were also not uncommon in the first months after the war. Germans were often still living in the homes that were being taken over by the new Polish arrivals. This resulted in arrangements in which Germans and Poles were forced to temporarily share the same living space while experiencing very similar struggles for survival. This trope has also found its way

60 Tokarczuk, "Syndrom Królewny Śnieżki," 163. The cited source is a reversible book, and it includes both the original Polish version (157–66) and the German translation of the essay, titled "Das Schnewittchensyndrom und andere niederschlesische Träume" (164–75). My translation is from the original Polish: "Polega on [Syndrom Królewny Śnieżki] na dziwnej i nie do końca przyjemnej świadomości, że oto weszło się w czyjąś intymną przestrzeń. Zupełnie jak uciekająca przed złą macochą Królewna, która znalazła się w domu krasnoludków podczas ich nieobecności. Zobaczyła zastawione stoły, zaścielone łóżeczka, wszystko gotowe na przybycie swych właścicieli, nie zaś dla obcej królewny, intruza. Gdy próbowała odpocząć na łóżku, okazywało się, że jest dla niej za krótkie. Gdy próbowała zjeść coś z ich talerzy, były zbyt małe. Niby więc wszystko było w porządku, ale nic nie pasowało, wszystko wydawało się obce i dziwne, jakby z innego wymiaru. W tej wersji bajki, w której my uczestniczymy po wojnie, krasnoludki odeszły i nie wróciły, pozostawiając nam swoje pokoje i sprzęty, domy i ulice, wzgórza i ścieżki, a my musimy je teraz oswoić."

61 The fairy tales collected by the Brothers Grimm and others are themselves evidence of multiple border crossings—from their oral transmission all over Europe, northern Africa, and Asia to their multiple migrations, translations, and adaptations in the modern period. See Darnton, "Peasants Tell Tales," 11–12, 21.

62 For an analysis of this residual fear, see, for example, Weber, "Angst in der polnischen Deutschlandpolitik nach 1945," esp. 134–36.

into literature. For example, a German and a Polish family must share a house in Tokarczuk's novel *House of Day, House of Night* until the Germans are expelled.[63] Anecdotes of this nature are sometimes also included in historical accounts that discuss the political and social circumstances of this Polish-German cohabitation.[64]

Even after the Germans had left, and fear of their return had receded into the background, the current inhabitants continued to experience the disconnect between the place they occupied and the place they still perceived as belonging to the Other. Besides the physical devastation that served as a constant reminder of the catastrophic war the Germans had waged, there was also material evidence of another kind of difference: the built environment looked unfamiliar, buildings and household items bore German inscriptions, and one could find books, papers, and documents in German, often an inaccessible language to the new arrivals. In this sense, both the destructive forces and the productive cultural traces of a German presence were inscribed into the landscape, and a post-German reality was visible in daily life.[65] Thus, "Snow White" must have not only *felt* that things did not quite fit or that she had just stepped into another dimension; she was also confronted with material evidence of the unintelligible stories and secrets in the place she had just set foot. In many ways, these traces of a former presence could neither be fully appropriated nor denied. The world as many experienced and memorialized it in stories was disrupted so fundamentally that it resisted appropriation.

Border poetics entails working through these memories and their ramifications for the present. And with the increasing temporal distance, it becomes possible to reconsider the varying and changing affiliations in more cosmopolitan terms. The practice therefore also constitutes a claim in the sense proposed by B. Venkat Mani in the context of Turkish-German literature. Mani argues that the negotiation of different identities needs to be reinscribed positively as "cosmopolitical claim," in which cosmopolitanism "does not manifest itself in a complete absence of identification with a nation, ethnicity, or culture and certainly not in declarations of absolute detachment or rootlessness." On the contrary, Mani continues, Turkish-German authors "are astutely cognizant of the cultural and political geographies of their polis, but they are not hesitant

---

63   This story is told in the chapter "To the Lord God from the Poles" (*House*, 231–38); "Panu Bogu—Polacy" (*Dom*, 306–14).

64   See, for example, Thum, *Die fremde Stadt*, 134. See also Halicka, *Polens Wilder Westen*. Halicka shows that Germans and Poles who were forced to live together had little sympathy for one another, and instances of compassion were rare. Poles who had been expelled from the Eastern provinces, however, were often more sympathetic to the Germans because they had suffered more under Soviet occupation and less under German rule (158–62). For a documentary film that chronicles both positive and negative encounters and interpersonal contacts during the expulsion process, see Badura, *Schlesiens Wilder Westen*.

65   Kuszyk, *Poniemieckie.*

82 ♦ BORDER POETICS

to unsettle and radicalize the definition of belonging to that very cosmos and the polis through their writings."[66] In my understanding, cosmopolitical claims are therefore also claims to agency; they are deeply held political commitments and expressions of ethical responsibility that motivate interventions in the space one inhabits. In this sense, cosmopolitical claims can also manifest as moments of resistance.

The point of resistance requires elaboration, but it seems necessary to first clarify the distinction between appropriation and cosmopolitical claim. With the aim of coming to a more nuanced understanding of different processes of appropriation, historian Thomas Serrier has developed a typology of forms in which new spaces and material objects may be appropriated into a culture. Beata Halicka applies this typology to her analysis of the postwar settlement of Poland's "Wild West"—that is, Germany's former eastern territories—and this typology can also help clarify the distinctiveness of border poetics.[67] For Serrier, "cultural appropriation" ("kulturelle Aneignung") comes in the form of either "exclusionary" ("exkludierende") or "inclusive appropriation" ("inkludierende Aneignung"). The former strives for a new beginning and attempts to symbolically, or in actuality, suppress or deny the previous presence of the Other. The latter acknowledges the Other's contribution to the space one now inhabits and aims to establish a sense of continuity with the past.[68] Exclusionary cultural appropriation was the dominant mode in the formerly German areas during the first three decades after the war. It resulted in hard and divisive political and mental borders that aimed to create a stable and homogenous society.[69] For reasons explained in the previous chapter, these borders have become gradually more porous since the 1970s, but it was not until 1989/90 that Germans and Poles were able to approach their shared past together.

Inclusive cultural appropriation has two subforms, according to Serrier: "administrative appropriation" ("verwaltende Aneignung") and "creative appropriation" ("schöpferische Aneignung"). Administrative appropriation entails the acknowledgment of a place's history and the realization that its cultural heritage must be preserved, even if it is not one's own. Creative appropriation goes one step further and refers to the recognition of cross-cultural connections, which brings about a sense of co-ownership, shared responsibility, and appreciation for the shared cultural heritage.[70] These notions of the different forms and stages of appropriation can help trace the development from viewing the border as a dividing line to the emergence of a German-Polish transborder consciousness. Following this trajectory, creative appropriation

66   Mani, *Cosmopolitical Claims*, 6.
67   Halicka, *Polens Wilder Westen*, 183–85.
68   Serrier, "Formen kultureller Aneignung," 20–22.
69   Serrier, "Gedächtnistransfer," 158–59.
70   Serrier, "Formen kultureller Aneignung," 22.

has laid the ground for border poetics because it supports narratives that challenge the exclusionary discourses of the past. The appropriation narrative also has its limitations, however, because it is, at its core, still prefigured on difference. Border poetics grows out of a desire to simultaneously maintain and suspend difference, and it therefore must go beyond even the last stage of creative appropriation.

Although border poetics in a certain sense emerges out of inclusive appropriation, I suggest that the effect of border poetics is conceptually closer to Mani's notion of a "cosmopolitical claim." Cosmopolitical claims more explicitly foreground processes of becoming and cosmopolitanization and the participation in an inclusive political process. Where the notion of appropriation may appear one-sided and forgo questions of agency, the expression of a cosmopolitical claim implies an opportunity for resistance—both by the thing that is being claimed, because it maintains its difference, as well as by the ones making the claim, because they must both insist on and suspend their own difference in order to make the claim at all. In this simultaneous suspension and maintenance of difference lies a moment of transdifference. At the same time, the German-Turkish claim-making Mani describes differs in important ways. This is due to the actual physical and political border between Germany and Poland and the history and relations connected to this border. As noted above, Halle has pointed to this difference with the notion of "interzones," noting that "Polish-German is spatially close yet understood only haltingly as a common place, while the Turkish-German is geographically distant, certainly not contiguous, but understood as connected and even continuous."[71] In light of the strained relations between Germany and Turkey since 2016, I am uncertain whether this juxtaposition still holds, but it is undeniable that there is a sense of distance and mistrust in Polish-German relations and that, generally speaking, the space is not perceived as "connected and even continuous." This reality is based in large part on the fact that throughout the centuries, Germany and its predecessor states have made various territorial and material claims on Poland and the East, and such negative connotations cannot be ignored when speaking of claim-making. Still, the "cosmopolitical claims" articulated through border poetics are quite different from any of the concrete claims of the past: they are mutual, they express new and flexible forms of attachment and belonging, and they aim at integrating difference without dissolving it permanently.

The cosmopolitical claim-making described here is an expression of critical cosmopolitanism, and it demands transborder thinking—not only in spatial but also in temporal terms. I have already alluded to the important role that memory plays in the process of claim-making, and "Snow White syndrome" encapsulates the psychological impact of the past quite fittingly. Memory, a "phenomenon of conceptual border zones," as Azade Seyhan has described it, is both collective and individual, circulates locally and globally, responds to

---

71   Halle, *The Europeanization of Cinema*, 4.

84 ♦ BORDER POETICS

the particular and the universal, and "dwells at the crossroads of the past and the present."[72] In the Polish-German context today, memories often relate to the Second World War and its aftermath, especially experiences of flight and expulsion. Even now, almost eighty years after the end of the war, feelings of alienation and uncertainty as well as a desire to fill blank spots still matter. The end of the Cold War, the recognition of the finality of the German-Polish border (1991), Poland's entry into the European Union (2004), and accession to the Schengen Zone (2007) have created new opportunities for contact and conversations about the past. These opportunities include access to documents, collaborations and dialogue between German and Polish scholars and communities, and more open conversations among various civil society actors and across different generations. Combined with a sense of urgency to redefine one's place in the newly constituted Europe and in the world at large, understanding the past within a broader European and global context became an important aspect of the search for a new sense of belonging for both Germans and Poles.

Books and libraries are essential for developing a shared memory and sense of history, although collaborations between authors, translators, and publishers often suffer from a lack of funding.[73] Many cultural organizations and artists also contribute to this process through events and projects, such as a literary cruise along the Oder and Rhine Rivers organized by the Kleist-Museum in Frankfurt an der Oder and the Heinrich-Heine-Institut in Düsseldorf in 2004. The cruise brought authors, translators, and publishers together, and readings took place at stops along the way. The project resulted in an anthology in which many contributions address questions of memory and that includes works by Tanja Dückers, Inga Iwasiów, and Olga Tokarczuk.[74] The ongoing activist art project "Nowa Amerika" with its capital "Słubfurt" is another fitting example. Located in the border towns Frankfurt an der Oder and Słubice, the project was initially conceived to facilitate a better understanding between the Polish and German inhabitants of this region.[75] In part II of this study, I discuss literary works that all, in one way or

---

72 Seyhan, *Writing outside the Nation*, 31. See also Friedman's reading of Seyhan and the connection between memory and borders in "Migration, Diasporas, and Borders." In chapter 3, I ask how literary texts operate in this space in which memories are territorialized and specific to a certain space and at the same time widely accessible and universalized through global circulation.

73 Katharina Raabe, then editor for Eastern European literature at the Suhrkamp publishing house, comments on the significance of libraries. Raabe, "As the Fog Lifted." For details about the various collaborations between authors, translators, and publishers, see Makarska, "Übersetzen," esp. 5–6.

74 Jordan and Wyrwoll, *Oder—Rhein*. I discuss Iwasiów's contribution to the anthology in chapter 3, "Disruption."

75 May-Chu, "Reimagining the German-Polish Borderlands."

another, revolve around questions of memory and the recovery, and reevaluation, of a painful past.

Border poetics requires a productive engagement with the past and the conflicting collective memories in the present. Borderlands are sites of memory, and they occupy a central space in discussions about entangled memories and the difficulty of a shared European memory or even "cosmopolitan memory"; that is, "collective memories that transcend national and ethnic boundaries."[76] In the European context, many memories are defined by the experiences of the Second World War and the Holocaust, but owing to the plurality of experiences, they often compete across national or regional contexts. The resulting tensions and disconnects create a fractured memory landscape in which memories can be "shared" ("gemeinsam") but are more often "parallel" or "divided" ("geteilt"), to follow a categorization proposed by Hans Henning Hahn and Robert Traba in the context of German and Polish sites of memory.[77] In light of growing conflicts over the uses and abuses of history, the idea of a shared memory, or what Michael Rothberg has described as "multidirectional memory" in which memories are in a mutually influential dialogue rather than in competition with one another, is challenging.[78] Cosmopolitical claim-making as formulated through border poetics also aims to bring together the burst pieces of memory, even if doing so is an incomplete process.

Border poetics works against the appropriation and political instrumentalization of memory by committing to a process that is both "multiperspectival" (Rumford) and self-critical. Border poetics advances dialogues between different memory regimes in favor of creating a cosmopolitan imagination that unsettles hegemonic narratives and overcomes memory contests. This results in a manifold anchoring of memory that acknowledges one's own position in a fractured narrative and at the same time affords the Other the opportunity to enter that narrative to jointly revisit and reimagine it. This kind of hospitality of the imagination also acknowledges the incompleteness of any narrative that is closed off and does not allow for a critical examination from within and from without. Cosmopolitan memory can thus also be described as both a

---

76   Levy and Sznaider, "Memory Unbound," 88. See also Levy and Sznaider, "Cosmopolitan Memory."

77   In shared sites of memory, both the remembered content and the function of the site of memory are equivalent or very similar for both collectives. Parallel sites of memory refer to different actual objects of remembrance, but those fulfill very similar functions in a given society. Divided sites of memory are the most common: while the object of remembrance is the same in both societies, the event or person is remembered differently or fulfills a different function. See Hahn and Traba, "Wovon die deutsch-polnischen Erinnerungsorte (nicht) erzählen," 22–23.

78   Rothberg argues that differences in memory discourses cannot be resolved and that they therefore need to be in a dynamic exchange: *Multidirectional Memory*, 3.

86 ♦ Border Poetics

disruption of old narratives and an investment in new ones. The difference can be neither fully appropriated nor dissolved.

Authors in Germany and Poland have been responding to this new imperative in various ways, and there is continued interest in the literary exploration of the shared German-Polish history.[79] Novels by Polish and German authors that have been published since the 2010s appear to indicate a continuation of this trend.[80] It comes with the territory—quite literally speaking—that these broader historical contexts are articulated through the lens of a specific locality or social unit. Literary texts about the borderland take stock of the past by critiquing the incomplete and contradictory narratives in which it is encoded, as the next chapter demonstrates. Such narratives often interrogate collective memory by showing how it is refracted through individuals and their relations with one another. For several decades, many Polish authors have been examining the multicultural history of the border regions and have brought multiple and often suppressed narratives into the conversation. This approach is clearly evident in Olga Tokarczuk and Inga Iwasiów, who are prominently featured here, but it applies to many other authors, several of whom are known across borders.[81] German-language authors, by contrast, frequently explore questions of guilt and responsibility across multiple generations. They are invested in a critical examination of family histories that are sometimes, but not necessarily, related to their own family history. Tanja Dückers, Sabrina Janesch, and Günter Grass are discussed in more detail within the scope of this book, but multiple other examples can attest to this ongoing trend in German literature.[82]

Borderlands/la frontera/Grenzland/pogranicze

This study focuses on Polish and German border stories but is also driven by the desire to suggest a horizon that can be expanded into other contexts. I therefore conclude this chapter with some thoughts on border poetics as a lens to bring locally situated texts, such as Polish and German borderlands literature, into a shared world literary space. German-Polish border poetics creates worlds that have been crossed by borders, but the narratives that hold

---

79 In 2015 this interest was still growing, according to Barbara Cöllen, "Polsko--niemieckie tematy."

80 Among these works are Joanna Bator's *Gorzko, gorzko* (2020), Artur Becker's *Der unsterbliche Mr. Lindley* (2018), Dörthe Binkert's *Vergiss kein einziges Wort* (2018), Martyna Bunda's *Das Glück der kalten Jahre* (2019), Susanne Fitz's *Wie kommt der Krieg ins Kind* (2018), and Szczepan Twardoch's *Pokora* (2020), to name but a few.

81 For example, Joanna Bator, Artur Becker, Paweł Huelle, Stefan Chwin, Wojciech Kuczok, Artur Daniel Liskowacki, Czesław Miłosz, Magdalena Parys, Andrzej Stasiuk, Dariusz Muszer, and Szczepan Twardoch.

82 For example, Ulrike Draesner, Jenny Erpenbeck, Susanne Fitz, Julia Franck, Ruth Fruchtmann, Reinhard Jirgl, Per Leo, Stefan Wackwitz, and Christa Wolf.

these worlds also have the ability to cross borders. Borderlands can connect different times and places, and this sentiment has been powerfully expressed by Gloria Anzaldúa in *Borderlands/La Frontera: The New Mestiza* (1987). In her book, Anzaldúa describes the diversity and heterogeneity of those who inhabit the permanent borderland between the United States and Mexico. Not only does the work shed light on various iterations of borders and border crossings within a narrative, but its wide circulation and reception also demonstrates how literature can transmit ideas across borders and inspire global alliances. Anzaldúa's text has been influential far beyond the U.S.-Mexico context, and it also inspired my own thinking about border poetics, the concept's importance to the study of world literature, and its connection to German and Polish literature.[83]

Using literary critic Gerard Genette's differentiation between story and discourse, it can be said that *Borderlands/La Frontera* is evidence of border poetics both on the level of discourse (i.e., how a narrative is told) and of story (i.e., what is being told). First, the book is not easily categorized and transgresses multiple genre boundaries as it moves between history writing, theoretical reflection, mythology, poetry, and autobiography. Second, it acknowledges, but at the same time transcends, the locally and historically specific context and makes visible the psychological and corporal impact of a variety of border crossings by addressing global issues of gender-based oppression, social injustice, solidarity, and queerness. Anzaldúa blends the exploration of "physical borderlands" with that of "historical, psychological, sexual, spiritual, and aesthetic borderlands" and connects the latter with the former in a kind of translation process that reveals different kinds of hybridity.[84] Addressing the specific situation of Mexican-Americans, *Borderlands/La Frontera* exposes numerous intersecting systems of oppression, sources of agency, and frameworks of identification, such as nationhood, ethnicity, disability, and gender.

For Anzaldúa, the borderland is both a physical space and a mental state; it is an embodied infliction that is passed on through multiple generations. At the same time, it is a place of continuous negotiation and engagement with contradictions, and it therefore also has significant subversive and empowering potential. The place where two worlds collide is an "open wound," but it is also the homeland, a cultural borderland, and a "third country."[85] In contrast to Homi Bhabha's "third spaces," difference is not dissolved in Anzaldúa's "third country." As Bhabha explains in an interview, cultural hybridization "displaces the histories that constitute it, and sets up new structures of authority, new political initiatives.... The process of cultural hybridity gives rise to

---

83   On the broad impact of Anzaldúa's book, see, for example, Cantú, "Comparative Perspectives Symposium." The special issue of *Signs* includes perspectives on Anzaldúa from Spain, the Canary Islands, Poland, the Czech Republic, and other places.

84   Friedman, *Mappings*, 95–96.

85   Anzaldúa, *Borderlands/La Frontera*, 24–25.

something different, something new and unrecognisable, a new area of negotiation of meaning and representation."[86] Anzaldúa's notion of the "third" is related more closely to that of transdifference and the maintenance of difference in the form of a permanent wound. This distinction is important, because just as betweenness in this study is not an empty space, it is likewise not a "third space" in the sense of "something new and unrecognisable." The "third" of *la frontera* may be a new constellation that offers opportunities for new alliances and affords agency, but it is not unrecognizable and relies heavily upon a rootedness in specific historical as well as mythical, cultural, and political conditions. At the same time, there is a sense of ambiguity that is central to Anzaldúa's notion of the borderland as a "third country."

Importantly, Anzaldúa makes a distinction between borders and borderlands: borders are regulating mechanisms "set up to define the places that are safe and unsafe, to distinguish us from them. A border is a dividing line, a narrow strip along a steep edge." Yet, borders are also porous, and they create extended between-spaces, which are borderlands. For Anzaldúa this borderland "is a vague and undetermined place created by the emotional residue of an unnatural boundary. It is a constant state of transition."[87] Borders not only demarcate the outer limits of a unit of supposed sameness; they also carry within themselves the very difference that they are trying to keep out. Thus, the purportedly bounded systems of reference that create a border at the places where they meet or collide are already "blurry" systems in and of themselves.

One can extend this understanding of the borderland to any site where seemingly bounded systems meet; for example, to the notions of "German" or "Polish," or "German culture" and "Polish culture." As is widely acknowledged, homogeneous "cultures" do not exist, and these terms can only serve as convenient shorthand here. Border poetics explores the porousness of borders and the blurriness of borderlands, and it imagines new ways of joining the particular with the universal. In this sense the borderland constructed through border poetics is not a no man's land but rather a space of excess and of potential everythingness, or the "more than" articulated by Halle.[88] It is a realm of heightened blurriness, mobility, and transborder exchange. It may be illuminating here to read the phrase "no man's land" with a shift in emphasis: from a "no man's land" that belongs to no one to a "no *one* man's land" that has the *potential* of existing as a diverse and shared space and that can be home to multiple identities. This space is not free of conflict and tension; it is a space that insists on negotiation, resists particularist claims, and pushes against established boundaries and hard borders. Herein lies the cosmopolitan vision advanced by border poetics: it is a vision that is expressed in

86   Bhabha, "Interview," 211.
87   Anzaldúa, *Borderlands/La Frontera*, 25.
88   Halle, *The Europeanization of Cinema*, 166.

various kinds of narratives and that uses different strategies to shape both the story and the discourse of a narrative. The next two chapters explore some of these strategies and thereby illustrate and challenge the theoretical interjections made in this chapter.

The critical engagement with borders through concepts such as borderland, la frontera, Grenzland, and pogranicze, as well as terms marking other borderlands elsewhere, has cosmopolitan potential also because it suggests that these spaces can be transformed. We can imagine them as alternative sites of interaction, where history can be told in new ways that emphasize shared experiences and transborder alliances. Border poetics draws attention to the narratives that result from liminal constellations and fleshes out the connections between and across them. Anzaldúa's *Borderlands* shares with the novels in this study a demand for imagining things differently, for developing a cosmopolitan vision of the world. This vision contends with reality, and it is fueled by a desire to draw attention to injustices and inequalities. Some scholars have pointed to correspondences between the US-Mexico border and the German-Polish border.[89] I am less interested here in a direct comparison and more in taking the border as what Agier has called an "object of reflection" that allows for viewing borderlands/la frontera and Grenzland/pogranicze as continuous, if different, spaces.[90] Such an expanded view is instructive for articulating the need for a cosmopolitan imagination without creating a hierarchy of experiences of oppression or suggesting that these borderlands are commensurate. The power of Anzaldúa's work and her applicability beyond the US-Mexico context lies in dismantling binaries and destabilizing established power structures through interventions and reinventions of these structures. Border poetics helps articulate connections between different people and contexts without losing sight of their differences.

89   Political scientist Peter Andreas compares the US-Mexican and the German-Polish borderlands with regard to the disparities in border policing that existed in the 1990s and until 2004, when the German-Polish border marked one of the outer limits of the EU. Andreas, *Border Games*. American studies scholar Grażyna Zygadło draws on Andreas's study and applies Anzaldúa's ideas about the borderland to Poland and its place in Europe. She argues that in the 1990s, Poles became the Chicanos of Europe and that both share "a distinct border identity" (30). Zygadło highlights the economic disparities between Germany and Poland in the 1990s, which were significant; but the level of poverty and border violence was never comparable to that of Mexico, and these inequalities were also overcome quickly, as the UN Development Index shows. Zygadło also calls for solidarity, especially among women, based mainly on a narrative of shared victimhood and subjugation (33) and does not refer to the narrative of resistance, subversion, and creativity that Anzaldúa also tells. Zygadło, "'Where the Third World Grates against the First.'"

90   Agier, *Borderlands*, 8.

Part II

Reading Border Poetics

3: Disruption: Fictions of Memory by Inga Iwasiów, Sabrina Janesch, and Tanja Dückers

Heute weiß ich, daß alles zuguckt, daß nichts unbesehen bleibt,daß selbst Tapeten ein besseres Gedächtnis als die Menschen haben. Es ist nicht etwa der liebe Gott, der alles sieht! Ein Küchenstuhl, Kleiderbügel, halbvoller Aschenbecher oder das hölzerne Abbild einer Frau, genannt Niobe, reichen aus, um jeder Tat den unvergeßlichen Zeugen liefern zu können.

Today I know that all things are watching, that nothing goes unseen, that even wallpaper has a better memory than human beings. It's not God in his heaven who sees everything. A kitchen chair, a clothes hanger, a half-filled ashtray, or the wooden replica of a woman named Niobe can serve perfectly well as an unforgetting witness to our every deed.

—Günter Grass, *Die Blechtrommel*, 247/*The Tin Drum*, 177

ACCORDING TO THE NARRATOR in *The Tin Drum*, all things are watching; they record everything; they have a memory. While I discuss Günter Grass's novel in the next chapter, this epigraph is nonetheless fitting here. Not only does it prompt us to think about the nature of memory, but it also frames storytelling as the task to elicit memories from people and things, to rerecord what has been previously recorded and has been forgotten, to resubmit to the present what would otherwise remain locked in the past. Drawing out these memories from inanimate objects or even people is no easy undertaking. It requires deciphering, translating, interpreting, creating relations between previously unrelated memories, and filling gaps in knowledge with imagination. Memory, in short, demands storytelling, and stories that heed this demand are at the center of this chapter. Following Genette's distinction between story (content) and discourse (form), the focus here is primarily on how border poetics unfolds on the content plane of narratives.

In this chapter, I argue that border poetics is particularly well suited for so-called fictions of memory because memory itself is a "phenomenon of conceptual border zones," as Azade Seyhan has argued.[1] Seyhan explains that memory inhabits a space "between the past and the present." She adds that

---

1   Seyhan, *Writing outside the Nation*, 31.

94 ♦ DISRUPTION: FICTIONS OF MEMORY

this temporality links memory closely to culture because both memory and culture share a diachronic structure in which the past provides the framework and the point of origin for what, she notes, Benedict Anderson has described as "imagined community." Drawing also on semioticians Yurij Lotman and B. A. Uspensky, Seyhan speaks of culture as "a record of community memory" and argues that "insofar as culture is memory, it is embedded in the past and will have to be retrieved in symbolic action."[2] In her comparative study, Seyhan examines the diasporic and transnational narratives produced by Mexican-American authors in the United States and authors of Turkish descent in Germany as acts of remembrance that lend "coherence and integrity to a history interrupted, divided, or compromised by instances of loss"; that is, it is a way of coping with the disruptions caused by having to leave one's home.[3]

The authors I discuss in this book are not necessarily writers in exile or diaspora, although moments in the lives of some, such as Günter Grass, might qualify them as such. Nevertheless, their belonging is not always clear: even though their passports may mark them as either "German" or "Polish," these writers navigate real and fictional spaces in which such generalizations hold little explanatory power. Their writings "originate at border crossings" in the most literal sense.[4] They stand out with a strong "metanarrative impulse," producing narratives that are "both creative and experimental and self-reflexive and theoretical. In other words, questions of speech and writing, fiction versus nonfiction, history and story, and official history and communal memory themselves become subjects of 'fiction.'"[5] Similarly, the authors in this book have in one way or another personally experienced German-Polish border crossings, and they have taken them as points of departure for narratives about figurative boundaries and the transgression of these boundaries. Memories—which draw on real border experiences but are at the same time temporally, spatially, or psychologically detached from the actually existing space—inform and shape the stories that I examine in the following pages.

Fictions of Memory

According to the Oxford English Dictionary Online, a narrative is "an account of a series of events, facts, etc., given in order and with the establishing of connections between them."[6] In this sense, narratives are created by remembering and trying to lend some kind of meaning to the past, be it in the form of written texts or cultural artifacts such as memorials, exhibitions, or different

---

2   Seyhan, *Writing outside the Nation*, 15–16.
3   Seyhan, *Writing outside the Nation*, 4.
4   Seyhan, *Writing outside the Nation*, 4.
5   Seyhan, *Writing outside the Nation*, 13.
6   Oxford English Dictionary Online, "narrative, n." OED Online. March 2023. Oxford University Press. www.oed.com.

kinds of media. Birgit Neumann explains that the term "fictions of memory" can refer to "literary, non-referential narratives that depict the workings of memory," but it has also been applied more broadly to "the stories that individuals or cultures tell about their past to answer the question 'who am I?,' or, collectively, 'who are we?'"[7] I am operating here primarily with the first, more restricted meaning as it pertains to literature, but it is important to note the interconnectedness of literary fictions and broader social discourses. In reference to Paul Ricoeur's writing on mimesis, Neumann agrees that the nature and functions of memory must always be understood within a culturally specific context, and this cultural specificity also shapes the way in which memory is represented in literature. At the same time, literary texts also "create new models of memory" because they can challenge and modify discourses: "They combine the real and the imaginary, the remembered and the forgotten, and, by means of narrative devices, imaginatively explore the workings of memory, thus offering new perspectives on the past."[8]

The "fictions of memory" I am about to discuss explore past events as well as how those events are recalled and adapted to meet the needs of the present, which includes both remembering and forgetting, competing and countervailing memories within one and the same generation, and the transmission of memories across multiple generations. The stories unfold either from one individual's perspective or through multiple voices and narrative perspectives. The recovery of the past usually involves interactions among several social units (e.g., families, friends, neighbors), as well as the narrator's evaluation of their actions across different times and places. Through these processes and fueled by the passing of time and changes in public discourse, memories and their evaluations also change. The works under examination here highlight that memory is a matter of constant negotiation, presenting it as a "multidirectional" phenomenon in which different memories mutually impact one another without necessarily being in competition, as Michael Rothberg (cited in chapter 2) has theorized. This means that authors frequently construct their protagonists, plotlines, and relationships in ways that undermine stereotypical and one-sided representations. Instead, they offer unusual viewpoints and narrative perspectives that are variously interpolated and intertwined with more conventional ways of remembering the past, and they thereby critique and complicate established narratives.

This is not to say that all the works in this study are perfect examples of what I describe as border poetics. At times, some of them process disruptions or negative aspects of the past in flawed ways; for example, by ignoring historical or current conflicts, dismissing differences, or neglecting important nuances. Such an idealistic harmonization lacks a self-critical distance and may put these works on the verge of what Berthold Schoene calls "cosmo-kitsch"

---

7   Neumann, "Literary Representation of Memory," 334.
8   Neumann, "Literary Representation of Memory," 334.

96 ♦ Disruption: Fictions of Memory

(cited in the introduction). As the previous chapter has shown, border poetics aims for a space of "transdifference" (Breinig and Lösch) that fosters the articulation and accommodation of disruptions. It does not, however, ignore or dissolve difference. It only suspends it long enough to allow for the imagination of an alternative mode of being and a more inclusive memory to arise. In this context, I find it helpful to refer to Neumann's description of the role of literature, which is "never a simple reflection of pre-existing cultural discourses; rather, it proactively contributes to the negotiation of cultural memory."[9] Following this argument, border poetics, as a form of critique, must be considered for its impact on actual borders by way of their discursive construction and the range of border experiences it records and illuminates.

Based on the description above, we can think of memory as a register of a broad spectrum of border crossings, both structurally and in terms of the content it chronicles. For Seyhan, these inscriptions resurface through "the labor of remembrance that reclaims the lost experience of another time and place in language and imagination."[10] In fictions of memory, border poetics can help articulate these border crossings and potentially destabilize existing discourses about borders by building on a symbiotic link between topographical, temporal, and symbolic borders and border experiences. These intersecting border experiences reveal the dynamic relationship between the particular and the universal. On the one hand, the narratives are anchored in historically, politically, or socially specific border experiences. On the other hand, border poetics expands such experiences beyond their particular contexts by complicating them with universally articulated questions. This expansion of the particular may be understood as the necessary "symbolic action" that Seyhan describes, and it can help recover and articulate what has been lost or disrupted in the past. In addition, this process gives greater context to a fractured memory, making it more accessible and helping to reveal connections between different particulars; that is, between various people and places.

Border poetics translates into aesthetic form the complex and often contradictory constellations of different identities, allegiances, and affiliations that are present within individuals and societies. It explores these constellations, often through ambiguous narrators or protagonists and entangled narrative perspectives, and thereby contributes to new insights into the past (in the sense described by Neumann above). This expanded and more nuanced understanding of the past undergirds a critical cosmopolitanism. Within these alternative times and spaces, discontinuities can be temporarily suspended in an effort to fill in some of the blank spots in personal, regional, or local trans-border histories that have resulted from forced and voluntary migrations alike. In the following, I illustrate how border poetics addresses many of these discontinuities in three novels. I examine the nature and significance of border

---

9   Neumann, "Literary Representation of Memory," 335.
10   Seyhan, *Writing outside the Nation*, 4.

poetics as an engaged practice that connects the world of the text (world-making) with the world outside the text (worlding). These new connections challenge the reader's imagination to advance a cosmopolitan reimagination of past and present border spaces. My analysis also raises the question whether and how the worlds that are constructed in and by these texts challenge hegemonic border narratives. The novels in this chapter are *Bambino* by Inga Iwasiów, *Katzenberge* (Cat Hills) by Sabrina Janesch, and *Himmelskörper* (Celestial Bodies) by Tanja Dückers. In each of these examples, protagonists struggle to negotiate a field of conflicting meanings. They either strive to confront the burdens of the past or try to ignore them, all to better orient their lives toward the present and future. Either one of these strategies makes the transborder connections in their lives visible.

All texts that I present here are marked by severe disruptions—in history, in the protagonists' own lives, or in the memories they are working through. The following readings ask how these narratives deal with disruption, to what extent these efforts are evidence of or might advance a cosmopolitan imagination, and how borders and border experiences can be made productive as sites of transborder mobility and exchange through this narrative process. I also identify some areas in which these works may be lacking a truly critical transborder perspective: border poetics within the same text may be practiced in one area but still fail to deliver in another, owing to the author's own limitations or biases. These tensions do not mean that I am dismissing such works as somehow not cosmopolitan enough. Rather, I am interested in understanding the discomfort produced by this lack and to examine it foundations. I ask whether the narratives indeed achieve a broadening of perspectives that can effectuate the worlding of the reader and contribute to the reconfiguration of existing discourses about borders. Or do they reinforce existing boundaries despite their best intentions? In short, how far do the authors of these novels take border poetics, and how far does border poetics take their stories?

Knotted Histories in
Inga Iwasiów's *Bambino* (2008)

Inga Iwasiów, born in 1963 in Szczecin, is a renowned Polish writer, literary scholar, and activist. She is a professor of literature at the University of Szczecin and an important voice in the fields of gender studies and feminist literary criticism. Besides being a prolific writer and academic, she also publishes regularly in the Polish press, especially the newspaper *Gazeta Wyborcza*, where she comments on political and cultural developments pertaining to topics such as women's rights and migration. Her broad interest in borders and different manifestations of boundaries is evident in her scholarly and literary activities as well as her past work for the bimonthly literary and cultural journal *Pogranicze* (Borderlands). The Szczecin-based journal existed from 1994 to 2012, and Iwasiów served as its editor in chief from 1999 until its end.

98 ◆ Disruption: Fictions of Memory

Iwasiów's literary career began in 1998 with the publication of the prose collection *Miasto-ja-miasto* (City-I-City). Since then, she has published poetry, short prose, a theater play, and several novels, including the critically acclaimed *Późne życie* (Late Life) in 2023. Her first novel, *Bambino*, which I examine here, appeared in 2008, and it was short-listed for the *Nike* award—Poland's most prestigious literary prize. *Bambino* is set in Szczecin, formerly German Stettin, a port city in northwestern Poland. The story begins in the 1950s, when the city was still being rebuilt and establishing a new identity after the Second World War. It ends in summer of 1981, shortly before the Communist Polish government cracked down on the opposition movement Solidarność and placed the country under martial law. The novel also includes memories and flashbacks to earlier time periods that help explain the protagonists' backgrounds and motivations. *Bambino* is the first installment in a very loosely connected trilogy. It was followed in 2010 by *Ku słoncu* (Toward the Sun), which covers the 1980s and 1990s, and in 2012 by *Na krótko* (For a Short While), which begins in the early 2000s. Although Iwasiów is a highly regarded author in Poland, her major works have yet to appear in German or English, and only excerpts from *Bambino* are available in English translation.[11]

Bambino tells the story of Maria, Janek, Ula, Anna, and Stefan, who are from different parts of Poland, and who come to Szczecin with hopes for a better future. Their lives become entangled when they meet by chance in the 1950s in a milk bar ("bar mleczny") named Bambino.[12] The nonlinear narrative, which spans three decades and is told over forty-two chapters, explores how the protagonists' life stories have been impacted not only by the multiple and violent changes in geopolitical borders but also by figurative boundaries, especially those of ethnicity, language, gender, class, and religion. The novel explores how the past, including suppressed traumatic experiences, secrets, and blank spots, affects human relations. *Bambino*'s first four chapters are devoted to the backgrounds and the family histories of four of the five main

11 An excerpt of *Bambino*'s introductory chapter (translated into English by Antonia Lloyd Jones), as well as short samples from other novels, are available on Iwasiów's website, https://ingaiwasiow.info/the-author/. Two chapters from *Bambino* (translated into English by Karolina Hicke and Karolina May-Chu) appeared in a special issue of the journal *TRANSIT*. See Iwasiów, "Bambino (2008): Excerpts from the Novel." Some nonfictional essays are also available, such as "Die Ungeliebten," which examines Szczecin's historical and cultural identity.

12 A bar mleczny is an affordable Polish eatery known for serving mainly dairy- or flour-based vegetarian dishes. During Communist times, milk bars offered subsidized food to workers and often functioned as a kind of cafeteria. Today milk bars continue to provide traditional Polish fare at affordable prices and are eligible for government subsidies. They are popular with the wider Polish population and among tourists. When Tanja Dückers describes a milk bar as "a kind of soup kitchen" ("eine Art von Almosenküchen," 151) in her novel *Himmelskörper*, which I discuss later, it trivializes this broader social and cultural context of the institution.

protagonists, and they explain why and how each of them came to Szczecin. As the narrative progresses, the reader learns more about the characters' personal stories and how the differences between them impede their ability to create a shared space to overcome the burdensome aspects of their pasts. By bringing together these different lives, the novel weaves an intricate web of human connectivity that reveals how personal histories and affiliations, as well as rituals of intimacy, feelings of belonging, and solidarity are influenced by global events and their resulting border changes. And while the ideological and social structures inevitably shape these protagonists' lives, translator and scholar of Polish literature Ursula Phillips rightly points out that *Bambino*'s main focus "is much more on the internal, emotional and existential experiences of individuals and their intimate relationships, on the private rather than the public."[13] *Bambino* examines the inner life of each of the characters as well as the social relations between them, and it shows how deeply personal lives, bodies, and relationships are impacted by past experiences, pain, and trauma.

Refracted through the prism of the ever-present past, many different types of borders and border crossings are articulated by Iwasiów. The myth of Poland's "recovered territories" promulgated from above in the service of building a homogeneous Polish society after the Second World War also applied to Szczecin. *Bambino* makes clear that this myth could hardly reflect the national, ethnic, and regional heterogeneity on the ground. Even more, the prescribed collective memory led to a suppression and silencing of past breaks and disturbances, which eventually resurface as internal and interpersonal conflicts in the present. Figurative boundaries, especially those of class, language, gender, and religion, further complicate the disruptions caused by geopolitical or territorial border crossings. All of these multiply intersecting and shifting geopolitical and symbolic processes of bordering and border transgression are inscribed into the novel's leitmotifs of the thread, both large and small ("nić" and "nitka") and the knot, also large and small ("węzeł" and "węzełek"). Each "thread," that is, each life or storyline, delineates an individual's boundaries and defines that person's identity. The protagonists and the narrator are equally involved in constructing this knotted narrative. While the protagonists want to rid their lives of complications, they struggle to gain or maintain control over the narrative of their lives. The narrator comments on this struggle and provides further information and insights to the reader, showing that there are no firm boundaries or simple threads, no linear trajectories to follow. Rather, each individual is already a complicated conglomeration of threads—a tangle of many past and present experiences, relations, and circumstances. Threads and knots thus reflect both the content and the form of the novel, driving home my earlier point of the knot as a contact zone, or rather a complex, multidimensional, and intertwined structure in

---

13 Phillips, "Generation, Transformation and Place," 20.

100 ♦ Disruption: Fictions of Memory

which the individual threads do not disappear but become inseparable from other threads.[14]

Flashbacks, foreshadowing, changing focalizations, narrator commentary, and meta reflection enhance the "knotty" structure and provide insights into the protagonists' feelings and motivations as well as into the narrative's constructedness. This is, for example, the case in chapter 7, "Knots." This chapter introduces the gradual merging of the lives of Maria, Janek, Ulrike, and Anna, who meet in the milk bar. In this chapter, the narrator also introduces the leitmotif of the knot to reflect on different kinds of intersecting and conflicting attachments that guide every person's lives:

> In such a city, people meet by chance, in new constellations. People made up by chance. Let's say, most often at work. Anna and Ula's workplace is "Bambino," where they end up after several other milk bars. Bambino, bambino, bambino. Janek, sweet upon first sight, but still a man, is their customer, Marysia Ula's tenant. Bambini, bambino. It is a chance arrangement. The set will expand later. By an essential element. For life. They have something in common: they don't have here, in this city, any family. They build their lives, connecting only skin-deep with the people from here, making covenants, swearing oaths.
>
> They are one of the little knots one can try to untangle. Each one of them inside, within themselves. Between one another. With other people. They and those they have left behind. People are like knots: nobody knows what gets caught up in them and whether they can be untangled. Whoever thinks that this is material for myths or sagas is mistaken. Knots are knots. Nothing less, nothing more. Knots.[15]

Knots appear here as default modes of human existence, which is also why part of this quote has served as my epigraph for chapter 1, "Entanglements in German and Polish History, Literature, and Culture," in which I discuss the broader historical and cultural context of border poetics. *Bambino*'s border

---

14 This structure is a messier version of the playground climbing sphere with "many access points" that Coleman proposes as model. *The Right to Difference*, 45

15 Iwasiów, "Bambino (2008): Excerpts from the Novel," 147–48. The original reads, "Dla Anny i Uli miejscem pracy jest bar 'Bambino,' gdzie trafiają po zaliczeniu kilku innych barów. Bambino, bambino, bambino. Janek, też słodki na pierwszy rzut oka, ale i mężczyzna, jest ich konsumentem, Marysia lokatorką Uli. Bambini, bambino. Oto przypadkowy układ. Komplet poszerzy się później. O niezbędny element. Do życia. Mają z sobą coś wspólnego: nie mają tu, w mieście, rodzin. Uklepują swoje życie, stykając się naskórkami z ludźmi stąd, zawierają przymierza, składają przysięgi. // Są jednym z węzełków, które można próbować rozsuplać. Każde z nich wewnątrz, w sobie. Oni pomiędzy sobą. Oni z innymi ludźmi. Oni i ci, których pozostawili. Ludzie są jak węzełki: nie wiadomo, co się w nie zabierze i czy dadzą się rozplątać. Kto myśli ze można z tego zrobić mit lub sagę, jest w błędzie. Węzełki są węzełkami. Ni mniej, ni więcej. Węzełki" (*Bambino*, 66).

poetics builds on the premise of an inescapable human entanglement, which also includes the idea that these knots cannot be undone, no matter how hard one tries. The narrator suggests that incoherence and disruption are indelible parts of the human narrative, and this idea determines both the novel's structure and its plot. I suggest that *Bambino*'s border poetics lies primarily in opening up transborder connections through this knotted structure and the stories told about the protagonists. These knots are articulated not to create meaning or coherence but to provide new points of entry for other, more figurative border experiences and other kinds of difference.

Szczecin as Borderland

The setting of the novel is central to its border poetics. Szczecin is a port city near the Baltic Sea in northwestern Poland with about four hundred thousand inhabitants. It has a complicated and multilayered border history and is therefore an ideal locale for negotiating geopolitical and figurative border experiences and the relations and disruptions between different identities, times, and places. Szczecin was crossed by new borders in 1945, when the previously German city Stettin became part of Poland. The Oder River flows through the city, but just south of Szczecin, the German-Polish border deviates from the course of the river, running a few miles west so that Szczecin itself was not divided (in contrast to cities like Frankfurt an der Oder and Słubice, or Görlitz and Zgorzelec). Those who settled here after the war brought their multiethnic and linguistically, religiously, and culturally diverse attachments and affiliations with them, along with myriad strategies to balance contesting identities both within themselves and in their relations with others.

As was true for other formerly German areas, there was a lingering fear in Szczecin that Germans would eventually return and reclaim what they were forced to leave behind.[16] This led to a phenomenon that historian Gregor Thum has referred to in his study of the city of Wrocław (formerly Breslau) as "impermanence syndrome" or, as one of his sources says, a "psychosis of impermanence."[17] Jan Musekamp applies the term to the situation in Szczecin, and he uses it to describe the multiple processes of resignification that Szczecin has undergone.[18] Both the "*psychosis* of impermanence" (emphasis mine) and the previously discussed "Snow White *syndrome*" (emphasis mine) are based on medical terminology, and they describe related kinds of disruption with a psychological impact. While the first term refers to a disruption in time— that is, a disturbing feeling that everything can change in an instant, the latter suggests a spatial disorientation and discomfort that occurs when entering an unfamiliar space that has traces of an Other's presence. The protagonists

16   Weber, "Angst in der polnischen Deutschlandpolitik nach 1945," 136.
17   Thum, *Uprooted*, 171 and 189.
18   Musekamp, *Zwischen Stettin und Szczecin*, 122–26.

102 ◆ Disruption: Fictions of Memory

of *Bambino* are afflicted by both conditions, and this negatively impacts their ability to navigate the city and shape the literal and figurative spaces they try to claim for themselves. Throughout the novel, Szczecin gradually emerges as a microcosm of postwar Polish society and as a borderland in many different senses of the word.

Each of the novel's protagonists represents the notion of a multiply disrupted borderland in his or her own way, and the city intensifies these border biographies. The story of Ula or Ulrike merits a closer look here because it links *Bambino's* fictional world with that of the author. Ula is inspired by a woman named Teresa, a late friend of Iwasiów's family, whose loneliness, poverty, and illness preoccupies the author, as she explains in her autobiographical essay "Ingeleine, du wirst groß sein" (Little Inge, You Will Grow Up). As a friend of Iwasiów's grandmother, Teresa was a constant presence in Iwasiów's life, although she knew very little about her. What she does know is that Teresa was born in German Stettin and that she remained in the city after it became Polish. Later in life, Teresa suffered from gout, and because she was too poor to afford the proper medical care, this illness eventually led to the amputation of her legs. Unable to get a wheelchair, Teresa was confined to her apartment, and Iwasiów's mother looked after her until she died.

The essay was written within the framework of a project aimed at facilitating transnational European understanding, a literary cruise that took place along the border rivers Oder and Rhine in 2004 (mentioned in chapter 2, "Border Poetics"). Yet, in the first part of the essay, Iwasiów hesitates as to whether she should tell Teresa's story at all, even though she feels compelled to do so. She rejects the instrumentalization of painful stories and does not want to feed into German-Polish "Versöhnungskitsch" (reconciliation kitsch) narratives. With the present being so focused on the future, however, she insists on the importance of telling such stories of suffering and pain and of remembering the past: she concludes that while boat cruises such as the one she is on lead into the future, and even though wonderful stories lie ahead, stories like Teresa's—a "macabre and sentimental story about death in Szczecin, my beautiful city"—must continue to be told.[19] Teresa's story is

> Zeitgemäß und doch nicht zeitgemäß. Denn ich sollte meine biegsame Stilistik eher dazu nutzen, Grenzen zu überschreiten. Doch ich—nach all denen, die schon an diesen Orten waren—werde über eine Frau schreiben, die von den Grenzen überschritten wurde. So weit, dass diese ihren Körper in Stücke geschnitten haben. So buchstäblich, dass sie ihr ziemlich große Körperstücke weggenommen haben. Ich, eine postmoderne Literaturanalytikerin, eine Randgebietbewohnerin, die modische

---

19   Iwasiów, "Ingeleine," 139. My translation from the published German translation: "eine makabre und sentimentale Geschichte über das Sterben in Stettin, meiner wunderschönen Stadt."

DISRUPTION: FICTIONS OF MEMORY ♦ 103

Themen verachtet, werde anlässlich einer Schifffahrt die Geschichte einer Frau erzählen, die der Vergangenheit angehört; einer Vergangenheit, die—oh Ironie des Schicksals—in diese, der Zukunft zugewandten Zeiten verwickelt ist. Und (obwohl ich es nicht sollte)—ich werde es im Namen der Erinnerung tun.

[timely but also out of time. I should use my nimble style to cross borders. But I—after all those who have already been to these places—will write about a woman who was crossed by borders. So much so that they cut her body into pieces. So literally, that they took fairly large body parts from her. Me, a postmodern literary analyst, an inhabitant of the periphery, who despises fashionable topics, will use the opportunity of a boat cruise to tell the story of a woman, who belongs to the past; a past—oh irony of fate—that is entwined with these future-oriented times. And (even though I shouldn't)—I will do so in the name of remembrance.][20]

Iwasiów's essay makes clear that the pains of the past cannot be erased, even as the focus is on the future. *Bambino's* story follows this spirit: it is not a story of overcoming the differences and traumas created by borders, although the protagonists continuously try to do so. Rather, the story is about finding moments in the present in which those disruptions can be temporarily suspended.

Knots, Large and Small

The borderlands in *Bambino* take shape through attempts to forget as much as through processes of remembering. While the reader learns about the events that the protagonists recall from their pasts, the narrator also delves deeper into those moments of their lives that they are unwilling or unable to articulate or recall. In this way, other times and places in both former and present-day Poland come to play an important role in the novel, and they are "brought" into the city by protagonists who find themselves unable to detach themselves. Each of the first four chapters tells the story of one individual's family, his or her experiences during the war, and how that person came to Szczecin after the war. The novel thus begins by situating each character in a very precise moment, place, and social situation before gradually entwining the narrative threads. Maria, Anna, Ula, and Janek eventually meet in the seventh chapter, which is titled "Little Knots" ("Węzełki") to describe both the present state of each protagonist as well as their social relations.[21] Postwar Szczecin initially appears to be a place where they can begin a new life and finally focus on the present and future. Yet, little by little, their past traumas and the beliefs and prejudices from which they sought to emancipate themselves resurface and

20 Iwasiów, "Ingeleine," 134. My translation from the published German translation.
21 Iwasiów, *Bambino,* 64–67. For an English translation of this chapter, see Iwasiów, "Bambino (2008): Excerpts from the Novel," 146–48.

104 ♦ Disruption: Fictions of Memory

disrupt their lives. The protagonists remain deeply entangled with all the "baggage" they thought they had left behind, and this causes further complications in the present. I will introduce the individual characters to make these "knots" more visible.

Maria was born in 1940 near Drohobycz in Poland's eastern territories that were incorporated into the Soviet Union after the Second World War and are today part of Ukraine. After the end of the war, Maria's family considers going west, but they stay because they lack the proper paperwork and find it difficult to make a decision. When the Soviet Union closes its borders, they are no longer allowed to leave the country, and they lose the little decision-making power they had. The family lives in extreme poverty, and Maria grows up speaking Russian as her primary language. The family is eventually able to emigrate in 1957, but by that time the most attractive places in Poland had been taken, and they settle in an economically deprived rural area. At this point, Maria decides to strike out on her own and pursue an education in Szczecin. Yet, she comes to the city with an overwhelming sense of responsibility for her younger siblings and a deeply felt guilt for having abandoned her family. Maria is also homesick, a feeling that is encapsulated in her relationship to language. She struggles to learn Polish and does not feel at home in the language, which seems to continuously reject her. Still, she loves to read and finds that literature frequently facilitates border crossings and allows for a temporary escape. At the same time, she also encounters many impermeable borders—or to use Aamir Mufti's phrase, cited in the introduction, "border regimes"—that reinforce visible and invisible social boundaries. Maria rents a room from Ula, who works at Bambino. At the milk bar, she later meets Janek; the two fall in love, get married, and have a child.

Janek was born in a village near Poznań in the comparatively wealthy region of Greater Poland (Wielkopolska) in 1940. Despite being male and growing up with a relative economic advantage, Janek has a low social standing because his father's identity is unknown and he is considered a "bastard" ("bękart," 20). Janek's very existence is a scandal in his childhood community of traditional Catholics, and he is an outsider at school and among extended relatives. When his mother is forced to leave home to find work in the city, Janek grows up with his grandparents, who also know German and had worked for the Germans in various capacities before and during the war. After his grandmother's passing, Janek goes to Szczecin to find work and "become a man." In the city, no one cares about his fatherlessness, and he seizes the opportunity to make a career by cooperating with the Polish secret police. When he marries Maria, the two initially appear to have a perfect relationship and a comfortable life. Janek's collaboration with the Communist regime allows the couple to join the privileged class. Yet, over time, their pasts catch up to them: Janek develops an increasing sense of superiority over his wife and her poor family from the east. Maria struggles with alcohol abuse, and, after she dies, her friend Ula (Ulrike) takes in the couple's daughter.

Ulrike was born in German Stettin in 1930. Ulrike's father was an engineer and became an ardent National Socialist and a member of the Wehrmacht, Germany's armed forces during the Third Reich. When he does not return after the war, Ulrike and her mother presume him dead. Only much later does Ulrike learn that her father is still alive, and that he is living with a new family in West Berlin. Ulrike's mother is of mixed German-Polish descent, though she had long tried to forget her Polish side and had gone along with the Nazi regime. With nowhere else to go, Ulrike and her mother manage to avoid the expulsions and stay in Szczecin after the war. When her mother falls ill and dies in 1947, Ulrike remains in the city but conceals her German background, which includes changing her name to Ula.[22] Ula works in the milk bar, and when she is looking for someone to share her apartment, Maria becomes her tenant. Later, Ula begins a relationship with Stefan, a Polish Jewish Holocaust survivor from Warsaw. Like all relationships in the novel, theirs too is built on silences and omissions: although both can sense the truth about the other person, she does not mention her German past, and he never speaks about his life before or during the war. Their relationship ends in 1968, when Stefan is forced to leave Poland due to the antisemitic campaign led by the Communist authorities.

Anna was born in 1930. She is from the southern Polish resort town Wysowa-Zdrój in the Beskidy Mountains, about ninety miles southeast of Cracow (Kraków). The town became part of Habsburg Galicia during Poland's first partition in 1772; it was Polish during the interwar period, and during the Second World War it was occupied by Germany and incorporated into the General Government. Anna's father was a Polish bookbinder who completed some orders for the National Socialists and was murdered during the war. It remains unresolved whether the Germans murdered him because he was Polish or whether Poles killed him because they viewed him as a Nazi collaborator. As the circumstances of his death are unknown, and his body was never found, there is no death certificate. Anna and her mother thus have no legal right to the house in which the family used to live. After the war, the property is therefore passed on to the eldest son from the father's first marriage, who forces Anna and her mother out of their home. The patriarchal social and legal structures leave the widow and her unmarried daughter with no rights or protections. When Anna's mother remarries, Anna moves to Szczecin to pursue an education and begin a new life. She finds employment in the Bambino milk bar.

The initial four characters (a fifth, Stefan, joins the group later) are introduced in the first four chapters, and the remaining chapters complicate their narrative threads and the individual knots further. Guided and inhibited by their secrets and feelings of loneliness, pain, and desire, the protagonists

---

22 For an English translation of Ula's introductory chapter, see Iwasiów, "Bambino (2008): Excerpts from the Novel," 140–46.

106 ◆ Disruption: Fictions of Memory

struggle to build their lives and find themselves. The city in which they hope for a better future is itself marked by disruptions: everyone in Szczecin suffers from "Snow White syndrome" in their own specific way. If, like most, they came here after the war, they had to adapt to a strange place. For someone like Maria, this included learning a new language. If they were here before or during the war, like Ula, they needed to unlearn what they knew and reconfigure the space in accordance with the new reality, which for Ula meant hiding her German identity. Shedding her Germanness is all the more important for Ula because a permanent feeling of "ours-not-ours" ("nasze-nie-nasze") saturates the city. This symptom of the "psychosis of impermanence" is bolstered by the fear that the Germans will return one day and reclaim the city, a narrative that the novel shows to be part of the Communist propaganda.[23] The city has been culturally appropriated and appears in a "German-now-Polish version" ("w wersji niemiecko-teraz-polskiej"), but because the appropriation is imperfect, many elements in the city trigger memories of the past that all four—and later five—protagonists came here to forget.[24] Ruins from the war are still all around in the 1960s, and Maria's affirmation "To hell with the past!" proves to be more wishful thinking than an attainable reality.[25]

The narrative emphasizes that Maria, Ula, Anna, Janek, and the people they meet have crossed, have *been* crossed, and *continue to be* crossed by political, gendered, ethnic, religious, cultural, linguistic, and class borders. These border crossings have complicated the threads of their lives, and they have left visible and invisible scars on their psyches and their bodies. Ula, for example, vehemently insists on her independence from everyone, particularly men. Later, though, she gives herself up entirely in her relationship with Stefan. Stefan, in turn, never speaks about his experiences during the war, having survived the Holocaust by going into hiding in Warsaw. He suspects that Ula is German, but he tries hard not to be bothered by it. Similarly, Ula tries to detach herself from her German past and push aside her feelings of guilt and shame. Yet, these feelings are reawakened when Ula receives a letter from her presumed dead father in West Germany. Ula initially hides this news from Stefan. Meanwhile, Stefan is silent about his wife, who survived a concentration camp and now lives in Switzerland. She sends Stefan care packages but has no intention of ever returning to Poland.

---

23   Iwasiów, *Bambino*, 139. The novel explains that "ours-not-ours" leads to a lack of commitment to the city: "Nie inwestują, bo nie wiedzą, czy nie przyjdzie oddać" (They don't invest, because they don't know whether the time won't come to give it back). My translation. For a discussion of "Snow White syndrome" (Tokarczuk) and questions of belonging, see chapter 2, "Border Poetics."

24   Iwasiów, *Bambino*, 11. My translation.

25   Iwasiów, *Bambino*, 97. My translation. We will see in the next chapter how magical realism and the fantastic can help address even the formidable barrier of the past differently.

Ula and Stefan's life together is shrouded in secrecy and silence. And as much as they try to overcome their differences, their relationship is unable to withstand the heavy burden of the past. Even more than Ula, Stefan embodies the notion of a disrupted narrative and the blank spots in collective memory. He is the fifth main protagonist, but he is even more of an outsider than the others. The reader learns relatively little about him—much of it based on Ula's speculations—and he joins the four friends after their "knot" has already been tied. Stefan's presence in the story is therefore also an absence and a reminder of what was lost during the Holocaust. Iwasiów articulates this loss powerfully through obvious omissions, silences, and ellipses. Stefan thus symbolizes the difficulty of coming to terms with the past and the absence of Jewish life in postwar constellations, which is further amplified by the fact that he leaves Poland in 1968.

Even though this chapter focuses primarily on how border poetics is articulated on the level of story in a given work, it is worth returning briefly to my point that *Bambino*'s border poetics is also evident at the level of discourse and that one could examine its discursive strategies of knitting and weaving more closely. Iwasiów's syntax, for example, is characterized by a great variability in sentence length. Some sentences are very long, with multiple commas and coordinate and subordinate clauses. Meaning sometimes carries over between clauses that are at some distance from one another, interrupted by insertions and digressions, like in a stream of consciousness. Other sentences are very short, even truncated. They frequently initiate associations, and they elaborate on or emphasize previously stated information. The visible and invisible knots and entanglements and their accompanying secrets and lies are also enhanced by the novel's nonlinear narrative structure and the use of multiperspectivity and polyvocality. The voice of the narrator, who says she feels closest to Maria but expresses uncertainty whether this position can be upheld, is interwoven with the protagonists' voices.[26] The protagonists' intimately personal internal perspectives shine through in their actions and behaviors, which often lay bare their fears, anxieties, and hidden motivations. The many voices from the past that have impacted and scarred them in conscious or subconscious ways also reverberate in the present. This includes the propaganda heard at home or in school, the lessons and restrictive values inherited from mother or father, the social norms and oppressive mores transmitted by the church and the grandparents, and the protagonists' rebellion against, yet inescapable immersion in, these various voices and influences. Inner monologues and streams of consciousness reveal how worldviews, beliefs, and norms, especially gender norms, are transmitted and internalized, how they shape relationships, create patterns and traditions, and have a powerful and often damaging hold on the individual.

---

26   Iwasiów, *Bambino*, 66.

108 ◆ DISRUPTION: FICTIONS OF MEMORY

These multiple borders and border experiences intersect more and more as the disparate narratives of the protagonists' lives touch, and sometimes collide, in the city. *Bambino*'s protagonists are citizens of the cosmopolitan "border world" that is Szczecin, but there are only unfulfilled promises here. Maria, Janek, Anna, Ula, and Stefan can suspend difference for brief moments, but it always reinforces itself in new and often unexpected ways. While the five friends are excluded from "worlding" and do not benefit from any kind of cosmopolitan outlook, the reader gains a deep insight into the multiply layered ways in which human identity, belonging, and desire are entangled and connected in large and small ways in this borderland. Creating new forms of belonging relies in part on the suspension of difference, but the novel also paints a dark vision of cosmopolitanism by showing the difficulty of attaining this suspension and creating a space of transdifference.

Disrupted Spaces in
Sabrina Janesch's *Katzenberge* (2010)

Whereas Iwasiów's border poetics generates a starkly realist and fleeting cosmopolitan vision in which difference always comes back to reassert itself, Sabrina Janesch's *Katzenberge* can be read as a more optimistic outlook from a dark and violent past.[27] Janesch was born in West Germany in 1985 and is of German and Polish heritage. *Katzenberge* is her debut novel, and she addresses the German-Polish theme again in her second novel, *Ambra* (2012), which I discuss in the next chapter. Like Iwasiów's *Bambino*, Janesch's *Katzenberge* constructs "world" from the perspective of the borderland; it is locally bound and globally situated at the same time, linking historically and geographically specific events with more universally relatable liminal experiences. *Katzenberge* offers access to history and memory through different times and places, and it unsettles multiple kinds of boundaries on the levels both of story and of narrative discourse. While *Bambino* integrates figurative border experiences entirely in the realist mode, *Katzenberge* incorporates magical realism to articulate fluid identities and provide a transnational and transgenerational perspective on historical trauma, as Sabine Egger has argued. The reimagined past both serves as a "familial postmemory" and supports a much broader transnational Polish-German memory.[28] Similarly, Friederike Eigler has placed the novel within the context of changing notions of "Heimat" and identity into more fluid and deterritorialized concepts. By exploring different forms of belonging, the novel contributes to "the discursive transformation of formerly highly contested European border regions."[29] This transnational

---

27 *Katzenberge* has not been translated into English. All quotes from the novel are my translation.

28 Egger, "Magical Realism," 71.

29 Eigler, *Heimat, Space, Narrative*, 9.

perspective reveals the interrelatedness of German and Polish collective and individual histories and magical realism aids in rearticulating historical disruption.[30] The next chapter of the present book demonstrates that the fantastic or magical realism are effective discursive strategies for border poetics. For the time being, however, the main focus remains on the expression of border poetics through plot and story.

The world of *Katzenberge* is constructed from the double vantage points of the German-Polish and the Polish-Ukrainian borderlands; that is, two politically defined spaces that changed when Poland's eastern and western borders were both shifted westward after the Second World War. The protagonists at the center of *Katzenberge* are directly or indirectly affected by the resulting population shifts. Previous discussions of the novel have described *Katzenberge*'s borderlands as both geographical sites—places that one can experience perceptually—and delocalized symbolic spaces that hold contested and painful memories. These memories cannot be contained within nationally oriented frameworks, and Eigler argues that by integrating different perspectives and spaces, Janesch maps a transnational contemporary memory landscape. The main protagonist is not only of German-Polish heritage; she is also a representative of the young and globally oriented generation. Her position as a literal and allegorical border crosser fundamentally informs her storytelling.[31]

Mapping the Borderland

The novel maps the borderland as a confluence of material and symbolic spaces. Existing physical places provide helpful points of orientation for its three main plotlines. The frame narrative introduces the reader to the first-person narrator, Nele Leibert, who lives in Berlin and is of mixed Polish-German descent. The year is 2007, and Nele has come to the formerly German region of Lower Silesia in southwestern Poland to visit the cemetery where her grandparents Stanisław and Maria Janeczko are buried. She has just returned from her grandfather's birthplace in present-day Ukraine (formerly Polish Galicia), and she has brought back some soil from his homeland to spread on the graves. As Nele bikes to the cemetery, two inner narratives unfold. These narratives are assembled in the form of a nonchronological montage, and they offer a more detailed account of Nele's travels east to collect the soil, as well as the violent circumstances of her grandparents' settlement in Silesia. Nele's travels are triggered by her grandfather's passing some months earlier, and she hopes to find out who Stanisław Janeczko "really was" and preserve his story. Later, she is also confronted with the rumor that her grandfather had murdered his own brother, Leszek, which becomes an additional driving force in

---

30 Eigler, *Heimat, Space, Narrative,* 151–76.
31 Eigler, *Heimat, Space, Narrative,* 170–71.

110 ♦ Disruption: Fictions of Memory

her exploration of the past. Several blank spots in the family's history and different understandings of what constitutes reality increasingly undermine the idea that there is one authoritative truth to simply be discovered. I focus here on the plot, but it is important to point out that, just like in *Bambino*, the story is told through several narrative perspectives and voices. The next chapter shows in detail how the incorporation of different sources of information and insight functions as a central discursive strategy for border poetics.[32]

The physicality of spaces and traces is both established and questioned as Nele's journey takes her to places that have significantly changed since her grandfather had passed through, and that are imbued with memories, perceptions, and stereotypes in the present. Nele also finds material objects that are remnants of the past and that have acquired additional layers of meaning. The story is thus driven by a tension between the material and immaterial aspects of reality, and physically present objects stand in contrast to symbolic traces. This tension is already inscribed in Nele's last name, Leibert. Referring on the one hand to Nele's actual bodily existence, the very same body (*Leib*) is also in question. In an imagined conversation with her grandfather, Nele says, "Für etwas sonderbar hat man mich schon immer gehalten, aber seit ich von meiner Reise zurückgekehrt bin, Großvater, hält man mich für eine auratische Erscheinung. Obwohl man mich berühren, spüren kann, glaubt man mir meinen Körper nicht" (15; People have always considered me a little strange, but ever since I've returned from my trip, Grandpa, they think that I am some kind of auratic apparition. Even though I can be touched and felt, they don't believe my body).[33] Nele's physical journey east and her figurative journey into her grandfather's life have destabilized what had hitherto been taken for material reality.

Nele's journey first takes her to Wydrza in eastern Poland, where some members of her remote family still live, and then farther to Ukraine to visit Janeczko's birthplace and home for the first twenty-four years of his life: Zdżary Wielkie (later Zastavne), a village in the *kresy*, the Polish term that

---

32 In an analysis of *Katzenberge*, Florian Rogge has pointed out that Nele is not only a narrator and a protagonist; she also employs three different narrative voices: As narrator of the frame narrative, Nele tells the story and comments on the events; as narrator in the framed narrative, Nele travels and relates her feelings and impressions at the time, and these often receive ironic commentary from the Nele of the frame narrative. The third narrative voice is that of the grandfather—Nele tells her grandfather's story from his perspective but through her voice, as indicated by the recurring phrase "Großvater sagte" (Grandfather said). Rogge, "Galizien," 285.

33 Although this is not referenced explicitly, there are also affinities here between Nele and Nelly, the main protagonist in Christa Wolf's *Kindheitsmuster* (1976; *Patterns of Childhood*, 1980). Wolf's Nelly investigates her past by uncovering different layers of memory in a kind of archaeological process. Besides the symbolic unearthing of the past, Nele also engages in an archaeological process when she literally digs in the ground to find evidence of the past (204–7).

refs to Poland's former eastern borderlands.[34] Nele's eastward journey is the countermovement to Janeczko's forced westward movement more than sixty years earlier, when he was driven out of his village by a wave of violence from Ukrainian nationalists against the Polish population in 1943–44. He first flees to German-occupied Lwów (German Lemberg, today Lviv) by moving south and crossing the Bug River (which farther north also forms the current border between Poland and Ukraine). He then continues west to Wydrza, where he reunites with his family. When return to the Galician homeland becomes impossible after 1945, Janeczko; his wife, Maria; and others from their village continue farther west to Silesia, and they settle in the homes that have just been vacated by expelled Germans. They become affected by "Snow White syndrome," and they have a hard time feeling at home in the new and strange place.

Katzenberge is written in a realist mode; but with the help of fantastic elements, the novel also establishes another layer of reality that follows different rules of engagement. This reality is, for example, related to the workings of an ominous beast that appears throughout the story. The beast is at once a symbol of past horrors and an unquestioned material presence in the lives of several of the protagonists. It is accompanied by other supernatural beings, which can be interpreted as different iterations of the beast; for example, a wolflike creature (27) or an owl (173), which haunt the places in which Janeczko and Maria try to rest or settle. The beast lurks in the distance; its footsteps are audible (68); and it even attacks Janeczko and his first-born son, leaving physical marks on their bodies (104). On two occasions Maria performs a ritual to expel the beast from their house. Nele's sprinkling of earth on her grandparents' grave is also meant as a third and final expulsion ritual to banish the beast forever. The beast is not constrained to the past or the grandparents' lives, however. Nele herself encounters it on two occasions: on her way to the cemetery in the frame narrative and as a child many years earlier. Nele recounts her own childhood memory and her grandfather's reaction: Nele had spotted a large, black wolflike creature from the window of a train. Janeczko later responded to his granddaughter's report, "Es ist also wieder da" (27; So it is back), and Nele remembers his speculation "dass es sich vielleicht deshalb ausgerechnet mir gezeigt hätte, weil ich beide Teile vereinte, von drüben, von jenseits der Oder, und von hier" (27; that perhaps it had shown itself to me because I unite both parts, from over there, from beyond the Oder, and from here).

The fact that Nele has access to the beast is interpreted to be the result of her own transnational biography, a fact that might prove helpful in banishing the beast forever. Janeczko had last encountered the beast when his son was born: "Großvater sagte, als der Schrei seines zweiten Sohnes über die Felder hallte, sei das Biest in der Erde verschwunden. Geöffnet habe sie sich und es

---

34   I discuss this and other terms in chapter 1, "Entanglements in German and Polish History, Literature, and Culture."

112 ♦ Disruption: Fictions of Memory

mit Haut und Haaren verschlungen. Innerhalb weniger Sekunden habe sich die Krume geteilt und wieder geschlossen" (146; Grandfather said that when the cry of his second son echoed across the fields, the beast vanished into the earth. The earth parted and swallowed it whole. In just a few seconds, the crust had opened and closed again). Maria tries to make sense of her husband's experience: "Das kann vieles bedeuten. . . . Wer wisse schon, was diese Erde in sich trüge, mit wem sie verbündet sei und mit wem nicht. Ohne die dritte Bannung ließe sich nichts weiter unternehmen. Wir müssen damit rechnen, . . . dass es jederzeit zurückkehren kann. Jetzt oder in fünfzig Jahren" (148; It could mean a lot of things. . . . Who knows what this soil is carrying inside itself, who is its ally and who is not. Without a third expulsion ritual nothing could be done. We have to be prepared for its return. . . . Now or in fifty years). Maria, like her husband later, concludes that the border crossers in the family have a special relationship to the beast. She believes that for the time being their newborn son would provide them with the "Schutz des ersten polnischen Schlesiers, der in diesem Haus geboren wurde" (148; protection of the first Polish Silesian born in this house). She gathers: "Wir sind frei, Stanisław. Für viele Jahre. Janeczko atmete auf. Sein Kopf schmerzte. Zusammen schauten sie aus dem Fenster. Der Himmel war kornblumenblau, es würde ein guter Tag werden" (148; We are free, Stanisław. For many years. Janeczko was relieved. His head hurt. They looked out the window together. The sky was cornflower blue, it was going to be a good day).

Katzenberge's beast is a border crosser between worlds. It stands as a symbol for a past that is not completely past, and it serves as a stand-in for traumatic experiences and painful memories that are rooted directly in the earth or soil.[35] Not only does the beast come from and disappear into the earth; earth is also used to expel the beast. In the novel, earth is a symbol that connects different times and places as well as different understandings of what constitutes reality. The novel plays with the multiple meanings of "earth": as the world or planet; as the cultivable soil that forms the upper crust of that planet; or as that portion of land to which one has an emotional attachment— a homeland. These various meanings are also contained in the German word "Erde" and its Polish equivalent, "ziemia." "Erde" as a material object and a symbol exemplifies the particular and the universal, and it can yield familiarity as well as a strangeness that at times reveals itself as "beast."

Roots and Routes

Earth and world are central to the story of *Katzenberge,* and this brings to mind James Clifford's conceptualization of roots and routes: On the one hand,

---

35   See also Rogge's reflections on the significance of soil in the novel, especially the contrast between the rich Galician earth and the dry and barren soil of Silesia. Rogge, "Galizien," 293–94. Coleman analyzes this motif in *The Right to Difference,* 135–40.

earth is the place to which humans are connected, where they have put down roots; where they thrive and grow—or where they are forced to remain. At the same time, humans are also voluntarily or involuntarily mobile and experience the world always while "en route" from one location to the next—literally or symbolically, as travel, migration, or virtual or imagined movement.[36] Stanisław Janeczko experiences a sense of rootedness but also the disruption of that certainty in a corporeal way when he is forced to flee from his village to save his life. During the massacres he hides for hours in his wheat fields before he dares to continue. He feels "kühle, feuchte Erde, die durch das Hemd an seinen Bauch drang. . . . Janeczko rührte sich nicht, er war Teil seines Weizens, stimm- und reglose Wucherung des czarnoziem, der ölig schimmernden galizischen Schwarzerde" (238; cool, moist soil that penetrated his shirt and touched his stomach. . . . Janeczko did not move, he was part of his wheat, a silent and motionless growth of the czarnoziem, the oily and shimmering Galician black soil). This traumatic experience has also forever altered his relationship to this soil and shaken his belief in the organic and enduring union of people and their homeland: "Als Kind hatte Janeczko gedacht, dass sein Körper mit der Erde, auf der er lebte, untrennbar verbunden sei. Es hatte nicht lange gedauert, bis er feststellte, dass dies zwar sein mochte, dass man aber trotzdem die Erde verlassen und weiterleben konnte; unter Schmerzen zwar, aber es ging" (29; As a child Janeczko had believed that his body was insolubly connected to the soil upon which he lived. It did not take long for him to find out that this may be the case, but that one could nevertheless leave this soil and go on living; with great pains perhaps, but it was possible). The imagery of a connection or even a merging of body and earth recurs several times in *Katzenberge*. In the passage cited above, the boundary between body and soil becomes fluid, inextricably entwining the soil and those who live on it.

Janesch's description is reminiscent of images conjured by poet Tomasz Różycki, one of her literary inspirations, with whom she shares a "traveled topography," as Magdalena Baran-Szołtys points out: both authors have grandparents who either had to flee or were unable to escape from Galicia, and both have traveled from west to east to retrace these journeys and reconnect with a lost family history.[37] Różycki's poem "Spalone mapy" ("Scorched Maps") is a reflection on this journey to Ukraine. In it, the lyrical "I" seeks to connect with loved ones who have vanished, and several of the poem's images echo in Janesch's novel. In a guest post on the PEN America blog that accompanies Mira Rosenthal's English translation of the poem, Różycki explains that the work was inspired by the search for his family's former house. Just like Nele in *Katzenberge*, Różycki was only able to find "a brick cellar, half-buried, next

36   Clifford, *Routes*.
37   Janesch, "Interview mit Sabrina Janesch"; Baran-Szołtys, "Gonzo, Ironic Nostalgia, Magical Realism," 71.

114 ♦ Disruption: Fictions of Memory

to a dirt road that runs today over the spot where the house once stood."[38] The poem describes how, after finding nothing "but grass and leaves" (line 6) the lyrical "I" lies down, addresses the earth directly, and is literally embraced by it: "I said come out, // I spoke directly to the ground and felt / the field grow vast and wild around my head" (lines 12–14). As the lyrical "I" utters the words "you can come out, it's over" (line 9) to the ground, "bees began / to fly from everywhere" (lines 11–12).[39] *Katzenberge* ends with a similar sadness but also on an optimistic and reconciliatory note, when a bee lands on the scarf in which Nele had transported the Galician soil (272).

This more positive tone at the end of the novel does not diminish the extraordinary pain of the grandfather's experience and the relevance of the past for the present. Owing to the violent amputation from his homeland, Janeczko's sense of the world's wholeness is broken and replaced with a phantom pain that feeds on memories of this traumatic experience. Nele, as part of a globally minded generation and because of her mixed German and Polish heritage, feels less of a connection to a particular and clearly defined homeland. Although Nele can be thought of as a border crosser with conciliatory powers, she nevertheless experiences again and again how persistent real and imagined borders are, and how stereotypes, beliefs, and memories map the earth, shape convictions, and motivate actions. It seems fitting to recall here Beck and Grande's argument, outlined in the previous chapter, that the most challenging paradox for a cosmopolitan recasting of Europe is that "the national must be both overcome *and* preserved."[40] *Katzenberge* navigates this paradox: Nele's power lies not in resolving difference but in bringing multiple perspectives into a conversation across spatial and temporal divides. This creates a sense of world in which multiple local, territorial, social, cultural, or situational affiliations are connected to form a more cosmopolitan vision of the future.

As is also true for Tokarczuk's and Iwasiów's work, the "cosmopolitan vision" of *Katzenberge* is not to be misunderstood as a vision of harmonious coexistence but rather as a constructive tension of persisting difference. There is, for example, a significant disparity between Nele's and her grandfather's connection to the soil: in order to travel to Janeczko's birthplace, Nele has to cross the same river (the Bug) that Janeczko had crossed to save his life. But Nele's perception of the borderland is infused with a naive romanticism that is possible because *her* journey is voluntary and, despite some logistical difficulties, leisurely. Demystification sets in quickly, however, as the borderland reasserts itself and literally grounds her:

38　Różycki, "Guest Post."

39　Różycki, "Scorched Maps." In Polish, the poem has appeared under the titles "Spalone Mapy" and "Zapomniane Mapy" (Forgotten Maps).

40　Beck and Grande, *Cosmopolitan Europe*, 261.

Der Bug, sagte ich leise. Dann stieg ich aus. Schwarzes Wasser. Sonnenspiel auf Wellen, Strudel, die ihnen entgegenliefen, Sandbänke, die wie Finger in den Fluss hineingriffen. Dichte Weidenwände umgaben das Wasser, noch wenige Meter davor war nichts vom Bug und seinen Steilufern zu sehen gewesen. Ich verließ die Brücke und versuchte, mich seitlich ins Dickicht zu schlagen. Der Boden war feucht, und als mir einfiel, dass ich mich an den Zweigen der Weiden entlanghangeln könnte, rutschte ich aus, fiel auf die Seite, schlitterte einige Meter nach unten und prallte gegen einen Baumstamm. Ein hellbrauner Streifen Lehm zog sich dort, wo ich ausgerutscht war, durch die Erde.... Meine ganze rechte Seite war bedeckt mit ukrainischem Lehm.

[The Bug River, I said quietly. Then I got out of the car. Black water. Rays of sunshine playing on the waves, water swirling against them, sandbanks reaching into the river like fingers. Thick walls of willows surrounded the water, just a few meters back one had been unable to see anything of the Bug and its bluffs. I left the bridge and tried to enter the thicket sideways. The ground was moist, and just when I thought that I could hold on to the branches of the willows, I slipped, fell on my side, skidded several meters downward, and crashed into the trunk of a tree. A light brown streak of clay cut through the soil from where I had fallen.... My entire right side was covered in Ukrainian clay.][41]

To make her embarrassment even greater, Nele is immediately chastised by her Polish travel companion for attracting the attention of the Ukrainian border guards, who must now be paid off with an additional bribe. Despite such interruptions along the way, she finds some remnants of her grandfather's house, although its traces are as faint as the ones Różycki describes in his poem. Still, finding the site where the house once stood is essential because it allows Nele to bring some soil from her grandfather's homeland back to Silesia.[42] According to Claudia Winkler, this "almost slapstick moment" in which Nele slides down the banks of the Bug River encapsulates the novel's demystification of the lost homeland in the east in exchange for more symbolic claims through memories and stories.[43] I argue that this remaking also opens up the borderland for a cosmopolitan reimagination, and it is the kind of imagination needed for Nele to complete her mission. With Nele's help, the Galician soil has become mobile (just as its people had previously) and is transplanted to

---

41   Janesch, *Katzenberge*, 234–35. My translation.

42   See also Coleman's reading of *Katzenberge*, and how the mobile soil challenges ideas of nation and territory. Coleman, *The Right to Difference*, 137–38.

43   Winkler points to the discursive and spatial strategies with which Janesch transports *Heimat* into the realm of the symbolic, where it can be claimed through stories and memories. See Winkler, "Third-Generation Perspective," 93–95, especially 94; and 88.

116 ◆ DISRUPTION: FICTIONS OF MEMORY

Silesia. Under the prying eyes of the beast, she bikes to the cemetery to reunite her grandparents with the earth they had come from. The road is bumpy, however, and by the time Nele is ready to spread the soil on the graves and ban the beast forever, she realizes that she has lost most of it along the way. Nele cannot make borders disappear or reconcile the past, but she is forced to embrace the imperfect moment, use her imagination, and spread only the remaining fragments of dried earth on the graves. Yet, despite its limitations, Nele's journey was important: She searched for the past, discovered the many interpretations of her family's story, sensed its implications for the present, and found a suitable symbol—soil—to embody all of it and feel real at the same time. She thereby not only creates but also embraces a perceptual experience, and this practical orientation is crucial for contemporary cosmopolitanism.[44] In doing all of these things, and by admitting that myths, gossip, beliefs, customs, and "small" histories have an impact on world-making, Nele, and by extension Janesch, contributes to creating a "memory culture that spans borders."[45] The borders in *Katzenberge* are manifold, including those between Germany, Poland, and Ukraine today; between Silesia and Galicia of the past; between 2007 and 1943; between and through generations; and between different conceptions of reality.

Katzenberge puts forth a cosmopolitan vision of Europe: the novel's border poetics lies in recovering and keeping alive the memories of a traumatic past, but it does so with a practice-oriented and optimistic gesture that Amir Eshel has called "futurity."[46] In *Katzenberge*, there is the timid hope that the past may be a good place to begin practicing the cosmopolitan imagination by paying attention to the smaller and marginalized but interconnected histories. This possibility is also hinted at in the novel's concluding paragraphs. After completing her mission, Nele returns to her aunt's house, shakes the dust from her grandmother's scarf onto the lawn, and places it on the railing. The novel's final sentences echo Maria's and Janeczko's feelings after the last sighting of the beast cited earlier—a moment of hope for a new beginning (148). Nele says, "Auf der größten Blüte des Tuches landet eine Biene und wärmt sich in der Sonne. Der Himmel ist kornblumenblau, es wird ein guter Tag werden" (272; A bee lands on the scarf's largest flower and warms itself in the sun. The sky is cornflower blue, it will be a good day). The focus of these last lines may be only on the day ahead, but perhaps we can also think back to Różycki's poem,

44   Kim, *Cosmopolitan Parables*; e.g., 39, 42.
45   Beck, "Re-Inventing Europe," 112.
46   According to Eshel, futurity entails an examination of the political, cultural, and ethical implications of past events for the present and the future, and it imagines alternatives; Eshel, *Futurity*. While my reading focuses on the novel's utopian and future-oriented gesture, Eigler has noted that *Katzenberge* represents a "post-memorial space" that is firmly grounded in the European present. Magical realism makes the "specters of the past" visible and helps reimagine space as transnational. Eigler, *Heimat, Space, Narrative*, 176.

in which the bees come out when it is safe to do so. Perhaps it is therefore possible to carry this sentiment forward and to draw this optimistic conclusion from Nele's essentially incomplete mission to reconcile the past with the present and to not regard it as a failure.

Reality keeps reminding us that this future is, of course, fragile. Janesch and Iwasiów are well aware of this fragility when they lay bare the threads that simultaneously connect and separate people. In both novels, material objects and real places matter greatly, but just as important are ideational borders and imagined boundaries. These are suspended temporarily at best, and new borders often emerge where old ones fade away. Still, it is precisely the awareness of this fragility that is central to the cosmopolitan imagination and a driving force of border poetics. We can see the same processes and caution at work in Tanja Dückers's novel *Himmelskörper*, which I discuss next. Yet, the novel also reveals some challenges that lie in the attempt to articulate a genuinely cosmopolitan vison.

Clouded Memory in
Tanja Dückers's *Himmelskörper* (2003)

Tanja Dückers was born in West Berlin in 1968. She is a writer and freelance journalist, and her long list of publications includes essays, poetry, children's and young adult fiction, short prose, and several novels. In her journalistic work, Dückers engages with diverse aspects of German politics and society, and her articles appear regularly in major German newspapers and magazines, including *Die Zeit, Der Spiegel, Süddeutsche Zeitung, taz, Frankfurter Rundschau, Berliner Zeitung,* and *Berliner Morgenpost.* She advocates for human rights and is an outspoken supporter of refugee support organizations, including "Weiterschreiben.jetzt," a network that was founded in 2017 and through which German writers collaborate with writers from regions affected by war and unrest. *Himmelskörper* (Celestial Bodies) is Dückers's second novel, and it was published in 2003, one year after Günter Grass's novella *Im Krebsgang (Crabwalk,* 2002) reignited the debate whether it was acceptable for Germans to be portrayed not only as perpetrators but also as victims of the Nazi regime.[47]

Im Krebsgang and *Himmelskörper* both tell a story related to the events of January 1945 and the sinking of the German military transport ship *Wilhelm Gustloff* by the Soviets. The ship had carried mainly German civilian refugees trying to escape the advancing Soviet troops but also some military personnel. In an interview, Dückers explains her shock when she learned that Grass was writing a book on the same subject and her relief upon realizing that they

---

47   *Himmelskörper* has not been translated into English. All quotes from the novel are my translation. For a comparative analysis of *Im Krebsgang* and *Himmelskörper* with a focus on the topic of flight and expulsion, see Palm, "'Neuer deutscher Opferdiskurs'?"

118 ♦ Disruption: Fictions of Memory

had approached the topic quite differently. Even though Dückers concedes that two narratives about an event do not have to be mutually exclusive, she goes on to criticize Grass for being partial and too emotionally involved. While such a perspective "makes sense" for someone of Grass's generation, Dückers insists that she possesses "the necessary historical distance" and can "see the facts." Perhaps to further distinguish herself from the world-renowned Grass, Dückers adds that she "feels" her version to be "more correct and more historically accurate" and deems Grass to be too emotionally involved.[48] The focus on emotion as a point of criticism of Grass's work is puzzling considering not only that Dückers *feels* her version to be more appropriate but also the great value she places on accessing history emotionally. This claim to the historical truth and the idea that there is a safe historical distance from which one can see the emotionally unencumbered facts is not only complicated by the reality of many current memory debates but also by Dückers's own concept of "sensual historiography" ("sinnliche Geschichtsschreibung"). According to the author, this kind of historiography relies precisely on shrinking the distance between historical fact and personal experience and on a more intimate look at the entanglements of individual and collective memory.[49]

Himmelskörper itself is an engaging narrative that explores memory culture in compelling, if at times overly didactic, ways (which is something it has in common with Grass's novella). The *Gustloff* tragedy serves as background, but the primary focus is on processes of remembering and forgetting, questions of responsibility, denial, and the transmission of trauma across multiple generations, all of which make the novel a fitting case study for a number of memory studies concepts.[50] *Himmelskörper* also exemplifies a generational

48   Haberl, "Tanja Dückers." In the interview, Dückers says, "Sein Blick ist der seiner Generation. Es macht schon Sinn, dass Grass parteiischer, pathetischer und emotionaler ist, weil er involvierter war. Ich dagegen habe die nötige historische Distanz und sehe die Fakten. . . . ich empfinde meine Version als richtiger und historisch treffender" (His perspective is that of his generation. It makes sense that Grass is more partial, dramatic and emotional, because he was more involved. I on the other hand have the necessary historical distance and see the facts. . . . I feel that my version is more correct and more historically accurate).

49   Interview by Sabrina Ortmann, cited in Ächtler, "Topographie eines Familiengedächtnisses," 295.

50   The novel invites a reading through the lens of memory studies. One can, for example, find reflections on the differentiation between collective and individual memory (Maurice Halbwachs); cultural memory and its distinction from communicative memory (Aleida and Jan Assmann); or absences that have turned into *lieux de mémoire* (Pierre Nora). For a helpful overview of these and other major concepts and theories in memory studies, see Erll, *Memory in Culture*, esp. 13–37. *Himmelskörper* also offers insights into narrative and emplotment, forgetting and recollecting, rituals and cues, media of memory, and processes of transformation and remediation of memory and postmemory. At times these concepts are invoked quite overtly, which may add to the novel's didactic tone.

shift in German memory culture; namely, the emergence of a new generation of authors. For Harald Welzer, these grandchildren of the perpetrator generation ("Tätergeneration") stand in contrast to writers of the second generation, who have often grown soft and wish to reconcile with their parents. Welzer has credited this new generation, and Dückers specifically, for refraining from this problematic "mild consent" ("mildes Einverständnis").[51] Mila Ganeva has noted, however, that often these "grandchildren assume a remarkably warm and compassionate attitude when they reconstruct, imagine, or simply invent the stories of their grandparents." Despite the "shocking discoveries, uncomfortable questions, and painful confrontations with traumatic events," *Himmelskörper*'s main protagonist and narrator avoids confrontation or accusation and focuses on uncovering the family history.[52] Indeed, the narrator's lack of critical distance and self-reflection and the absence of other instances in the text that could challenge her perspective negatively impact the novel's border poetics. The engagement with politically defined spaces is uneven, difference tends to be reified rather than questioned, and implausible characters and plotlines hamper the novel's obvious intention to create a multidirectional and transnational memory network. Despite its many merits, these deficiencies bring the novel closer to "cosmo-kitsch" (Schoene) or "reconciliation kitsch" (Bachmann) than border poetics.[53]

Memory's Borderlands

Himmelskörper is told in the first person from the perspective of Freia (whose real name is Eva Maria Sandmann), a doctoral student in meteorology. At the beginning of the novel, presumably in the early 1990s, Freia is on her way to an academic conference. There she will present on cloud classification models and issue a call to international scientists to create a new and comprehensive cloud atlas. At the time of this trip, Freia's personal life has been in turmoil for several weeks. Her grandfather recently passed away, and her grandmother is very sick. Moreover, soon after the trip, Freia learns that she is pregnant, and this triggers in her a desire to know "in was für einen Zusammenhang, in was für ein Nest ich da mein Kind setze" (26; into what kind of context, into what kind of nest I am placing my child). This concern prompts her to embark on a mental journey into her family's past, including her own childhood and youth, and to examine how this history has shaped her family's life.

The reader learns that Freia grew up in a middle-class family in a West Berlin suburb with her twin brother, Paul, and her parents, Renate and Peter. Johanna (Jo) and Maximilian (Mäxchen), her grandparents on the mother's side, visit the family frequently. Jo and Mäxchen met in Gotenhafen (today

51 Welzer, "Schön unscharf," 63. My translation.
52 Ganeva, "Väterliteratur to Post-Wall Enkelliteratur," 160.
53 See my discussion in the introduction.

120 ♦ Disruption: Fictions of Memory

Gdynia, Poland) on the Baltic coast, where they lived from 1939 until their expulsion in 1945. While Mäxchen was still at war, Johanna and her young daughter, Renate, together with Johanna's sister, Lena, fled the advancing Soviet troops. They left Gotenhafen on a minesweeper called *Theodor* on January 30, 1945—the same day on which the *Wilhelm Gustloff* also departed from there. While Soviet torpedoes sank the *Gustloff*, resulting in the deaths of around nine thousand people, the *Theodor* arrived at its destination.[54] The sinking of the *Gustloff* serves here as a point of crystallization that allows for a reflection on guilt, silence, and forgetting, as well as on processes of memory and the transgenerational transmission of trauma. It is also serves as a red flag that draws attention to a family secret and the novel's central question: Why were Jo, Lena, and Renate not on the *Gustloff*? How did the three manage to get a coveted spot on the smaller, much safer, and better equipped minesweeper *Theodor*? In short, how did they manage to survive?

As Freia grows up, she slowly realizes that her grandparents could not have been, and in fact were not, the innocent bystanders of their own stories. Instead, they were ardent Nazis, and their privileged position and ties to the National Socialist German Workers' Party (NSDAP) had granted them a spot on the *Theodor*. In the chaos of advancing Soviet troops, of quick retreat and fast evacuation, however, even their prearranged journey was no longer guaranteed. The two women and the child arrive late on the overcrowded dock, and the barely five-year-old Renate secures for the family the last spots on the *Theodor* by denouncing a neighbor and her young son for wavering in their loyalty to the Nazis. According to Renate, the neighbors were then sent to the *Gustloff*, while Johanna, Lena, and Renate were allowed to board the *Theodor* (247–50). While Jo and Mäxchen express pride in their daughter for having saved their lives, Renate is plagued by a lifelong feeling of her own and her parents' guilt, as well as a sense of shame over their continued inability to critically examine their past. The constellation of multiple generations, their different deeds and silences, their acknowledgments and denials of guilt, and their varied ways of dealing with the past are shown to have an effect on the present, where they cause conflict, miscommunication, and, in the case of Renate, depression, and ultimately suicide.

Intertwined with this plot that investigates an individual family's history and historical responsibility within a larger historical context is a love story in which Wieland, Freia's first boyfriend at the age of seventeen, subsequently falls in love and begins a relationship with her twin brother, Paul. While this

---

54 The sinking of the *Gustloff* is today known as one of the deadliest maritime disasters in history. In German public discourse it was long a taboo topic because it represented the problematic notion of Germans as victims. With his novel *Im Krebsgang*, Grass broke this taboo. See Hage, "Das tausendmalige Sterben," 185. In private discourse, however, such a taboo never existed. Palm, "'Neuer deutscher Opferdiskurs,'" 49.

part of the plot, where questions of gender and sexual identity are at the center, makes Freia come to life as a more complex character, it also connects back to questions of the German past in two ways: first, it turns out that Wieland's elderly father is a war veteran and Wagner-loving Nazi (110); and second, during their relationship, Freia and Wieland travel to Warsaw (151–76), where Freia tries to investigate her uncle's suicide. And although Wieland eventually disappears from the siblings' life, his memory carries on into the narrative present. The novel ends about two and a half years after Freia's trip to the conference with which the story began. In the meantime, both grandparents have died, Freia has given birth to a daughter, and Renate has taken her own life. Now, two years after their mother's death and the sale of their childhood home in Berlin, Freia and her brother are in Paris and decide to write a book together that would contain the family's memories (315–18). Their idea is to transform the vast number of stories and inherited material objects (including photos, entrance tickets, and even Freia's ponytail) into a more manageable format ("Transformationsarbeit," 270), and they resolve to archive their memories in the form of a book that will be titled "Himmelskörper."

Through Freia's eyes, the reader gets an intimate view of her growing understanding of memory as a fraught process. She begins to question certain details of her grandparents' stories, tries to understand what has been forgotten and left out, and learns that subjective versions of events do not always measure up against historical facts and evidence. This journey into her family's past and her scientific research into clouds are intimately connected. In particular, cirrus perlucidus, an extremely rare and hardly visible cloud (11–12), appears as a leitmotif and main metaphor. Freia searches all over the world for cirrus perlucidus so that she can include it in the international cloud atlas. This cloud is so translucent that it is "eigentlich nicht mehr Objekt und doch noch nicht ganz entmaterialisiert" (24; no longer an object, yet not quite dematerialized). It has frayed and fleeting borders and stands for the volatility of memory and the intangible connections between different generations—an interpretation that the novel conveniently provides for the reader: Freia's desire to better understand her family history is accompanied by several journeys, one of which brings Freia and her mother to Gdynia. Unsurprisingly, it is here, standing in the harbor from which her family fled in 1945, that Freia finds the long-sought cirrus perlucidus. As if to ensure that the cloud metaphor is not lost on the reader, Freia also contemplates a colleague's idea about an academic conference on clouds as medium of storage ("Geschichtsspeicher") for history ("Geschichte") and for stories ("Geschichten"), respectively.[55]

Similar to the motif of knots and threads in *Bambino*, the less subtle discussion of cirrus perlucidus serves as a metareflection on processes of remembering and the nature of memory, and it provides insights into what Freia describes as the "schwebende Grenze zwischen 'subjektiver' und 'objektiver'

---

55 Dückers, *Himmelskörper*, 307. For an analysis of clouds as metaphor in the novel, see Stüben, "Erfragte Erinnerung," 182–85.

122 ◆ Disruption: Fictions of Memory

Geschichte, zwischen Faktum und Empfindung" (307; floating border between subjective and objective history, between fact and feeling). It reflects Dückers's belief in literature as a kind of sensual historiography and the desire to bring together "subjective" and "objective" history. The fluidity of these boundaries is articulated throughout *Himmelskörper*, and it is enhanced by the fact that Freia's identity is not solely determined by the historical burden of being German. She must also negotiate spaces that are universally related to growing up, her relationship with her twin brother, and questions of intimacy, love, and loyalty, as well as the pressure to conform to gender expectations and define her sexual identity.

Topographies of Absence

Even though various real and figurative boundaries entwine in the flexible memory landscape of the novel, the universally inflected ideas are not always convincingly connected to the particularity of the German-Polish borderland. Often the German-Polish plotlines lack specificity, and the binary treatment of Polish and German spaces diminishes the novel's intended openness. Other scholars have viewed these aspects more positively. Dagmar Wienroeder-Skinner counts Dückers among those authors whose writing exhibits a "genuine and very personal interest in their Polish neighbors," pointing out that "the inclusive character of the literature written by younger authors is one step towards reconciliation."[56] From a narratological perspective, Norman Ächtler has credited *Himmelskörper* for its artistic complexity. He interprets it positively that German and Polish spaces are represented as diametrically opposed, arguing, with reference to Michel Foucault, that this aids in the establishment of Poland as a space of "counter-memory."[57] This "cartographic polarity" on the structural level cannot do without certain stereotypes and schematic depictions, but Ächtler values Dückers's attempt to establish "a new, genuinely literary form of historiography."[58]

Examining the novel with a focus on border poetics, however, I find that the promise of inclusivity is only partially fulfilled, and that the polarity of spaces must be regarded as problematic. First, Polish spaces may be constructed as realms of "countermemory," but the Polish-German dualism also reinforces existing boundaries and constructs Poland as the space of the Other. Eigler has noted in disagreement with Ächtler that this construction essentially favors "a (albeit critical) German perspective."[59] Second,

56 Wienroeder-Skinner, "Attempts at (Re)Conciliation," 276–77.
57 Ächtler, "Topographie eines Familiengedächtnisses," 281; 276–77; see also 282–96.
58 Ächtler, "Topographie eines Familiengedächtnisses," 288 and 296. My translation.
59 Eigler, *Heimat, Space, Narrative*, 150.

the novel's spatial composition is not only made up of polar opposites, but there is a notable asymmetry in how these spaces are developed. The novel remains focused on Freia, who sees herself as part of a "lang[e] Kette" (26; long chain) and "dichtes Netzwerk" (254; dense network), but the details of this network remain elusive. Freia and Renate's seemingly intimate connections to Poland and the Polish language lack plausibility, there is little engagement with Polish perspectives or spaces, and Polish voices are conspicuously absent from the narrative.

Poland is introduced via two main plotlines: the first involves Gotenhafen, where Renate was born and from where she and her mother fled in 1945. Renate spent the first four years of her life there, and shortly before Renate's suicide, she and Freia visit the now Polish city Gdynia together. The second plotline relates to Warsaw via Uncle Kazimierz, a central but absent character. He is the reason why the family visits Poland often during the 1970s and 1980s and why Freia travels to Poland's capital at the age of eighteen. Renate is fluent in Polish, and her daughter, Freia, seems to have some proficiency in the language as well. Why or how they know Polish is never explained, however. Instead, the Polish language appears as a convenient attribute to make Freia and her mother appear less "German" and more cosmopolitan. The intention was perhaps to support a reconciliatory stance toward Poland and remind the reader of the Germans' historical responsibility, but the lack of any proper engagement with the Polish language or an explanation of why the two women speak Polish at all does more to underline how firmly rooted this novel is in the German viewpoint and how little it engages with Poland.

Places matter greatly for my assessment of the novel's superficial treatment of Poland. Freia's grandmother Johanna was originally from Königsberg (today Kaliningrad in Russia), but her father had sold the family business there in 1938 to join the merchant marine. At the end of 1939, the family moves to Gotenhafen, where Johanna meets and marries Maximilian (123). In 1940, they have a child: Freia's mother, Renate. The reader learns in passing that Maximilian's last name is Bonitzky (78), but there is no indication of a Polish connection in the family, nor that Polish was spoken at home. In addition, Renate does not meet her father until she is four years old, and it is unlikely that the mother spoke Polish, given her upbringing in a German/Prussian city like Königsberg. It can be construed with some effort that Maximilian's sister married a Polish man and they had a son named Kazimierz. Kazimierz is introduced to the reader as Freia's favorite uncle of German-Polish background. These family relations are never explicit, however. The reader learns only that Kazimierz and his parents fled to Warsaw after the war and that he grew up with an aunt in Warsaw after his parents died (157).

Renate and her parents, in turn, flee Gotenhafen and settle in Minden, in West Germany. Maximilian and Johanna had been members of the NSDAP, and while they insist that they were not "Nazis," Freia observes critically that

124   ♦   Disruption: Fictions of Memory

even fifty years after the war, they have no qualms identifying as "treudeutsch" (126; true German). Throughout their lives, Johanna and Maximilian harbor anti-Polish sentiments that they express in their talk of Poles as thieves (246) or of Polish mismanagement ("Polen-Wirtschaft," 155). Despite her parents' hostility toward Poles, Renate keeps in touch with Kazimierz, although it is unclear how and when this contact was reestablished and maintained. She also takes several secret trips to Poland. All these circumstances notwithstanding, the reader learns that Renate is fluent in Polish (154). Even more, she possesses *native* fluency, and during the trip to Gdynia she converses with everyone in accent-free Polish, making Freia wonder whether it made her mother happy when people thought of her as Polish (292). Renate's native proficiency in Polish is highly implausible and would at least require some explanation, but none is even implied in the novel. It is also revealed that Uncle Kazimierz, who is six years older than Renate, loved the German language, which he had learned from Renate as a child (167), yet there is no mention about the family's life in Gotenhafen or how five-year-old Renate taught her older cousin German.

Freia's knowledge of Polish is also dubious, and her precise level of proficiency is unclear. As a child, she does not know Polish, and Kazimierz needs to translate for the children when they visit a theater in Warsaw (155). And when Freia visits Gdynia with her mother as an adult in the 1990s, she is unable to read even a small commemorative plaque, except for the year 1944 (297). Nevertheless, when Freia travels to Warsaw four years prior (in 1986) to investigate Uncle Kazimierz's suicide, she insists that she knows "a little" Polish (154) and that she had to brush up on her apparently marginal but existing Polish skills (173). Her "gebrochenes Polnisch" (164; broken Polish) is sufficient to interview people who knew Kazimierz. The reader never finds out anything about Freia's effort to learn Polish or when and how she might have picked up enough to carry on a conversation. Freia's and Renate's ability to communicate in Polish could cast both women as border crossers with mixed identities. This option, however, is never explored, and neither Renate's nor Freia's Polish proficiency explains itself through their biographies—on the contrary, it even seems highly unlikely.

Because none of the Polish-German connections in the novel are explained plausibly, they remain flat. While it is entirely credible that Freia does not have insights into all aspects of the past, and while the narrative perspective limits what the reader can know, Freia also shows no sign of having to negotiate a conflicted (or even a nonconflicted) German-Polish identity. She never says that she is of mixed German and Polish descent, nor does she in any way think about her personal role in the Polish-German border story. The plot does little to explain Renate's and Freia's connection to Poland, and any references to the Polish side of the family remain vague: "diese und jene entfernte Großtante oder -cousine, denen meine Mutter sporadisch schrieb, diesen oder jenen alten Kumpel, mit dem wir in Warschau mal ein Bier trinken gewesen waren"

(159; here and there a distant great-aunt or cousin, to whom my mother wrote sporadically; here and there an old friend with whom we had once met up for a beer in Warsaw). Instead, Renate's and Freia's "Slavic looks" are meant to convince the reader. Freia's mother is "sehr schlank und hübsch mit ihrem feingeschnittenen slawischen Gesicht, den blonden langen Haaren und den blauen Augen" (14; very slender and pretty with her delicate Slavic face, her long, blond hair, and blue eyes), and she also has a "blasse[s] slawische[s] Gesicht" (167; pale Slavic face). Freia characterizes herself in a similar way: "Ich entsprach eher dem östlichen Typ mit puppenhaftem Gesicht, hohen Wangenknochen und bleicher Haut. . . ." (156; I looked more like the Eastern type with a doll face, high cheekbones and pale skin). While the racism that is embedded in the grandparents' language is problematized throughout the novel, Freia never critically examines her own stereotypes; nor is this done by other narrators or protagonists. Freia is oblivious to her own assumptions, which puts serious limitations on the persuasiveness of the German-Polish transborder network that the novel aims to create.

Places also matter as travel destinations and often serve as "containers" for ideas of Poland and the East more generally. Altogether, there are three visits to Poland that Freia remembers in more detail, and each of these visits represents a specific stereotype about Poland and the East. The first stereotype is that of the "wild East," embedded in Freia's memory of a family trip to Silesia when Freia was a child. Here, Poland appears as a place where one can be free and escape the constraints of civilization and familial obligations.[60] This romanticized image of Poland stands in stark contrast to Freia's perception of Warsaw during her second trip around 1986 (following Kazimierz's suicide). The city appears depressing and gray, a place of victims and absences. Freia is overwhelmed by the abundance of reminders of the Second World War through memorials, buildings, and empty spaces, and she notices everywhere the traces of German atrocities. Ächtler notes that Freia experiences Warsaw as an assemblage of what Marc Augé has described as "non-places."[61] While this trip is an opportunity for Freia to contemplate German responsibility and guilt, she also replaces what Ächtler has described as the "cliché of a free and wild East" with the stereotype of Poland as gray, backward, and depressing.[62]

Freia's experience in 1986 differs significantly from the third and final trip in the 1990s, during which she and her mother visit post-Communist Gdynia together. Yet, even then, Freia perceives the city as an exaggerated and outdated version of the West. She is struck by the bright colors and speculates that they must have been introduced after the fall of Communism. The color

---

60   Dückers, *Himmelskörper*, 16–17. For an analysis of this visit, see Ächtler, "Topographie eines Familiengedächtnisses," 288.

61   Ächtler, "Topographie eines Familiengedächtnisses," 290–91.

62   Ächtler, "Topographie eines Familiengedächtnisses," 288. My translation.

126 ◆ Disruption: Fictions of Memory

palette is a stark contrast to the gray tones she encountered during her earlier journey to Warsaw, but now she surmises that this is what an "LSD-Trip" (293) must be like. Stereotypes of a formerly gray and now overbearingly colorful and garish East notwithstanding, Freia notes that the town has a global and vibrant flair and that she feels as if she were in a "Polish Mallorca" (295), the Spanish island in the Mediterranean that is famously overrun with partying German tourists every summer. Renate remarks that the place seems to have overcome its traumatic past (306). Freia's discovery of cirrus perlucidus during this trip appears like a confirmation of her mother's assessment: the past is still present here but only as a faint trace.

The missed opportunity to integrate a Polish voice in the novel is especially apparent with regard to Uncle Kazimierz. Freia's memories of her uncle set him up as a chaotic and drunk, yet lovable, Pole, who took her to a bar to drink vodka when she was only fifteen (166). This memory of her uncle comes to Freia on her 1986 trip to Warsaw, during which she hopes to understand her uncle's recent suicide by speaking to people who knew him (157). Throughout his life, Kazimierz was affected by political border shifts. Even after the war, he was an outsider in Polish society because he was of German-Polish descent. By cooperating closely with the Communist regime, however, he managed to have a career as a TV moderator (169), which granted him some fame and privileges. Kazimierz's biography would lend itself well to explorations of national, ethnic, or regional identities and the complicated ways in which they overlap and come into conflict with one another. Yet, his character remains underdeveloped, and, in fact, absent. He does not appear in the novel except as part of Freia's memories. He is even doubly absent when Freia recalls for the reader the conversations she had *about* him.[63] In Freia's own memories, he is drunk and chaotic but fun because he does not reprimand the children for playing in his disorderly office (154–55). As an adult, Freia tries to understand why her grandparents disliked Kazimierz, even though the grandparents make no effort to mask their racism and prejudice against Poland and the Poles. Nevertheless, she longs for a rational explanation—a desire that appears to be satisfied much later, when Renate reveals that Kazimierz knew why and how the family was able to escape on the *Theodor*, and that her parents feared he might incite their daughter against them. For Renate, the relationship to Kazimierz has a healing function; she can talk to him, and she sees in him an older brother (301). Ächtler notes that because he is Polish and a victim of the Germans, his forgiveness can also alleviate the guilt she feels.[64]

Reader responses to the novel might perhaps provide additional insights into its "worldliness" or a lack thereof. German popular reception of

---

63   During her visit to Warsaw, Freia talks to eleven people who knew Kazimierz, yet according to her, none of them has anything new to tell her (173). Other witnesses appear unpleasant and stereotypical; e.g., with greasy hair and dirty clothes (164).

64   Ächtler, "Topographie eines Familiengedächtnisses," 289.

Himmelskörper was mixed, but few reviewers made any comments on the role of Poland or the Poles.[65] In 2014, the novel was translated into Polish and published under the title *Ciała Niebieskie*. In one of the few Polish reviews that had been published as of 2023, renowned literary critic and writer Kinga Dunin writes that the book is "not bad," but that the Polish plot "seems artificial, but perhaps it had to be there for the sake of completeness—readers here, however, will find it irritating."[66] Scholars have generally credited Dückers for her exploration of the difficult and flawed processes of remembering and forgetting, the transgenerational transmission of memory and trauma, and Dückers's particular contribution as an author of the third generation.[67] Some scholars have drawn attention to the novel's deficiencies regarding the Polish plot, such as Eigler, who has commented that Dückers's "fledgling orientation toward the East does not result in any substantive engagement with Germany's eastern neighbor. Rather, the narrator's trips to Poland seem to render the country and its people even more opaque."[68] Izabela Drozdowska-Broering likewise criticizes Dückers's half-hearted and predictable engagement with Poland, speculating that it may be in part due to her lack of Polish-language skills. She argues that the novel is filled with clichés and shows no genuine engagement with Poland and the Poles, and that an open dialogue with the Other is forgone in favor of political correctness. Interestingly, in a personal interview with the author that can be found in the appendix to her study, Drozdowska-Broering even addresses the topic of "reconciliation kitsch" and "kitsch" more generally. Understandably, Dückers rejects the notion that her novel might be read as "kitsch."[69]

All this is not to say that Dückers does not have a "genuine and very personal interest" in Poland.[70] Still, I find the engagement with Polish history and culture in *Himmelskörper* rather unconvincing. The novel's exploration of memory and its boundaries through the German-Polish borderland and the interweaving of questions of gender and sexuality into the narrative hold a promise of border poetics. As I have shown, however, its fulfillment is hampered by stereotypical descriptions and the binary construction of Germany

---

65   For example, the reviews summarized in the online cultural magazine *Perlentaucher* criticize the novel for using platitudes (Susanne Balthasar) or note an implausible psychological motivation as well as a reliance on banalities (Stefanie Peter). Wolfgang Schneider from the *Neue Zürcher Zeitung* remarks on the book's "slavophile clichés and familiar postsocialist tristesse" (my translation). See "*Tanja Dückers.*"

66   My translation. In her very short note, Dunin writes, "Jest tu też wątek polski–który wydaje się sztuczny, ale może dla dopełnienia musiał się pojawiać, dla tutejszego czytelnika będzie jednak szeleścił papierem." Dunin, "Czytelnia Krytyki Politycznej."

67   Welzer, "Schön unscharf," 62–63; Ächtler, "Topographie eines Familiengedächtnisses"; and Stüben, "Erfragte Erinnerung."

68   Eigler, *Heimat, Space, Narrative*, 149–50.

69   Drozdowska-Broering, *Topographien der Begegnung*, 119, 125–29, and 211–26.

70   Wienroeder-Skinner, "Attempts at (Re)Conciliation," 276.

128 ♦ DISRUPTION: FICTIONS OF MEMORY

and Poland. *Himmelskörper* does not propose a model for what a shared European or cosmopolitan memory could look like, even if it could be only temporarily sustained. While the novel successfully articulates the intricacies of individual memory across three generations of Germans, it fails to engage with Polish memory discourses. Dückers emphasizes Polish suffering under German occupation and the destruction of Polish cities, but the novel remains steeped in a German perspective. The impression that there is very little questioning of established boundaries or self-Other designations, at least with regard to German-Polish themes, is enhanced by the fact that the only voice in the novel is Freia's and that any other perspective is always refracted through her. Poles are largely absent from the story, and the family's connections to Poland are vague. The novel's lack of complexity and nuance in effect means that the Other, once posited as such, has no means of disrupting and challenging the privileged German narrative. Paradoxically, while Freia's scientific cloud atlas is a universal project that depends on the collaboration of international scientists, the memorial space remains cordoned off from challenging perspectives. The novel emphasizes that memory and processes of remembering are communal efforts, but the narrative does not engage with other voices or views and remains safely on its side of the border.

Border Crossings

Himmelskörper, Bambino, and *Katzenberge* show different ways of expressing border poetics on the level of story—in the progression of events, their temporal and spatial coordinates, in the way in which stories establish coherences between places and people, and the strategies they use to respond to breaks and disruptions. Each text discussed here offers a distinct approach to borders and bordering practices, but they share a central concern with questions of collective and individual memory and how a past that is refracted through multiple lenses shapes the present and future. These fictions of memory tell stories of people who have crossed literal political and territorial borders, and how people, while remaining in place, have been crossed by borders that have moved, but also how these border crossings intersect and entangle with figurative border crossings. Nevertheless, the novels vary in the degree to which border poetics is produced effectively. Despite its nonlinear narrative and the exploration of real and figurative boundaries, *Himmelskörper* lacks convincing elements to disrupt existing frameworks, and it is an example of border poetics only in a limited sense. *Bambino* and *Katzenberge,* on the other hand, each create polyvocal narratives in which different perspectives interact to create a complex story that unsettles familiar constellations of centers and margins and self and Other. In all three novels, border crossings are impulses for stories—stories that articulate the border both as a dividing line and as a zone of contact and exchange. These stories negotiate the breaks and disruptions that characterize the German-Polish past. By not smoothing out or resolving such breaks, the novels—some more successfully than others—reveal the knotting, threading, and unraveling of stories and memories across literal and figurative boundaries.

4: Belonging: Defocalized Narratives by Günter Grass, Sabrina Janesch, and Olga Tokarczuk

> ... jestem czystym patrzeniem, czystym wzrokiem i nie mam ciała ani imienia. ... mogę zobaczyć wszystko naraz albo tylko najdrobniejsze szczegóły.
>
> ... I was pure sight, without a body or a name. ... first I could see everything, then only tiny details.
>
> —Olga Tokarczuk, Dom dzienny, dom nocny, 7 / House of Day, House of Night, 1

WHO IS THE NARRATOR in this epigraph? Can "pure sight" tell a story? And how is it possible to have an overview of everything but also perceive every tiny detail? To answer these questions, this chapter turns to the discursive production of border poetics in narratives. In other words, I am less concerned here with the *what* of the story, as I was in the previous chapter, and more with *how* the story is told in order to stage actual and figurative boundaries and their multiple and variegated transgressions. The narrated events remain important, but the goal of this chapter is to examine the role that narrative structure and formal choices play in border poetics, for example, when points of view intersect, overlap, or compete. The above excerpt from a dream at the opening of Olga Tokarczuk's novel *House of Day, House of Night* introduces a peculiar narrative perspective, but its underlying attitude is shared among the novels discussed in this chapter. All of them are simultaneously told as broad overviews granted by an omniscient perspective and as small, detailed, and personalized views of the world that are the privilege of a first-person narrator. To achieve this contradictory position, narrators defy boundaries of space, the body, or knowledge, thereby approaching the fourth-person narrator that Tokarczuk envisions in her "Nobel Lecture," and which I discussed earlier.[1]

The guiding concept for this chapter is that of belonging. If perspective is assumed to be a view *from* somewhere, anchoring a narrator's belonging, then what do we make of a narrative perspective that has no fixed location

---

1   I discuss Tokarczuk's concepts of the fourth-person or "tender" narrator in chapter 2, "Border Poetics."

and that displays a simultaneous access to every detail as well as its wider, even universal context? Belonging is multiple, ambiguous, and flexible, and it is made possible by leaving the boundaries of realism. As I explain in more detail below, magical realism or the fantastic lend themselves particularly well to border poetics because they unsettle the conventional boundaries that anchor belonging. Certain choices in narrative perspective and focalization foster border poetics by drawing attention to ambiguity, defocalization, and resistance to hegemonic discourses. In certain ways, these texts convey a sense of being "born translated" by challenging the reader to think of belonging as encompassing multiple sites and scales at once.[2] The second part of the chapter shows how these discursive strategies are at work in Günter Grass's *Die Blechtrommel* (1959; *The Tin Drum*, 1961 and 2009), Sabrina Janesch's *Ambra* (Amber, 2012), and Olga Tokarczuk's *Dom dzienny, dom nocny* (1998; *House of Day, House of Night,* 2002).

Border poetics questions boundaries and allows for mobile and flexible expressions of affiliation. Thus, the creation of blurriness and indeterminacy of perspective are among its most effective discursive strategies. Narratives have different ways of avoiding or limiting clarity, including ambiguous (or unreliable) narrators and protagonists, unusual and frequently changing points of view, and the articulation of multiple and often contradicting voices and narrative perspectives.[3] I draw on two main paradigms when considering the spatial and ideational locus (or even multiple loci) from which a narrative is presented to the reader. One is that of "focalization," while the other is "point of view" (or "perspective"). Burkhard Niederhoff has summarized the semantic and conceptual distinctions between the two as a difference between, on the one hand, access to and transmission of knowledge (focalization), and, on the other hand, an emotive or cognitive inflection of that knowledge (point of view). Drawing on Gerard Genette's narrative theory, Niederhoff explains that focalization is "a selection or restriction of narrative information in relation to the experience and knowledge of the narrator, the characters or other, more hypothetical entities in the storyworld." It does not provide as much insight into the "subjective experience of a character," but it creates "other effects such as suspense, mystery, puzzlement, etc." Point of view, by contrast, provides the more subjective insights by conveying how "events . . . are perceived, felt, interpreted and evaluated by [a character] at a particular moment." In contrast to earlier attempts to replace the concept of point of view with that of focalization, Niederhoff ultimately proposes a model in which both paradigms coexist, "because each

---

2   Walkowitz, *Born Translated*. See also the introduction to the present book.

3   Importantly, multiperspectivity is not merely a summative addition of perspectives. Rather, the same event is presented from different perspectives, without one perspective being the authoritative one. See Nünning and Nünning, "'Multiperspektivität,'" 375–77.

132 ♦ Belonging: Defocalized Narratives

highlights different aspects of a complex and elusive phenomenon."[4] In addition to point of view and focalization, I also draw on the concept of "voice" when it is important to emphasize who or what "speaks."[5]

In practice, however, and perhaps especially in the practice of border poetics, point of view, focalization, and voice cannot always be clearly distinguished. It may also be difficult to identify *who exactly* experiences, focalizes, or speaks. For example, who is the narrator in Günter Grass's *Tin Drum*? Can we trust anything he says? Is there one narrator or several? And what of the drum and the glass-shattering screams—what part do they play in telling the story? I will get to these problems later, but it is precisely this ambiguity that irritates the reader and helps undermine hegemonic discourses, thereby advancing a cosmopolitan imagination. To understand this process, three questions guide my analysis: *Through whom or what* does the reader *perceive* the events by way of the narrator (focalization)? *Who experiences* (point of view), and *who speaks* (voice)? In many ways, these questions pertain to ontological boundaries—they ask about the sources and limits of knowledge, and their answers depend heavily on the story world's conditions and rules: How does the narrator or the protagonist know what they (claim to) know? What restricts or facilitates their knowledge? How is it possible for them to experience the things they experience? I ask these questions in addition to those pertaining to the identity or position of the narrator or protagonist to better understand the multiplicity of border crossings and to peel back further layers of narrative ambiguity.

The texts I examine here share at least one characteristic regarding the source of this ambiguity: they violate our expectations about the plausibility of the narrative knowledge presented. These story worlds lack rational explanations because they are created in the narrative modes of the fantastic or magical realism. I argue that these modes produce multiple forms of attachment and detachment, and that this multiplicity contributes to border poetics. I explore more details of this conceptual blending below, but I also want to emphasize here that I regard magical realism and the fantastic as *modes* of writing, based on Matias Martinez and Michael Scheffel's understanding of "mode" as a category that describes a narrator's distance from the narrated events ("Mittelbarkeit") and the distinct perspective that is given to a narrative ("Perspektivierung des Erzählten").[6] Additionally, Claudia Pinkas regards mode as a structural principle of narratives that can be present across different genres, periods, and media and that can interact and mix with other narrative

---

4   See Niederhoff, "Focalization"; and Niederhoff, "Perspective—Point of View."

5   Gerard Genette introduced the category of voice to distinguish between a narrator who is also the protagonist (i.e., a narrative that is focalized *through* the protagonist) and a protagonist *on* whom the story is focalized, and who has a "voice," but who is not the narrator. Genette, *Narrative Discourse*, 189–99.

6   Martinez and Scheffel, *Einführung*, 47.

modes.[7] Viewing the fantastic and magical realism as modes of narration stresses their flexibility and broader applicability. Narratives that draw on these modes create connections across times, genres, and languages, producing effects that support border poetics.

Cosmopolitan Modes:
The Fantastic and Magical Realism

Fully aware that there are important differences between magical realism and the fantastic, I consider these two concepts jointly here, based primarily on how they relate to questions of borders. The fantastic and magical realist modes can be present in a text to varying degrees, and my main interest is in the ambiguity that supernatural or irrational events and elements create in a narrative. Narrative perspective is an important source of this ambiguity, as Wendy Faris explains:

> In magical realism, the focalization—the perspective from which events are presented—is indeterminate; the kinds of perceptions it presents are indefinable and the origins of those perceptions are unlocatable. That indeterminacy results from the fact that magical realism includes two conflicting kinds of perception that perceive two different kinds of event: magical events and images not normally reported to the reader of realistic fiction because they are not empirically verifiable, and verifiable (if not always ordinary) ones that are realism's characteristic domain. Thus magical realism modifies the conventions of realism based in empirical evidence, incorporating other kinds of perception. In other words, the narrative is "defocalized" because it seems to come from two radically different perspectives at once.[8]

What Faris describes here as defocalization corresponds to my earlier discussion of Stefan Chwin's notion of the "defocalized identities" that inhabit the German-Polish borderland and that have brought about "a new borderlands literature" (see chapter 1, "Entanglements in German and Polish History, Literature, and Culture"). In both instances, the term refers to a blending of different perspectives as well as a concern with the transgression and destabilization of borders. My translation of the adjective "nieostra" in Chwin's original expression as "defocalized," rather than as the more direct "blurry" or "blurred," is meant to echo Faris's word choice and account for the parallels between the border-crossing potential inscribed in certain modes of narration (such as magical realism) and the condition that, for Chwin, is a result of the

---

7   Pinkas, *Der phantastische Film*, 93.
8   Faris, *Ordinary Enchantments*, 43.

134 ♦ Belonging: Defocalized Narratives

particular constellation of the (Polish-German) borderland.[9] Moreover, to me, "defocalized" also expresses a more universal and figurative indeterminacy of the borderland that stems from its inherent violence but also its empowering potential, such as analyzed by Gloria Anzaldúa. The novels I discuss in this chapter are vivid illustrations of this confluence of associations.

By using the terms "magical realism" and "the fantastic," I refer to narratives with elements or phenomena that cannot be rationally explained. This conceptual blending is not meant to obscure the idiosyncrasies and separate histories of magical realism and the fantastic but rather to emphasize that border poetics focuses on multiple and simultaneous forms of affiliation and that those can be expressed equally well through the fantastic and through magical realism. In particular, I point to three major links between fantastic or magical realist modes of narration and the practice of border poetics: first, all three emphasize an ambiguity that is maintained by the continuous subversion and transgression of boundaries; second, they prioritize defocalized forms of existence and knowledge, which they express through multiple or unusual perspectives and polyvocality; and third, they resist and undermine established boundaries and support the creation of new forms of belonging. Let me briefly elaborate on this relation between ambiguity, defocalization, and belonging.

Ambiguity and doubt are fundamental elements of magical realism and the fantastic. In his writings on the fantastic, philosopher and literary critic Tzvetan Todorov elucidates the sources and the effects of this ambiguity. He argues that the fantastic emerges in narratives at a particular moment of insecurity and indeterminacy; namely, when an event occurs that cannot be explained by the laws that govern the familiar world. Confronted with such an event, the protagonist, narrator, or reader must decide whether the occurrence can be explained rationally (e.g., as an illusion, a dream, or a sign of a particular mental state) or whether there are supernatural causes for the event. If this question can be answered, we are no longer in the realm of the fantastic but are instead either entering the uncanny (if the event can be rationally explained) or the marvelous (if a different reality exists within which the event was possible). In a fantastic narrative, no such conclusive assessment can be made, and both rational and supernatural explanations remain equally likely.[10] Todorov further argues that, because the fantastic mode unsettles conventional conceptions of reality and questions what is considered normal and normative, it "requires doubt."[11]

Some scholars have reasoned that an important difference between magical realism and the fantastic lies precisely in the relationship to the issue of doubt. While the fantastic mode is suspended in a state of uncertainty and

---

9   Chwin, "Grenzlandliteratur," 5. The German version of the essay refers here to "unscharfe Identität."

10   Todorov, *The Fantastic*, 25–26.

11   Todorov, *The Fantastic*, 83.

ambiguity over the occurrences, as Todorov describes, Amaryll Beatrice Chanady contends that this kind of doubt is unknown to magical realism because it takes for granted the simultaneous existence of the natural and the supernatural.[12] By contrast, Faris insists that the reader may very well experience doubt and that doubt may also derive from the fact that "magical realism disturbs received ideas about time, space, and identity."[13] It is therefore difficult to draw a clear distinction between the fantastic and magical realism based on the ambiguity/nonambiguity binary, especially when considering that doubt, disruption, or indeterminacy can manifest not only at various levels within a narrative but also in their relationship to the extradiegetic world, such as a reader's response to a text. Moreover, I argue that the experience of doubt (by the reader, protagonist, or narrator) can be regarded as a location of the cosmopolitan potential of these narratives; that is, the possibility that the assumed unchangeability of existing boundaries needs to be reconsidered. This questioning of borders, their destabilization and utopian reconceptualization, explains the affinity between nonrealist modes of narration and border poetics.

Borders are at their very core about structuring belonging and about inhibiting or facilitating the ability to practice a subjectively felt sense of belonging. As has already become evident, belonging is a fluid concept that can change as different borders come in and out of focus. And, as stated earlier, magical realist narratives are "defocalized" because they result from two simultaneous and radically different kinds of perception.[14] These dissonant perceptions can derive from different positions, and those, in turn, can also be conceived of as different kinds of belonging or affiliation. We can again see parallels to Chwin's view of the defocalized identities that inhabit the Polish-German borderland: different positions are in tension with one another because the subjectively experienced sense of belonging (regional, local, or personal) does not align with the political reality of the current national border. Both conceptualizations of defocalization—as identity (Chwin) and as perspective (Faris)—point to a disruption or at least a destabilization of ideas of fixed belonging. In border poetics narratives that are situated in the Polish-German borderland and written in the magical realist or fantastic mode, these two meanings of defocalization merge, and they support and enhance one another.

I regard border poetics as an idiom of the cosmopolitan imagination, in part because it is attentive to the fact that belonging or identity are always

---

12   Chanady, *Magical Realism and the Fantastic*. Chanady also criticizes that the difference between the fantastic and magical realism is frequently not taken seriously, and her work focuses on what may trigger insecurity or doubt (12). She explains that the fundamental difference between magical realism and the fantastic is whether the crossing of a commonly accepted ontic boundary is perceived as problematic (the fantastic) or not (magical realism) (23).

13   Faris, *Ordinary Enchantments*, 7.

14   Faris, *Ordinary Enchantments*, 43.

136 ◆ Belonging: Defocalized Narratives

complicated by multiple overlapping and intersecting determinants, including (but not limited to) language, ethnicity, class, and gender. The practice broadens and integrates such differently defined border experiences because the border trope itself is flexible enough to pull together different notions of defocalization. Conceptualizing these intersecting affiliations and contested belongings is a narrative challenge, but magical realism and the fantastic both break open rigid structures and destabilize dominant discourses. By holding the rationally conceivable and the supernatural in balance, these modes create narrative borderlands—indeterminate and fluctuating in-between spaces that are open to different interpretations and claims. These in-between spaces are characterized by what Breinig and Lösch call "transdifference"; that is, the simultaneous suspension and maintenance of difference. I have already discussed this form of ambiguity in chapter 2: "Border Poetics," but I want to recall the vocabulary of transdifference here to account for the effects produced by modes like the fantastic and magical realism. Transdifference "interrogates the validity of binary constructions of difference without completely deconstructing them," and it "runs 'through' the line of demarcation drawn by binary difference."[15] Both magical realism and the fantastic likewise depend on that state of suspension of difference: while traditional realist narratives depend on a binary understanding of reality (either something can be rationally explained and is real, or the opposite is the case), the fantastic disturbs this understanding. This irritation is assuaged only when preconceived notions of reality are temporarily suspended, and alternative spaces of interaction are accepted. These alternative spaces offer opportunities to imagine new connections with others and negotiate new forms of attachment. We can conclude from this that magical realism fosters cosmopolitanism, as Kim Anderson Sasser has proposed: Belonging is a central concern in cosmopolitanism, and because magical realism is a response to "challenges to belonging of any kind," the two concepts are closely linked.[16]

Magical realism and the fantastic also share with border poetics the impulse to imagine spaces in which hegemonic structures are questioned, and resistance and solidarity can develop. Speaking of opposition within the notion of transdifference, Lösch has argued that the temporary suspension of difference can generate resistance to mechanisms of inclusion and exclusion and trigger social movements.[17] Applied to the practice of border poetics, disruption and defocalization provide an opportunity to discover and articulate new solidarities across and against the rigid boundaries that regulate belonging. And there are several reasons why border poetics may be drawn to

---

15   Breinig and Lösch, "Introduction: Difference and Transdifference," 23.

16   Sasser, *Magical Realism and Cosmopolitanism*, 38–39. For an exploration of belonging in connection with magical realism from a sociological perspective, see Tzanelli, *Magical Realist Sociologies of Belonging and Becoming*.

17   Lösch, "Begriff und Phänomen der Transdifferenz," 31.

magical realism as a powerful means of expressing resistance and solidarity. First, the mode has gained particular prominence within the larger history of Latin American postcolonialism as a challenge to Western cultural dominance and literary realism. This tradition remains an important reference point for theoretical reflections on magical realism, but the concept has also expanded beyond this context. Many scholars and writers today regard magical realism as a particular genre, style, or mode of writing that is "concerned not specifically with postcolonialism, but with issues of subversion and oppression regardless of political circumstances."[18] Second, and more broadly, magical realism has subversive potential as a counterpoint to realism. Lois Parkinson Zamora and Wendy Faris have ascribed this potential to the mode's specific relationship with ideology and ideological commitments. They argue that although magical realism is not free from ideology, its stance is less hegemonic than realism's because "its program is not centralizing but eccentric: it creates space for interactions of diversity. In magical realist texts, ontological disruption serves the purpose of political and cultural disruption: magic is often given as a cultural corrective, requiring readers to scrutinize accepted realistic conventions of causality, materiality, motivation."[19] It is not magical realism alone that is deemed to have subversive potential, however. Tzvetan Todorov also describes resistance as an inherent feature of the fantastic—it resists censorship, social norms, and mores. He suggests that "the function of the supernatural is to exempt the text from the action of the law and thereby to transgress the law."[20] In both modes, then, these transgressions can be viewed positively as challenges to the limitations of "reality" and established boundaries in the name of more open, cosmopolitan spaces.

This type of resistance and transgression goes hand in hand with cosmopolitical claim-making; that is, the deeply held political commitments and expressions of ethical responsibility that motivate interventions in the spaces in which one lives.[21] Fantastic elements and plots can simultaneously push back against established boundaries and make claims on borderlands in order to reconfigure them in more equitable and porous ways (often with the help of otherworldly creatures or powers). The fantastic explores the attachment (wanted or forced) to a particular bounded space or concept but also the defiance of that boundary and the exclusions it produces. The double move of resistance and claim-making may lead to the creation of (imagined) communities that share similar desires and motivations to transgress boundaries— communities into which the reader may feel invited. But such invitations need not be pleasant nor positive. A reader will hardly feel that an overwhelming hospitality emanates from the narrators in *The Tin Drum* or *Ambra*. These

18   Upstone, "Magical Realism and Postcolonial Studies," 155.
19   Zamora and Faris, "Introduction," 3.
20   Todorov, *The Fantastic*, 159.
21   Mani, *Cosmopolitical Claims*. See also my discussion in chapter 2.

138 ◆ Belonging: Defocalized Narratives

cosmopolitan invitations can—and perhaps should—come as provocations, expressed with aggression, anger, or pain. In a sense, the cosmopolitan imagination requires the exposing of negative structures and behaviors; it derives from an unbearable discomfort with the status quo.[22] Against such discomfort, belonging can be imagined as a positive claim rather than an entry permit only issued (or not issued) at the pleasure of those guarding the border.

In the remainder of the chapter, I illustrate my points by looking more closely at three novels and how they express border poetics through narrative perspective, focalization, and voice. In both Günter Grass's *Die Blechtrommel* and Sabrina Janesch's *Ambra*, the city Danzig/Gdańsk plays a central role in disrupting stable notions of belonging and identity. Ethnicity is both a choice and an external attribution with disastrous consequences. At the same time, the narrators claim their own spaces (successfully or unsuccessfully) within this disruption. In Olga Tokarczuk's *House of Day, House of Night*, the same applies also to gender. And in all three novels, the narrative is defocalized not only because of the borderland's present and historical conditions but also because the sources of knowledge are entirely unclear, making the position of the narrator an implausible one within any realist framework.

Obstinate Narrator(s) in Günter Grass's *The Tin Drum* (1959)

Even though the novel was written much earlier than the other works considered in this study, Günter Grass's *Die Blechtrommel* (*The Tin Drum*) cannot be omitted, and I propose that it is one of the earliest examples of border poetics in the German-Polish context. The novel tells the story of Oskar Matzerath, who was born in 1924 in what was then the Free City of Danzig and under the protection of the League of Nations. At the beginning of the novel, Oskar is a patient in a mental-care facility in 1950s West Germany. He looks back on his life, which has been shaped by the major historical events of the twentieth century, including the rise of National Socialism, the Second World War, and his family's postwar expulsion from Danzig. The novel is precise with regard to historical events, specific landmarks, and geographic locations. The actual political and geographic borderland, however, is a staging ground for various other boundaries and border crossings that render a defocalized topography. Oskar is a highly ambiguous individual with a number of fantastic characteristics. For example, he is born with the full mental capacity of an adult. Even more astonishingly, he wills his body to stop growing on his third birthday, resuming his growth only at the age of twenty-one, which coincides with the end of the war. Oskar also possesses two narrative devices or "instruments" that can be regarded as narrators in their own right: He has a tin drum that

---

22   Walkowitz has described it as "ethical discomfort" in *Cosmopolitan Stlye*, 20. See also the introduction to the present book.

BELONGING: DEFOCALIZED NARRATIVES ◆ 139

he never puts down, and he can produce high-pitched shrieks that can shatter glass across great distances.

Much of the novel's border poetics can be traced to the plot and its historical context and setting in which characters are constantly forced to negotiate multiple actual and figurative boundaries—most importantly, national and ethnic ones. At the same time, the novel's discursive strategies—its narrative structure and formal choices—play a significant role in unsettling these boundaries. The variations in narrative perspective, voice, and focalization mediate, replicate, and cut across the disruptions of the twentieth century and their consequences. Supernatural events and Oskar's seemingly magical powers underscore this effect of ambiguity, and they destabilize the reader's notion of what constitutes rationally conceivable reality. Since its publication in 1959, the novel has maintained its popularity and relevance, not least because it resists simple interpretations and questions one-dimensional understandings of belonging and affiliation. And, while much has already been said and written about this German classic, including multiple analyses of its German-Polish themes, a reading through the lens of border poetics brings in new perspectives and draws attention to defocalization and the transgression of boundaries as gestures of a self-critical cosmopolitanism.[23]

Danzig/Gdańsk as Borderland

The Tin Drum is set in a multifaceted borderland that makes defocalization almost unavoidable. Akin to Anzaldúa's borderlands, the novel's setting is in a "constant state of transition," and its protagonists "cross over, pass over, or go through the confines of the normal."[24] Large parts of the novel take place in Günter Grass's hometown, Gdańsk, at a time when it was the Free City of Danzig and had a majority German-speaking population. The author was born there in 1927, the year in which Oskar in the story world celebrates his fateful third birthday. Over the course of the centuries, this port city on the Baltic Sea had been under Polish, Prussian, or German rule, but it had also been a Free City at different moments in history. With the German invasion of Poland in 1939, Danzig's Free City status was abolished, and it was incorporated into the German Reich. After the Second World War, it became part of Poland and was integrated into the Polish national narrative.[25] Throughout its history, Danzig was also influenced by diverse populations settling in or passing through the important port town. These include ethnic Kashubians from the nearby Kashubia region (Polish Kaszuby; German Kaschubei; Kashubian

---

23 For readings of Grass's works that focus on their German-Polish context, see, for example, the scholarship of Norbert Honsza and Maria Janion.

24 Anzaldúa, *Borderlands/La Frontera*, 25.

25 Additional aspects of Gdańsk's history are discussed in the previous chapter, in the context of Tanja Dückers's novel *Himmelskörper*. See also Loew, *Danzig*.

140 ♦ Belonging: Defocalized Narratives

Kaszëbë). Kashubia is a "cultural landscape" rather than a clearly demarcated territory, and the Kashubians are Western Slavic people, as Roland Borchers explains. In the early Middle Ages, Kashubians settled an area bordered by the Baltic Sea and the Bay of Gdańsk to the north and northeast, stretching south to the town of Konitz/Chojnice, and extending east to the area just outside of Danzig/Gdańsk. The Kashubian language is an independent, nonstandardized West Slavic language that consists of several dialects and is today considered a regional language in Poland. Throughout history, Kashubia was alternately under German or Polish influence or divided among Prussia, Germany, and Poland. Thus, Kashubians were subject to either Germanization or Polonization well into the twentieth century.[26] Despite homogenization attempts during the Communist period, Kashubians have since reemerged as a distinct community actively involved in shaping the politics of the Pomerania province and preserving Kashubian language and culture.[27]

Günter Grass felt deeply connected to the Kashubian language and culture, and his obituary in a major Polish newspaper points out that he always referred to himself as Kashubian.[28] Grass also embodied the region's multiethnic and mixed character: His father was a Protestant of German origin and his mother a Roman Catholic of Kashubian-Polish origin.[29] Oskar Matzerath in *The Tin Drum* has a similarly mixed, albeit uncertain, heritage: his biological father could be either his mother's current German husband or her Polish lover; Oskar's mother herself has a Kashubian mother and a Polish father. Just as the family prepares to flee Danzig after the war, Oskar's grandmother Anna gives a pithy summary of what it means to be Kashubian. She explains her decision to stay behind in a kind of Kashubian-inflected German, though this is mostly lost in the English translation: "Denn mit de Kaschuben kann man nich kaine Umzüge machen, die missen immer dablaiben und Koppchen hinhalten, damit de anderen drauftäppern können, weil unserains nich richtich polnisch is und nich richtich deitsch jenug, und wenn man Kaschub is, das raicht weder de Deitschen noch de Pollacken. De wollen es immer genau haben!" (*Die Blechtrommel*, 547; "Because Kashubes don't move around a lot, they always stay put, and hold their heads still for others to whack, because we ain't really Polish and we ain't really German, and Kashubes ain't good enough for Germans or Pollacks. They want everything cut and dried"; *The Tin Drum*, 397). But as the novel makes clear, things are never cut and dried.

The region's geography, history, and ethnic composition provide important coordinates of the particular that is so central to border poetics. Such details are important for the plot, but they also shape the novel on a discursive level as they inform belonging and therefore perspective or voice. At the same time,

26 Borchers, "Kaschubei."
27 Modrzejewski, "Die kaschubische Minderheit," 2.
28 Redkult, "Günter Grass nie żyje."
29 Garland and Garland, "Grass, Günter," 302.

BELONGING: DEFOCALIZED NARRATIVES   ◆   141

the complexity of these details and the changing history point to the porousness and fluidity of borders. As we will see, even the setting itself takes on such a strong and individual character that it emerges as a protagonist in its own right; for example, when places are anthropomorphized, function as depositories of different voices, define a character's point of view, or provide their own narrative perspective.[30] Setting—here and in the other novels discussed in this chapter—is therefore more than a stage on which the story unfolds: it also determines *how* the story is told; that is, from multiple perspectives and through different voices. Part of this effect can be ascribed to fact that places themselves are enveloped in narratives. And these narratives change depending on the political circumstances, as the case of Gdańsk vividly shows. Peter Oliver Loew explains, for example, that in the myths of the Cold War years, the city was portrayed as either distinctly German or Polish, depending on political needs. These narratives have today been replaced by the myth that Gdańsk has always been a multicultural city, perhaps to make it a more attractive place for tourism and business. And while in reality, "in its history the city had a decidedly monocultural character,"[31] Loew also points to the myth of a genius loci, which supports today's multicultural narrative. This myth ascribes a certain "spirit of place" to the city that derives from its contact with others and a long tradition of openness, independence, and prosperity. The genuis loci is an insistence on the city's special and distinct character—a unique quality of defiance and independence that is a source of pride and a model for others. This spirit is said to have inspired resistance against numerous Polish kings as well as the Communist regime. The narrative of defiance seems questionable, and Loew asks provocatively why the very same city spirit was unable to prevent Prussian annexation or the National Socialist takeover.[32] Certainly, *The Tin Drum*'s main protagonist and narrator, Oskar Matzerath, has little interest in contributing to such mythologies. He stages his own resistance and thereby forces his readers and audience to deconstruct simplified views of the past.

Nevertheless, we can find in the novel a clear articulation of some kind of genius loci. Grass's Danzig is a mix of German, Polish, Kashubian, and Jewish cultures, which are embodied by different protagonists and which is present in the streets, buildings, and artifacts of the city. But Grass's variation of the genius loci is hardly that of a harmonious multiculturalism: Germans embrace National Socialist ideology and murder their Jewish and Polish neighbors; streets and buildings are destroyed. The city itself is devastated in the process,

---

30   We can observe anthropomorphization also in Janesch's *Ambra* and in Tokarczuk's *House of Day, House of Night*. Another example that draws on the German-Polish theme is Szczepan Twardoch's novel *Drach* (2014), which is told from the perspective of the earth. In my view, Tokarczuk's notion of the tender narrator could also be interpreted as a transformation of space into a narrator, or that of a narrator into a more spatially defined entity.

31   Loew, "Trzy mity," 140. My translation.

32   Loew, "Trzy mity," 138–40; and Loew, *Danzig*, 278.

142 ◆ Belonging: Defocalized Narratives

but it will survive in spite of everything because it is stubborn and obstinate, just like Oskar. Oskar presents his audience with a city that does not lend itself to appropriation by a German longing for the lost homeland in the East, nor does it easily fit into the official narrative of a mythologized Polish past. Rather than embodying some kind of undying "city spirit," what emerges in *The Tin Drum* might be better described as an anti–genius loci that disrupts the reader's spatial and moral coordinates. It is a defiant and mysterious character that we meet in literature again and again.[33] This spirit absorbs the conflicted loyalties and bizarre attachments and entanglements of its inhabitants and keeps them present. It also resists absorption into any single narrative, and wherever Oskar goes, he is involved in disturbing any attempt at such co-optation: he drums and screams until the surfaces literally crack and crumble. These cracks break up existing structures, but they also reveal connections.

The Tin Drum could be described as an example of the "temporal and spatial collage" that Ganguly speaks of.[34] It not only successfully articulates a very specific border experience and historical situation but also draws on material artifacts, ideas, human life events, fears, and behaviors to create a universal language that transcends particulars. In the introduction to the novel's most recent English translation (2009), Grass himself hints at this confluence of the local and the universal, although he claims to have been unaware of it when he wrote the novel. He recounts a meeting with the publisher Kurt Wolff in Zurich in 1959. During their conversation, Wolff tells Grass of his plans to publish *The Tin Drum* in America, to which Grass responds skeptically, "'The setting is so provincial, not even Danzig itself, but a suburb. The novel is filled with German dialect. And it concentrates solely on the provinces—'Say no more,' he [Wolff] broke in. 'All great literature is rooted in the provincial. I'll bring it out in America.'"[35] Despite Grass's hesitation, Wolff clearly situates the novel in a more global, or at least Anglo-American, context. Perhaps triggered by his conversation with Wolff and inspired by the novel's international success, Grass himself later reflects on the local as a site of the universal, and he connects it to his own upbringing. Danzig's suburb Langfuhr (today Wrzeszcz) is Grass's birthplace and an important setting in many of his works. In his 1963 novel, *Hundejahre* (*Dog Years*, 1965), he notes that this place contained

---

33   I show later that Janesch also treats the city's spirit as elusive and stubborn in her novel *Ambra*, where it cannot be incorporated into a smooth narrative. Paweł Huelle's 1987 novel *Weiser Dawidek* (*Who Was David Weiser?*, 1994) is a response to Grass's novella *Katz und Maus* (1961; *Cat and Mouse*, 1963). It is set in the Danzig suburb of Langfuhr and is similarly resistant to being co-opted for any simple narrative about the past. This anti–genius loci can also be applied to other places: my reading of Olga Tokarczuk's novel *House of Day, House of Night* shows that the locus (here the Silesian countryside) likewise resists its assigned "spirit."

34   Ganguly, *This Thing Called the World*, 85. I discuss Ganguly in more detail in the introduction.

35   Grass, *The Tin Drum*, vii.

the whole world: "Langfuhr war so groß und so klein, dass alles, was sich auf dieser Welt ereignet oder ereignen könnte, sich auch in Langfuhr ereignete oder hätte ereignen können" (*Hundejahre*, 374; "Langfuhr was so big and so little that whatever happens or could happen in this world, also happened or could have happened in Langfuhr"; *Dog Years*, 309).[36] This often-cited passage conveys an understanding of locality as a confluence of universal and particular experiences, and *The Tin Drum* is a compelling example of this entangled approach to world-making. The novel shows that the local is indeed "the place where the metahistorical components and ontological conditions of human existence unconceal themselves most clearly," to recall again Søren Frank's observation.[37] This articulation and entanglement of multiple contexts and perspectives brings about a defocalized and worldly narrative that both informs and sustains the novel's border poetics.

The World according to Oskar

Günter Grass constructs Danzig/Gdańsk as a repository and incubator of both particular and universal experiences, and this stance is fundamental for shaping the novel's narrator(s) and protagonists, as well as the often contradictory perspectives through which events are presented to the reader. But who is the narrator of *The Tin Drum*? Who is the protagonist? Whose story is being told and from which perspective? At first glance, the answers to these questions appear straightforward: Oskar Matzerath is the main protagonist and narrator, retelling the story of his own life. In the frame narrative, the first-person narrator and main protagonist are identical—voice and point of view are aligned in Oskar Matzerath. By contrast, the framed narrative is focalized through the protagonist and is told in the third person. This, however, is also where the novel's defocalization originates: The narrator of the frame narrative is the same person as the protagonist of the framed narrative, but the first-person narrator also speaks of himself and his earlier life in the third person, thus conjuring a distance between his present and his past self. At the same time, he repeatedly breaks down that very distance when he switches back and forth between first-person and third-person narration throughout the novel. Questions of perspective, focalization, and voice are thus more difficult to answer than it initially appeared, as can be seen by taking a closer look.[38]

---

36   For another exploration of this quote and Grass's "rewriting" of the city of Danzig, see Loew, *Danzig*, 253–56.

37   Frank, "Place and Placelessness," 75.

38   As a reminder, "point of view" or "perspective" refers to a protagonist's perception, interpretation, or experience of events, while "focalization" follows Gerard Genette's definition and describes the degree and quality of insight a narrator has into the workings of the story world and its inhabitants.

144 ◆ BELONGING: DEFOCALIZED NARRATIVES

Oskar Matzerath is *The Tin Drum*'s main protagonist and narrator. The frame narrative is set in a mental-care facility ("Heil- und Pflegeanstalt") in 1950s West Germany, where Oskar is a patient. Oskar is the first-person narrator and protagonist of this frame story that details his life in the institution and his writing process. As he looks back on the past and writes down his life story, the framed narrative unfolds. This framed narrative is told in the third person, but it is still focalized through Oskar. On many occasions, however, the first-person narrator from the frame narrative intrudes into the framed narrative and challenges the protagonist—that is, his past self. During these transgressions, the first-person narrator comments on Oskar's behavior and gives the impression of a split personality. This intermingling of narrative perspectives, focalizations, and voices creates a strange dissonance and irritation. The narrative constantly moves between the knowledge and attitudes of Oskar the narrator and Oskar the protagonist. In both roles, Oskar knows more than a human in a rationally conceived reality could feasibly know, such as the circumstances of his own birth.

All in all, Oskar is a mysterious being.[39] As omniscient first-person narrator, he is in "violation of mimetic epistemology" because he knows much more than a traditional first-person narrator could know.[40] Oskar is also able to focalize multiple perspectives and know the motivations and thoughts of others. With these insights, he weaves an intricate narrative web in which he holds (and manipulates) all the strings. He also comments on himself and on the past, frequently transitioning between perspectives and constantly crossing the boundary between internal and external focalizations. Combined with the ambiguity of Oskar's character and his questionable motivations, this narrative stance exposes how easily political, moral, and epistemological boundaries can be manipulated. As one reviewer observed, Oskar is an "incarcerated maniac, self-created dwarf, paranoiac, possessor of supernatural gifts, vindictive genius, fallen angel, miniature tyrant, obsessive beater of the titular drum. Oskar is all of these things and none of them; the ultimate unreliable narrator."[41] Oskar himself raises doubts about his trustworthiness as narrator, not least when he begins his story with the word "Zugegeben" ("Granted"): "Zugegeben: ich bin Insasse einer Heil- und Pflegeanstalt, mein Pfleger beobachtet mich, läßt mich kaum aus dem Auge; denn in der Tür ist ein Guckloch, und meines Pflegers Auge ist von jenem Braun, welches mich, den Blauäugigen, nicht durchschauen kann" (*Die Blechtrommel*, 9; "Granted: I'm an inmate in a mental institution; my keeper watches me, scarcely lets me out of sight, for there's a

---

39   Søren Frank highlights the mobility and unsettledness of Oscar by ascribing to him an "exilic point of view from below," as well as, citing Salman Rushdie, "a migrant's vision." See Frank, "The Migrant Vision," 167.

40   Heinze, "Violations of Mimetic Epistemology," 279–97.

41   McManus, "*The Tin Drum* Summarised the 20th Century."

BELONGING: DEFOCALIZED NARRATIVES ◆ 145

peephole in the door, and my keeper's eye is the shade of brown that can't see through blue-eyed types like me"; *The Tin Drum*, 3).

The narrator devotes the first chapters to telling the story of Oskar's origin, but like Laurence Sterne's Tristram Shandy, he digresses and begins some time before his own birth, raising more questions about the source of this intimate knowledge. Oskar's story begins with the first meeting between his Kashubian grandmother, Anna Bronski, and his grandfather, Joseph Koljaiczek. Counteracting the otherwise defocalized narrative, he is very precise in mapping this event, thereby also providing the time and exact location where Oskar's mother is conceived: "Man schrieb das Jahr neunundneunzig, sie saß im Herzen der Kaschubei, nahe bei Bissau, noch näher der Ziegelei, vor Ramkau saß sie, hinter Viereck, in Richtung der Straße nach Brentau, zwischen Dirschau und Karthaus, den schwarzen Wald Goldkrug im Rücken saß sie" (13; "The year was eighteen ninety-nine, she sat in the heart of Kashubia, near Bissau, nearer still to the brickworks, this side of Ramkau she sat, beyond Viereck, facing the road to Brentau, between Dirschau and Karthaus, with her back toward the black forest of Goldkrug she sat," 6).

Shortly thereafter, Joseph and Anna meet and have a sexual encounter. They get married, Anna Bronski becomes Anna Koljaiczek, and the couple moves from the countryside to Danzig. Here Anna gives birth to Oskar's mother, Agnes, just at the beginning of the new century.[42] This precision with regard to time and location continues throughout the novel. The narrative moves through a city of authentic landmarks, streets, and places. It is here, in Danzig, that Oskar is born in 1924; here he grows up; and from here he and the remainder of his family are expelled at the end of the Second World War. And while these spatial and temporal coordinates anchor the novel in the real world, this realism and seeming clarity in belonging is called into question by a series of grotesque and fantastical events that throw everything out of focus and shatter what has been set up as the real world. These irritations appear on the level of story but they are amplified discursively.

Oskar the narrator is crucial to this defocalization because he is an unusual being that manipulates reality. The major historical events can be verified, but the story world also has its own chronology and events, and Oskar spins them to irritate and undercut German collective memory. This is the case, for example, during a big Nazi rally, when Oskar hides underneath the grandstand and disturbs the carefully choreographed propaganda event with his drumming. In a carnivalesque scene, under the seductive and irresistible influence of Oskar's drum, the marching band first breaks into a waltz and later a Charleston, and the attendees begin to dance at the rally, falling from one mass hysteria into another.[43] Oskar quite literally retells history from below: He may not be a player in the official orchestra, but from underneath the grandstand he

42 *Die Blechtrommel*, 23–24; *The Tin Drum*, 13.
43 *Die Blechtrommel*, 151–55; *The Tin Drum*, 107–10.

146 ♦ Belonging: Defocalized Narratives

can manipulate it as he pleases. This unusual ability can be traced to Oskar's birth, which he recalls in detail, as well as a number of very conscious decisions he makes in the early days, months, and years of his life. He asserts, "Ich gehörte zu den hellhörigen Säuglingen, deren geistige Entwicklung schon bei der Geburt abgeschlossen ist und sich fortan nur noch bestätigen muß" (52; "I was one of those clairaudient infants whose mental development is complete at birth and thereafter simply confirmed," 35). As the newborn Oskar listens to his mother, Agnes, and presumed father, Alfred, discuss his future, he contemplates the options for his life. While Alfred envisions his son as the heir to his colonial-goods store ("Kolonialwarenladen"), his mother promises him a drum set for his third birthday. Uninterested in Alfred's middlebrow plans, Oskar impatiently awaits that fateful birthday, receives his present, and decides to stop growing at "ninety-four centimeters, or three foot one."[44] In order to provide his family with a rational explanation of his arrested growth, he throws himself down the stairs of his home, a tragedy for which Alfred gets blamed. Oskar is able to hide behind his physical appearance as a three-year-old and is never suspected of any mischief.[45] He maintains this stature until he is twenty-one and only decides to resume his growth during the family's expulsion from Danzig at the end of the war.

Within a realist framework, Oskar's mental capacities and deliberately chosen physical stature are puzzling, to put it mildly. Likewise, his identity, as well as his motivations and attachments, are unclear and take on a surreal air. First, it is known that his mother, Agnes, is half Kaschubian, but the identity of his biological father is not known with any certainty. Second, Oskar claims to be endowed with several remarkable talents, which further makes the reader wonder who he is and where these otherworldly abilities come from. Two unusual attributes are particularly relevant here, because they serve as narrative devices that supplement the narrative and provide alternate ways of telling the story. These voices or "instruments" underline the novel's unconventional narrative perspective: a tin drum that Oskar receives on his third birthday and that he plays incessantly and a high-pitched shriek that can shatter glass across great distances.[46] Both instruments are extensions of Oskar's self, and he uses them to enhance the narrative. As he gets older, these storytelling devices even

44　*The Tin Drum*, 390; *Die Blechtrommel*, 537.

45　Tomasz Lewandowski has interpreted the fact that Oskar intentionally stops growing as an act of hiding in the body of a three-year-old; Lewandowski, "Grass jako brakujące ogniwo," 241.

46　The drum and Oskar's high-pitched shrieks function as narrative voices. If the concept of narrative voice asks, "Who speaks," then both the drumming and his shrieks can be interpreted as extensions of Oskar's voice. At the same time, they also modify and enhance his voice. These narrative voices are, however, accessible to the reader only as they are mediated, interpreted, and manipulated by the narrator, who details both Oskar's intentions and people's reactions to his disruptions. The drumming and the shrieking are dissonant, loud, and provocative voices. One could also add that the drum help him make a living in a traveling variety theater. Oskar refers to his drumming as "work" and part of the narrative process. When he beats the drum, he tells stories and remembers, searches and explores, bears witness and records history. He uses the drum to access information, and without this access his world would not exist. He explains this existential significance of storytelling very early on: "Hätte ich nicht meine Trommel, der bei geschicktem und geduldigem Gebrauch alles einfällt, was an Nebensächlichkeiten nötig ist, um die Hauptsache aufs Papier bringen zu können, und hätte ich nicht die Erlaubnis der Anstalt, drei bis vier Stunden täglich mein Blech sprechen zu lassen, wäre ich ein armer Mensch ohne nachweisliche Großeltern" (23; "If I didn't have my drum, which, when handled properly and patiently, recalls all the little details I need to get the essentials down on paper, and if I didn't have the institute's permission to let my drum speak three or four hours each day, I would be a poor fellow with no known grandparents," 13).

Oskar's high-pitched shrieks are juxtaposed to his drumming. He uses this talent to defend his narrative labor against anyone who has either grown tired of his drumming or deems it inappropriate and attempts to take away his instrument: "Allein Sorge um den Fortbestand meiner Arbeit auf der Trommel hieß mich, meine Stimmbänder so zielstrebig zu gebrauchen" (77; "It was solely my desire to keep working on my drum that led me to use my vocal cords so single-mindedly," 53). Later in the novel, Oskar's screaming evolves from a defense mechanism into a narrative voice in its own right. While his drumming signifies the search for a uniform rhythm and the need to provide coherence and continuity to a narrative (albeit in a highly irritating way), his screams deconstruct narratives. On the surface, Oskar's screams shatter material objects, but he also destroys the narratives they embody and the institutions they represent.[47] He views his presentations as historical performances; for example, when he travels with the theater company: "Ich zersang nicht mehr simple deutsch-ordinäre Bierflaschen, nein, ausgesuchteste, schöngeschwungene, hauchdünn geatmete Vasen und Fruchtschalen aus französischen Schlössern zersang und zerscherbte ich. Nach kulturhistorischen Gesichtspunkten baute sich mein Programm auf" (432; "I no longer sangshattered ordinary German beer bottles, no, I reduced to shards with my song the most exquisite, gracefully curved, paper-thin blown vases and fruit bowls from French castles. My act was structured on a cultural-historical point of view," 311). In this process of destruction, however, Oskar also constructs new narratives and tells stories and, even more, anti-stories. He does not demolish random items in an unsystematic way. Rather, both the items and the sequence in which he destroys them are carefully choreographed to undo the meaning with which they have previously been endowed. Sadly

---

provides an impersonal point of view, as Lewandowski argues. Lewandowski, "Grass jako brakujące ogniwo," 241.

47   Frank, "The Migrant Vision," 165.

148 ♦ BELONGING: DEFOCALIZED NARRATIVES

for Oskar, few audience members are able to appreciate his narrative skills: "Wenn auch die feldgraue Masse im Parkett und auf den Rängen dem historischen Ablauf meiner Darbietungen nicht folgen konnte und die Scherben nur als gewöhnliche Scherben beklatschte, gab es dann und wann doch Stabsoffiziere und Journalisten aus dem Reich, die außer den Scherben auch meinen Sinn fürs Historische bewunderten" (432; "If the field-gray masses in the stalls and balconies could not follow my historical presentation and applauded the shards simply as ordinary shards, there were also occasional staff officers and journalists from the Reich who admired my historical sense as well as the shards," 311).

Who exactly admires his skills does not matter much to Oskar, who generally displays neither moral qualms nor sympathies. Instead, the consistent nonchalance of his observations exposes the destructiveness of National Socialist ideology and warfare and irritates the reader. Here Oskar as narrator seems to operate very much like Grass himself, at least according to Hans Magnus Enzensberger's observation in a review upon the novel's first publication: "What differentiates Grass . . . what legitimizes these blunt forays . . . is the total objectivity with which he presents them. . . . Grass does not seek out taboos; he simply doesn't notice them. It would be unfair to accuse him of deliberate provocation. He neither avoids scandal nor invites it; but that is precisely what will give rise to scandal: Grass doesn't have a guilty conscience; he takes what we find shocking for granted."[48] Oskar as narrator displays a similarly indifferent attitude toward the story world. It has even been argued that this "total objectivity" has allowed Grass to uncover the "banality of evil" prior to Hannah Arendt.[49]

With the help of a supernatural ability to "read" other people, the novel's narrator pushes the limits of what the "I" can know. Oskar/I can recognize other people's intentions and motivations, and he can access their memories and fears. This special ability is another attribute that aids his narration, and it is first made explicit in an encounter with a teacher who is trying to take away his drum:

> Vorerst hielt ich [die Trommel] fest, schloß die Arme in Pulloverärmeln um das weißrotgeflammte Rund, blickte sie an, blickte dann, da sie unentwegt den uralten schablonenhaften Volksschullehrerinnenanblick gewährte, durch sie hindurch, fand im Innern des Fräulein Spollenhauer Erzählenswertes genug für drei unmoralische Kapitel, riß mich aber, da es um meine Trommel ging, von ihrem Innenleben los und registrierte, als mein Blick zwischen ihren Schulterblättern hindurchfand, auf guterhaltener Haut einen guldenstückgroßen, langbehaarten Leberfleck. (98)

48 Enzensberger, cited in Grass, *The Tin Drum*, viii.
49 Lewandowski, "Grass jako brakujące ogniwo," 241.

[At first I held on tight, wrapped the arms of my sweater around the red and white flames of the cylinder, and stared at her; then, since she maintained the ancient stereotypical schoolteacher's gaze without flinching, I looked right through her, finding sufficient narrative material inside Fräulein Spollenhauer for three chapters of depravity, then tore myself loose from her inner life, since my drum was at stake, and as my gaze passed through her shoulder blades, registered the presence on her well-preserved skin of a mole the size of a gulden piece with long hairs sprouting from it. (68)]

It is evident in this passage that the narrator has access to everything, and he must choose which story to tell. He sees enough material for a steamy romance, but in the face of his teacher's attempt to discipline him, he opts for an irritating and disruptive tale. Oskar's reaction to the teacher's violation of his narrative integrity is instantaneous, but at first the damage is only slight. He produces a warning scream that leaves a small scratch on Fräulein Spollenhauer's glasses. Upon the teacher's renewed attempt to take away the drum, however, Oskar unleashes the full force of his shriek, which leaves Fräulein Spollenhauer with bloody eyebrows and an empty spectacle frame.[50]

The ambiguous narrative perspective, the changing focalizations, and the indistinctness regarding voice as well as the narrator's/protagonist's manipulations and deceptions distort and even dismantle any realist framework. Even more, they reveal realism's limitations and inadequacy in providing orientation and continuity and thereby pull the reader out of their comfort zone. Oskar is the wise fool, locked up in a mental institution. Told from the perspective of the 1950s, his story embodies and exposes Germany's highly ambiguous relationship with its Nazi past, its support of the National Socialist regime, the guilt and complicity of individuals in the system, and the contingency of existence. In all of this, Oskar is anything but a moral compass—he himself is deeply flawed, manipulative, and mischievous. Nevertheless, he passes through everything unscathed, disguised as a child, an innocent observer, when in reality he is the one who directs everything that happens around him. Folded into the historical space and time are questions of epistemic, ontic, moral, and other transgressions that paint a dark and irritating picture of human nature and of Germany in the twentieth century.

Oskar's shrieks and drumbeats have echoed far and wide through the world-literature space, and they also reverberate in Grass's other works. *The Tin Drum* was followed by the novella *Katz und Maus* (1961; *Cat and Mouse*, 1963) and the novel *Hundejahre* (1963; *Dog Years*, 1965). Together, these three texts make up the so-called Danzig Trilogy. Although each text in the trilogy stands for itself, there are intertextual references throughout. These range from recurring protagonists to cross-references to previous plots, as well as shared

---

50 *The Tin Drum*, 68–71; *Die Blechtrommel*, 98–101.

150 ♦ Belonging: Defocalized Narratives

themes or motifs. With the Danzig Trilogy, Grass pulled from and has contributed to an open narrative web that lends itself to new connections from within his oeuvre but also from the outside, such as the prominent example of Paweł Huelle's novel *Weiser Dawidek* (1987; *Who Was David Weiser*, 1991), to stay within the German-Polish context.[51] And, as the following section shows, Sabrina Janesch's novel *Ambra* is another text in this narrative network.

Spinning Tales in Sabrina Janesch's *Ambra* (2012)

Two years after her debut novel, *Katzenberge*, which I discussed in the previous chapter, Sabrina Janesch returned to the German-Polish theme in her second novel, *Ambra*. Similarly to *The Tin Drum*, the novel complicates questions of belonging through a radical defocalization of the narrative perspective and an unsettling of the boundaries and sources of knowledge. While *Katzenberge* already included fantastic elements, the magical realist or fantastic mode is much more fundamental to the functioning of *Ambra's* story world. Magic and fantastic elements drive the plot forward, they facilitate different points of view, and they create an alternative explanatory framework. Only through this new framework is it possible to bridge the gap between the past and the present and access events that did not become part of recorded history. These events have been forgotten because they took place among friends and family, in people's homes and communities, or because people have died before they were able to share their memories—such as the main protagonist's mother, who passed away when she was a child. The protagonist and narrator of the novel thereby not only claims her place in the historical narrative from an individualized point of view but also from a marginalized female perspective.

There are multiple echoes of *The Tin Drum* in this work. First and foremost, the setting is Gdańsk, which has led one reviewer to describe *Ambra* as the first literary exploration of the city by a German-language author since Grass.[52] Janesch uses magical realism and fantasy, a multiplicity of narrative perspectives, nonlinear narration, and frequent allusions to themes and motifs in *The Tin Drum* (as well as other works). The novel even begins with

---

51   I omit a longer discussion of Huelle's novel here because it connects more explicitly to Grass's novella *Cat and Mouse*. *Weiser Dawidek* is set in and around Gdańsk in the 1950s and tells the story of the mysterious disappearance of a Jewish boy. Weiser's captivating personality and his unresolved disappearance have invited comparisons to the figure of Joachim Mahlke in Grass's novella. There are also parallels in the narrative structure and setting. For a more detailed analysis, see Wozniak, "Günter Grass and Paweł Huelle," 119–31. Parallels between *Ambra* and *David Weiser*, as well as connections to other works of Danzig literature, have been pointed out by Wagner, "Literarische Grenzüberschreitungen," 199–206.

52   Platthaus, "Zu Besuch."

a not-so-subtle Grass reference: "Jeder Schlag auf jede Trommel und jeder Schrei, jedes zerbrochene Glas und jeder unlautere Gedanke findet Einlass ins Gedächtnis der Stadt" (Janesch, *Ambra*, 8; Each beat on every drum and each scream, each broken glass and each unsavory thought find their way into the memory of the city).[53] The ghost of *The Tin Drum*'s Oskar also appears to linger in the background when the main protagonist discovers her ability to read other people's minds and know the memories of all who have ever passed through the city. Similarly, the narration is facilitated by an "instrument" of sorts. The narrator does not beat a drum, nor does she scream and leave anyone with broken spectacles and bloody eyebrows, but she too has intimate knowledge of others' thoughts and fears, and she manipulates them to her advantage. Her "preposterous knowledge" of a rationally impossible omniscient first-person narrator is made possible by an amber pendant.[54]

The novel is set in the years 2009/10, and it has a frame narrative that begins where the framed story ends: the main protagonist, Kinga Mischa, is locked up in a room in her Polish relatives' apartment—a situation not unlike that of Oskar, who is held in a locked room of a mental-care facility when he begins to write. We learn that something has happened to Kinga's cousin, Bartosz Mysza (a traumatized soldier, who just returned from a tour of duty in Iraq), and his girlfriend, Renia Fiszer: "Renia und Bartosz waren verschwunden, einfach so, in die Stadt hinein, in ihre Gedärme waren sie gekrochen und nicht wieder aufgetaucht" (*Ambra*, 371; Renia and Bartosz had vanished, just like that, into the city. They had crawled into its entrails and were not seen again.) With this sudden and mysterious disappearance, Janesch enters an intertextual web that includes the vanishing of David Weiser in Paweł Huelle's eponymous novel, which in turn references Joachim Mahlke's disappearance in Grass's *Katz und Maus*.[55] In *Ambra*, the subsequent "interrogation" is led by Bartosz's mother, Bronka. Because she suspects Kinga to be somehow responsible for her son's disappearance, she kidnaps Kinga. Strategically keeping her son's machine gun in Kinga's sight, she demands to be told everything, to which Kinga obliges. Just like Scheherazade, Kinga proceeds to tell stories to save her own life. The longer she draws out the process, the more time she gains for herself and the more she can hope that Renia and Bartosz will return or that someone will begin searching for her. She claims that the events that have led to Bartosz and Renia's disappearance indeed originated several generations ago. In a series of embedded narratives, the story then weaves back and forth seamlessly between different times and places as well as between different narrative perspectives

---

53 No English translation of *Ambra* has yet been published. All translations are mine.

54 Heinze, "Violations of Mimetic Epistemology," 8.

55 Wagner, "Literarische Grenzüberschreitungen," 204. For intertextual references to *The Tin Drum*, see 199–201.

152 ♦ Belonging: Defocalized Narratives

and voices. At the end of the novel, the narrative frame closes, and Kinga is still in the room in which she first began to put her stories to paper.

The framed narrative begins in the recent past. The reader learns that Kinga Mischa has just graduated from a university and lives with her elderly father in a small German town in Lower Saxony. When her father dies in 2009, she unexpectedly inherits an apartment in Gdańsk. She travels to the city hoping that the property might solve her financial problems and to find out more about the Polish side of her family. Once there, she not only discovers why the family had been estranged but is also overwhelmed by a multitude of voices and stories that force themselves upon her. She becomes aware of her increasing power of clairvoyance and soon figures out that she has access to the city's memory through an amber pendant that contains a fossilized spider. The pendant was a gift from her father, but before it reached Kinga, it had been a matter of contention in her family for many generations. Through this pendant, Kinga becomes the voice and the repository of all haunted souls, and she channels not only her own family's history but also that of the entire city. And, because Kinga's access to other worlds also transgresses temporal limitations, she is able to recover voices that were lost to the present. It is once again the local in which "the metahistorical components and ontological conditions of human existence unconceal themselves."[56] And this unconcealing is again done by an impertinent narrator who is not worried about the other protagonists' traumatic experiences or desires: in order to make a living, Kinga uses her special talent of clairvoyance by joining "so eine Art Varietétheater. Aber nur für Mitglieder" (87; a kind of variety theater. But for members only). This theater features a "Kleinwüchsiger im Frack" (132; a small person in a tailcoat) and is in many other ways reminiscent of "Bebra's Theater on the Front," in which Oskar Matzerath showcases his glass-shattering gift.[57] Kinga's performances consist of reading other people's minds and, to their great discomfort, revealing their secret contents to the audience.

Kinga is a collector of stories and lost or suppressed memories that reveal how the personal is enmeshed with the political by way of intersecting and competing affiliations, such as national belonging, ethnicity, and gender. At the same time, these stories propose alternative kinds of knowledge and perception that destabilize conventional realist frameworks. They stand for a more comprehensive way of knowing—an omniscient perspective that goes far beyond human capacity. This kind of knowledge is made possible by the pendant, a magical item already hinted at in the novel's title.[58] The pendant

---

56   Frank, "Place and Placelessness," 75.

57   The scenes in the theater also bear resemblance to the "magic theater" in Hermann Hesse's novel *Der Steppenwolf* (1927; *Steppenwolf*, 1929) as well as Thomas Mann's novella *Mario und der Zauberer* (1929; *Mario and the Magician*, 1930).

58   "Ambra," a reviewer explains, is an old word for amber. It stems from the time when people believed that it was produced by fish rather than by tree resin. Platthaus,

BELONGING: DEFOCALIZED NARRATIVES ◆ 153

has been passed down through several generations, but Kinga is its first female owner. Over the course of the novel, it reveals itself as a narrative instrument that lends its owner a radically expanded perception. Furthermore, the magical pendant—or rather, the fossilized spider inside—not only brings multiple voices into the narrative but also emerges as a narrator with its own perspective and voice.

"Amber" generally refers to a gemstone made of fossilized tree resin, giving the reader at once a specific spatial orientation and a very expansive temporal frame. In terms of space, amber will make most German and Polish readers think of the Baltic Sea region, which is famous for this gemstone. The time frame, by contrast, is far more expansive and beyond human experience. The reader learns that millions of years ago, a spider was trapped by a drop of tree resin and has witnessed and recorded everything that has happened since (63). The pendant is thus a key instrument for collecting and bringing out different perspectives and voices to create a polyvocal, and once again highly defocalized, narrative. In particular, four main narrative perspectives or voices emerge throughout the novel: the setting (i.e., the city itself); the main protagonist, Kinga Mischa; the spider in the amber pendant; and a city scribe. There is also a hybrid voice that appears frequently over the course of the narrative and that represents a radical blending of two different perspectives and times: Kinga channels the traumatic memories of her cousin, Bartosz, that force themselves upon her through the spider narrator.

The City by the Sea

The setting of *Ambra* remains unnamed and is referred to only as "die Stadt am Meer" (the city by the sea). Nevertheless, it is clear from the beginning that the true identity of the place is Gdańsk.[59] And as in *The Tin Drum*, perhaps even more so, it rules over the narrative with its obstinate city spirit. Beyond being the setting, the city shapes the narrator's access to the story world, and it even appears to have its own—an all-encompassing—point of view. Danzig/Gdańsk speaks through other narrators and protagonists, but it also functions as a narrator in itself by spilling out the stories it has devoured over the centuries. The "city by the sea" has collected everything that has ever happened—including the exploits and stories of Oskar Matzerath. It is described as an organic

---

"Zu Besuch." Interestingly, the word for amber in contemporary German is "Bernstein," in Polish "bursztyn." I therefore suspect that the novel's title may initially be rather mysterious for readers who are not familiar with the word in other Latin languages, where it is closer to the English "amber."

59 The hardcover edition of the novel offers an illustration with scribblings of the name "Danzig" on the inside. Throughout the novel there are also plenty of clues, such as references to specific landmarks. By not mentioning the name in the text itself, Janesch omits the question whether the German or the Polish name should be used, and she avoids clear categorizations that do not exist in the story world.

154 ♦ Belonging: Defocalized Narratives

being with an ability to remember; it breathes, has a heart and intestines, and swallows people and their memories. It is determined by everything that has ever happened, and it is shaped by all peoples, times, and places that have ever passed through it. It then releases those stories back into the story world, mainly via the spider in the amber pendant and the narrator, Kinga Mischa, and it makes the past an enduring presence.

The anthropomorphization of the city does not necessarily make it a human protagonist or narrator but rather a supernatural being with human attributes. *Ambra*'s city is endowed with a genius loci—the spirit that transmits a distinct atmosphere and specific voice. While, as Loew has argued, this "spirit" is often evoked to lend a place narrative cohesion and emphasize its unique and special, mostly positive, character, in *Ambra* the genius loci resembles the anti-spirit that I also postulated for *The Tin Drum*.[60] It is stubborn and resists an oversimplification of the past, which prevents the city from being easily appropriated for any particular narrative. Instead, this place devours its people and their memories (89, 371); it digests them and then throws them back at a protagonist and narrator who has to deal with an unfiltered collection of thoughts, memories, and dreams. The city spirit communicates with the narrator Kinga Mischa through the amber pendant, and Kinga in turn channels the voices that (according to her own account) she can neither escape nor control. Kinga tries to manage the stories by telling them to the reader, by writing them down for her Aunt Bronka, and by disclosing them to the audience of her variety show. Within—or more accurately, *through*—this setting, multiple perspectives and voices blend and intertwine.

Kinga Mischa is the main protagonist and first-person narrator of the frame narrative, which provides the motivation for the narration, but the complexity of her family history and her own place (or placelessness) within this narrative are revealed only in the course of the narrative and only with the help of other voices and perspectives. Kinga is of mixed German-Polish heritage, but she was born and raised in West Germany with little awareness of her Polish relatives or her family history. Conflicting loyalties before and during the Second World War had torn the family apart, and some fled to Germany after 1945, while others remained in Poland. Her mother died shortly after Kinga's birth, thereby also erasing the female perspective on her family history. Kinga is able to recover this history only when she enters the "city by the sea" with the magic family heirloom. Growing up, Kinga is presented with only a vague and often mythologized version of her heritage. She is told that she is named after the Polish Saint Kunigunde, a princess who had to leave her homeland and live in a foreign land (19–20)—much like Kinga's parents had to do when their families were expelled from Gdańsk after the war.

---

60   Loew, "Trzy mity," 138–41. See also my earlier discussion of genius loci.

Kinga's last name, Mischa, is the Germanized form of the Polish name Mysza, which translates to English "mouse."[61] Actual mice are present throughout the novel, and the juxtaposition of "Kinga" and "Mysza" also draws attention to Kinga's double narrative perspective. On the one hand, she tells a story from below, from the perspective of a mouse, focusing on small details and family events. On the other hand, these stories are placed within the larger context of German-Polish history since the nineteenth century—the kind of history that is told from above, echoing the same kind of blending of narrative perspectives articulated by Tokarczuk in the epigraph to this chapter. Kinga is also true to her name because she rules over her narrative and directs it in her interest. While she presents herself as a reliable narrator with the best of intentions, she manipulates the other protagonists as well as the reader into believing her version of events. Yet, her account becomes increasingly untenable as other narrators speak up, and Kinga gradually appears to be motivated by jealousy and guided by self-interest. As more and more holes appear in her story, she grows more unreliable and mysterious, and by the end of the novel, the reader must wonder whether Kinga might be involved in her cousin's disappearance after all. The narrators who contribute to destabilizing Kinga's reign over the narrative are a German city scribe with the name Tilman Kröger and the omniscient spider narrator, whose voice often merges with that of Kinga. The city itself—as the depository of stories—emanates this multitude of perspectives and voices that do not allow for a smooth and harmonious narrative.

Webs and Entanglements

Ambra creates an open narrative web, in which clarity can never be attained. The fossilized spider in Kinga's necklace only slowly reveals itself to be the main narrator with a fantastic point of view. It embodies a state of spatial and temporal in-betweenness: it is a nonhuman animal caught within an inanimate object; it is frozen in time and space, but it is imbued with the magical power to record history and reveal it to its bearer, granting simultaneous access to all times and places. The pendant helps Kinga recover the past, and it filters her experiences in the city. At other times, however, the spider appears to narrate the events without intervention (and thus manipulation) from Kinga. Similar to Oskar's tin drum, the amber pendant serves as an instrument of narration that allows Kinga to recognize and articulate what would normally be

---

61   Animals and plants as well as the relationship between nature and culture play important roles in the novel and invite an ecocritical analysis or a discussion through the lens of animal studies. This crossing of boundaries between nature and culture and between species can also be read as an expression of border poetics on the level of story. Similar observations about the fluid boundary between nature and culture can be made about Tokarczuk's novel. Some of these "posthuman entanglements" within German and Polish literary relations more broadly speaking, specifically animals, objects, and plants, are discussed in Krzoska and Zajas, "Posthumane Verflechtungen," 213–25.

156 ♦ BELONGING: DEFOCALIZED NARRATIVES

inaccessible to her. To make sense of her experience, Kinga thinks back to her childhood. She remembers how her father explained to her the object's revelatory qualities: "Siehst du die Spinne? Sie hat sich alles gemerkt, alles was jemals um sie herum geschehen ist. An dieser Stelle widersprach Kinga, denn wie konnte man sich denn alles merken, was um einen herum geschah. Der alte Mischa lenkte ein und sagte, dass sie sich nur die speziellen Dinge merkte, und eines Tages würde sie, Kinga, schon dahinterkommen, was das sei: die speziellen Dinge" (22; Do you see the spider? It remembers everything that has ever happened in its vicinity. Here Kinga objected. How could one possibly remember everything. Old Mischa gave in and said that it only remembered the particular things, and that one day she, Kinga, would find out what those were: the particular things). It turns out that the particular things entail the personal family history and the movements and shifting loyalties within one family. They include the experiences of war and dislocation, of great historical events refracted through the everyday lives of individuals.

The forgotten and untold stories haunt Kinga from the moment she enters the city, and they increasingly bother her. To complicate things, the stories about her own family's past also mix with other peoples' pasts and memories. Kinga can indeed see and hear all the particular things around her. And in a city like Gdańsk, the multitude of particular things turns out to be quite overwhelming. According to Kinga, it is the spider that enables her to channel different voices. While the spider is the actual omniscient narrator, Kinga is frequently its voice. On other occasions the spider also seems to speak for itself and reveal things about Kinga that undercut her account. All the voices and memories are coincidental; every voice and memory reveals itself to Kinga simultaneously, regardless of origin. Her ability to access the thoughts of others is most notable when it comes to her cousin's experiences during his recent tour of duty in Iraq. Bartosz is plagued by his memories, which in turn take possession of Kinga. She channels Bartosz's perspective and then provocatively confronts him with things she could not possibly know. She does so to prove her mind-reading skills but also, the reader might suspect, to aggravate her cousin because she is jealous and enamored with his girlfriend, Renia.

In this polyvocal narrative, the transition from one perspective to another is not always clearly marked, which adds to the novel's defocalization. This fluidity is expressed on the formal level; for example, when the perspective switches seamlessly from a first-person narrator to third-person narration (as was also the case in *The Tin Drum*), or when the change from Kinga's to Bartosz's narrative voice occurs midsentence. Some transitions are also expressed visually on the page through a sudden switch to italics. These are used throughout the novel in episodes involving Bartosz's stationing in Iraq, which are channeled through Kinga but always told from his intimate first-person perspective. For example, in the following scene, Kinga meets Bartosz for the first time when he picks her up from the train station. She does not yet understand the origin of the different voices and images in her head, but she suddenly has access to Bartosz's memories of his fallen comrade Jarzębinski. The passage below reflects how this transition is represented visually on the page, with the second part set off from the first and printed in italics:

> Ich nickte, als ob ich verstehen würde, aber natürlich verstand ich überhaupt nichts. Bartosz rief etwas vom Vorplatz des Bahnhofs herüber. Wir schlossen zu ihm auf und ich
>
> *sah hoch am Himmel einen Geier kreisen, daran erinnere ich mich, und hätte der Beschuss nicht angedauert, ich schwöre, ich hätte das Vieh abgeknallt, weil es mich wahnsinnig machte, wie es da oben schwebte und geduldig kreiste, als würde es tatsächlich davon ausgehen, dass wenn alles vorbei war, man Jarzębinski einfach im Wüstensand liegen lassen würde* (41).

> [I nodded as though I understood, but of course I didn't understand anything. Bartosz yelled something over from the train station. We caught up to him and I
>
> *saw a vulture circle high above me, that's what I remember. Had the shelling not continued, I swear, I would have gunned that beast down, because it drove me crazy how it was hovering up there, circling patiently, as if it assumed that when all of this was over, we would simply leave Jarzębinski behind in the desert.*]

As the reader soon learns, this seeming change in perspective is in fact not so much a transition but a radical expansion of the main protagonist's perspective and its merging with Bartosz's point of view. Kinga instantly identifies this breaking down of the boundary between herself and others as a disturbance, and she refers to it as "mein kleines Problem" (my little problem). Initially, she is not sure where to place this experience, as it occurs immediately after her arrival, but it becomes more pronounced the longer Kinga lives in the city. More and more, she reenvisions distant times and places in the present, but she can only make old animosities and conflicts present, not solve them. This radical multiperspectivity brings many, and often conflicting, viewpoints into conversation, and it reveals the events of the past and people's different feelings and motivations, bringing them into an uncomfortable state of transdifference where existing boundaries and established stories must be reevaluated.

Kinga's retelling of Bartosz's story as well as her own family history does more than chronicle the events or ensure that Bronka does not kill her. Kinga also narrates back to life those who have been marginalized or ignored in the grand historical narratives, most notably the women in her own family. This process of world-making and -remaking also affects Kinga: by illuminating female strength and agency in her own family story and by connecting herself to the women, Kinga also narrates herself into existence. These women's reconciliatory powers helped them persevere and keep the family together through war, hunger, expulsion, and strife. While Kinga's grandfather identified as

158 ♦ Belonging: Defocalized Narratives

German and joined the Wehrmacht during the Second World War, which he did not survive, his brother was exempted from the military for health reasons, and he felt more allegiance with Poland. Their respectively German and Polish wives spent the war at home, reuniting a house that had been divided by these competing national loyalties. Joined in female solidarity, and in the absence of their men, they managed to raise a child together (Kinga's father) and survive the war. While this story can be read as an oversimplification and even romanticization of the role of women in war, it also signifies a lost part of Kinga's family history. In fact, owing to her mother's early death, it was buried so deep that Kinga needed a magical item to recover it. It is the spider that makes the story present—it holds all the narrative strings, and it weaves together different perspectives.

There is also a counternarrative to Kinga's story, which adds to the reader's mounting doubt regarding the veracity of her claims. Kinga's antagonist is the city scribe Tilman Kröger, a German who has been invited by city officials to write a book about the city and who therefore chronicles all the same events.[62] Kröger is frequently in the same places as Kinga, a fact that irritates Kinga and makes her resentful toward the writer. Kröger counters Kinga's narrative with his own interpretation of Kinga's life in Gdańsk and her relationship with Bartosz and Renia. But the seeming juxtaposition of Kinga's unreliable, personal, and female narrative "from below" with that of an official male narrative is itself ironized: The city scribe suffers from writer's block and never manages to put any words of the contracted official narrative on the page. Instead, Kröger becomes part of the tale spun by Kinga. Kinga's situation of being locked up in Bronka's apartment parallels that of the spider trapped in amber. Yet, while the spider offers a seemingly objective, or at least distanced, perspective, Kinga's narrative is biased and cannot be trusted. The rising doubt regarding Kinga's reliability increases as she appears to lose control of the narrative strings. By the end of the novel, Kinga knows that the narrative is slipping away from her. To end the story without revealing the truth about Renia and Bartosz, she must reassert her control. She puts an end to the story—and thereby to all stories—by burning the pendant with the all-knowing narrator inside.[63]

Through the many perspectives and voices, *Ambra* weaves a narrative that resembles that of a carefully constructed spiderweb. More accurately, the

---

62   Kröger can also be read as a self-ironic figure, referring to Janesch's status as official city scribe of Gdańsk in 2009. This writer-in-residence program is organized by the Deutsches Kulturforum östliches Europa (German Culture Forum of Eastern Europe), and it fosters intercultural dialogue and understanding. See Deutsches Kulturforum, "Stadtschreiber-Stipendium."

63   Amber burns easily and is therefore also called *Brennstein* (burn stone) in German. *Ambra* references the ritual burning of amber by shamans (61) and an old children's rhyme said at a game of hide-and-seek: "Bernstein, Brennstein, alles muss versteckt sein!" (372; Amber, burn stone, everyone must hide!)

multiple personal, spatial, and temporal entanglements—the very specific context of the German-Polish borderland entwined with seemingly distant times and places—make the narrative seem more like a cobweb that invites critical views of clearly defined borders. Epistemic borders play a particularly significant role, and the novel pushes the reader to consider what we can know, whether and how knowledge can be accessed, and by whom it is transmitted. These questions are put into sharp relief through the magical realist mode, driving home the point that marginalized or forgotten voices must be accessed through the imagination and that they provide important counterpoints to hegemonic, often too-simple narratives. We have also seen this strategy in *The Tin Drum*, where Oscar exposes other voices and perspectives—often unpleasant ones—through his drumming. Olga Tokarczuk's *House of Day, House of Night*, to which I turn next, tackles similar questions of the possibilities of knowing, and we can sense in this and the other works discussed here something of Tokarczuk's "tender narrator." It bears repeating here that this narrator has an all-encompassing narrative perspective that lets the reader see that everything is interconnected. It is the ethical narrative stance that aims to show that any decision or action has an effect elsewhere.[64]

Fluid Boundaries in Olga Tokarczuk's *House of Day, House of Night* (1998)

Of the works discussed in this study, Olga Tokarczuk's novel *Dom dzienny, dom nocny* (*House of Day, House of Night* [2002], henceforth referred to as *Dom* or *House*) is perhaps the most salient example of the practice of border poetics as I define it. The novel features an astonishing variety and complexity of transgressions and border crossings, including a play with narrative perspective and focalization, the transgression of gender boundaries, and an exploration of the unstable border between nature and culture, as well as the life of artifacts and otherwise silent objects. In postmodern fashion, *House* also breaks with genre conventions and thus underpins the significance of the interplay of form and content in the practice of border poetics. Tokarczuk's work is labeled a novel, but like Anzaldúa's *Borderlands/La Frontera*, it pushes genre boundaries and would be more adequately described as a collage of loosely connected stories and sketches, historical documents, a dream diary, and other texts, such as recipes and a tourist brochure. Like other works discussed here, *House* is structured by complicated and shifting constellations of various border spaces, both on the story plane and on the discursive level. Magical and mythological elements permeate the story and keep unsettling the narrative perspective in exemplary ways.

---

64   Tokarczuk, "Nobel Lecture," 21. See my longer discussion of this idea in chapter 2, "Border Poetics."

160 ♦ Belonging: Defocalized Narratives

With Tokarczuk's novel we return to the southwestern region of Poland, to Lower Silesia, whose significance I have already discussed in the context of Sabrina Janesch's novel *Katzenberge*. Tokarczuk endows this region with an almost mythical quality, creating a borderland in which past and present political borders entwine with symbolic boundaries. Lower Silesia provides the topography for many of Tokarczuk's intellectual activities and much of her literary oeuvre, which can be in part attributed to the author's personal experience with and in these border spaces. Tokarczuk was born in 1962 in Sulechów, Poland, less than 60 miles from the German-Polish border. Since the fifteenth century, this region had been part of the Margraviate of Brandenburg and later the Prussian province of Brandenburg until it became part of Poland after the Second World War. In the late 1990s, Tokarczuk moved to a small village outside Nowa Ruda, which is about 120 miles south of her birthplace. It is here, near the current Polish-Czech border, that *House* is set.

In the frame narrative, the unnamed first-person narrator, who is also an author, and her partner have just moved into a house in the Polish countryside. From here the narrator ventures out on trips in the region, visits with neighbors, enters the virtual reality of the internet, occasionally abandons any kind of corporality and visits other times and places in her dreams. The narrator adopts various perspectives to tell a series of individual stories. Some of these stories are connected by recurring characters, but for the most part, they share themes and motifs or are primarily tied together through their connection to the region. Here, Silesia's unsettling and unsettled history is a focal point, and *House* shows how traumatic experiences have impacted the lives of its inhabitants and have triggered in them the "Snow White syndrome"; that is, a sense of strangeness and alienation that derives from entering a foreign space.[65] As in other places, many postwar inhabitants were new to the region, resettling here from central Poland or arriving as expellees from the formerly Polish eastern territories. In addition, the novel is also set near the current Polish-Czech border, which means that besides the now historical and symbolic German-Polish borderland, a current geopolitical border also plays a role in some of the episodes.

Tokarczuk draws on the region's complex history and the multiple forces that can impact an individual's sense of belonging, and she uses them to create a complex literary landscape in which all borders are porous. This landscape is teeming with ghosts that cannot be expelled, uncontrollable animal spirits, everyday objects with a life of their own, and signs that are not easily deciphered. The fluidity of boundaries is further underscored by a sense of

---

65 Tokarczuk, "Syndrom Królewny Śnieżki." I discuss this concept in more detail in chapter 1, "Entanglements in German and Polish History, Literature, and Culture," but according to Tokarczuk, it afflicts those Poles who settled in these formerly German regions after the Second World War and moved into the homes and towns of its previous inhabitants.

simultaneity of time: stories from the early Middle Ages reverberate in contemporary questions of gender identity; a car left behind by a German aristocratic family during the expulsions has become an organic part of the landscape; a werewolf seen in drug-induced hallucinations brings back traumatic war experiences. The loosely interconnected episodes illustrate that no event, place, or person is isolated and that everything can be summarized as a series of recurring, universally human experiences, needs, and desires that connect humans across and against all borders. Taking a long view of history, *House* stresses that changing affiliations inform the identity of places and peoples and that these are variously inscribed into a landscape. Thus, the novel's relatively restricted geographical space becomes a site for exploring universally conceived figurative boundaries, including those between nature and civilization, man and woman, human and animal, dream and reality, and life and death. Tokarczuk uncovers what lies beneath the veneer of perceptible reality by looking closely at these different border-crossing experiences, and she leaves the realm of realism to access them. The mythological landscape of the novel does not merely bring previously marginalized narratives into the center; rather, it dissolves the dichotomy of center and periphery altogether.

The small town of Nowa Ruda in the novel is a microcosm, similar to that created by Günter Grass in his writings about the Danzig suburb Langfuhr. Irene Sywenky has described this microcosm in even more expansive terms as "a deeply mythological space that is both historical and timeless, connected to the real world and isolated from it." The novel is thereby also embedded within a network of world literature in which the town "has an uncanny resemblance to the apocryphal topographies of William Faulkner's Yoknapatawpha County and Gabriel García Márquez's town of Macondo."[66] This network does not lack specificity and particularity: through the creation of a mythological space, it facilitates the transcendence of multiple boundaries, including those of space, time, and gender. In the process, the local and the individual are reoriented toward a larger framework or context.

In a very productive way, the novel navigates a permanent tension between worldliness or transcendence of specificity, on the one hand, and belonging to a specific local context, on the other hand. Tokarczuk uses the supernatural and magical realism to recover and re-narrate history.[67] Ewa Wampuszyc explains that magical realism contributes to the transgression of boundaries because it disrupts dominant narratives by "unmasking their instability, rather than simply idealizing a place or past." She thus argues against reading the novel in the context of the literature of small fatherlands

---

66 Sywenky, "Representations," 74. I examine the idea of the "worlding" of Polish literature after 1989 and its alleged reorientation away from Polish themes and the dominant Romantic literary tradition in the introduction.

67 Kołodziejczyk, "The Uncanny Space of 'Lesser' Europe."

162 ◆ BELONGING: DEFOCALIZED NARRATIVES

or homelands, which, according to her, "promotes a poetics of nostalgia and return."[68] As discussed in the introduction to this study, however, literature of the small homelands has changed significantly after 1989 and is marked precisely by a critical engagement and distancing from a mythologized past.[69] It is therefore plausible to read the novel in the context of literature of the small homelands, as Dagmar Wienroeder-Skinner has done. She highlights its conciliatory and nonideological tone, which facilitates German-Polish reconciliation needed in a unified Europe.[70] Expanding on the German-Polish theme, *House* can also be examined in dialogue with Sabrina Janesch's *Katzenberge* within the context of a transnationalization of German-Polish memory and changed notions of "Heimat," as Eigler has done.[71]

Tender Narration

As was the case in the examples discussed earlier in the chapter, Tokarczuk's border poetics emerges through an intricate interplay of different narrative perspectives and voices. The first-person narrator not only reveals her own thoughts and dreams but also transforms herself into an omniscient narrator and channels the intimate perspectives of others. The novel's polyvocality stems from constant changes between first- and third-person narration and from focalization through different protagonists. The transitions between perspectives and voices are fluid, making the world visible as a complex network of spatial and temporal connections. Often the narrator also knows things that cannot be explained rationally, once again circumventing the aforementioned "mimetic epistemology" through dreams, mythology, and magical elements.[72] Even before her articulation of the concept of the tender narrator, Tokarczuk explained this approach to storytelling in an interview: "I tell the whole story as if I was looking at a map, that is, speaking from a point of view above it all, only I tell the story from the kitchen, from home. How it was to have two families in one kitchen, two women cooking and unable to understand one another. How it looked from that side, from the inside. An intimate view."[73] To tell a story adequately, Tokarczuk enters a space of transdifference: she suspends the dualism between inside and outside, between overview and detail. It is a paradoxical view, but it aims to simultaneously capture the birds-eye view and an intimate perspective without prioritizing one over the other.

The intimate focalizations (told in the third person) are made possible by the first-person narrator's self-positioning—and self-distancing—at the novel's

---

68 Wampuszyc, "Magical Realism," 368.
69 Czapliński, "The 'Mythic Homeland,'" 357–65.
70 Wienroeder-Skinner, "Attempts at (Re)Conciliation," 278.
71 Eigler, *Heimat, Space, Narrative*, 151–76.
72 Heinze, "Violations of Mimetic Epistemology," 8.
73 Wiącek, "The Works of Olga Tokarczuk," 141.

BELONGING: DEFOCALIZED NARRATIVES   ♦   163

outset. While the narrator describes a dream here, the multiple and changing points of view that follow suggest that the narrator is a subjectless, bodyless, nameless being that hovers high above the valley in which Nowa Ruda is located and that can observe, embody, and narrate everything. It is the scene that I hint at in the epigraph to this chapter. Here it is in greater detail:

> The first night I had a dream. I dreamed I was pure sight, without a body or a name. I was suspended high above a valley at some undefined point from which I could see everything. I could move around my field of vision yet remain in the same place. It seemed as if the world below was yielding to me as I looked at it, constantly moving towards me, and then away, so first I could see everything, then only tiny details.[74]

This flexible narrative perspective allows for the constant shifting between different protagonists: at one time zooming in to perceive every little facet and at other times zooming out to survey everything from a great distance. The distances covered refer also to temporal ones: just as we have seen in *Ambra*, the narrator of *House* is able to bring seemingly disparate times to life in the present:

> Then I discovered that I could see through time as well, and that just as I could change my point of view in space, so I could change it in time too. I was like the cursor on a computer screen navigating of its own accord, or at least oblivious of the hand that is moving it.[75]

As pure sight, the first-person narrator is unbounded by space and time—free to inhabit multiple and vastly different characters and channel their perspectives.

The narrator inhabits not only human perspectives but those of other beings as well. This all-encompassing view further illustrates Tokarczuk's poetology, which is based on a sensitive or feeling narrator who understands the interconnectedness and entanglement of all beings. The motif of the mushroom is an expression of this poetology: One chapter introduces a winter mushroom called velvet foot, which "lives on dead trees" (46). Because it grows outside

---

74   *House*, 1. The original reads, "Pierwszej nocy miałam nieruchomy sen. Śniło mi się, że jestem czystym patrzeniem, czystym wzrokiem i nie mam ciała ani imienia. Tkwię wysoko nad doliną w jakimś nieokreślonym punkcie, z którego widzę wszystko lub prawie wszystko. Poruszam się w tym patrzeniu, ale pozostaję w miejscu. To raczej widziany świat poddaje mi się, kiedy na niego patrzę, przysuwa się i odsuwa tak, że mogę zobaczyć wszystko naraz albo tylko najdrobniejsze szczegóły"; *Dom*, 7.

75   *House*, 1–2. "I zaraz odkrywam inną rzecz—że potrafię patrzeć także poprzez czas, że tak samo jak zmieniam punkt widzenia w przestrzeni, mogę go zmieniać także w czasie, jakbym było strzałką na ekranie komputera, która jednak porusza się sama z siebie albo po prostu nie wie nic o istnieniu poruszającej nią dłoni"; *Dom*, 8.

164 ◆ Belonging: Defocalized Narratives

the mushroom-picking season, it is overlooked by most mushroom hunt-ers. The narrator, however, appreciates its taste and prepares it for her friend Agnieszka, concluding the chapter with a recipe for the velvet foot croquettes she made.[76] The mushrooms in the novel frequently end up in recipes before or after initiating the narrator's reflections about life and death, darkness and light, and the unstable nature of being, conjured by images of darkness, damp-ness, and water. The chapter following "Velvet foot" is titled "Grzybość" in Polish, which is the author's neologism for what can be translated as "mush-roomness" in English, and which in Polish is notably "constructed to be gram-matically feminine."[77] The published English translation gives the chapter the more conventional title "On being a mushroom," whereas the German version captures the grammatical play through the likewise invented feminine noun "Pilzheit."[78] In this chapter the narrator imagines life as a mushroom, and what it would be like to grow on trees, without need for sunlight, and indifferent to humans or death. At the end of the chapter, the narrator concludes, "I would be generous to all insect life; I would give away my body to snails and maggots. I would feel no fear, I would never be afraid of death. What is death, I would think—the only thing they can do to you is to tear you from the ground, slice you up, cook you, and eat you."[79] Urszula Paleczek has noted that the mush-room "embodies the fluidity of the concepts of life and death," and this view is amplified by the fact that many of the mentioned mushrooms are poison-ous to some degree or can easily be mistaken for a poisonous variant.[80] In this sense, one could also read the mushroom as a simultaneous representation of belonging and disruption: While a mushroom is anchored in the soil through a far-reaching rhizome, such belonging can be easily disrupted by a foraging human. At the same time, a carelessly ingested poisonous mushroom can also "pluck" a human from life and return them to the soil. The narrator explores these different forms and manifestations of existence throughout the novel and invites the reader to think about the blurriness between categories of all kinds.

Defocalizing Gender

The narrator's radically defocalized perspective applies also to the category of gender, and the novel thereby expresses a pointed critique of patriarchal structures and heteronormative assumptions throughout the ages. This cri-tique is implemented on the level of plot and through narrative perspective,

76 *House*, 46–48; *Dom*, 65–68.
77 Paleczek, "Olga Tokarczuk's *House of Day, House of Night*," 51.
78 *House*, 48; *Taghaus*, 58.
79 *House*, 49. "Byłabym hojna dla wszelkiego robactwa; oddawałabym swoje ciało ślimakom i larwom owadów. Nigdy nie miałabym w sobie żadnego lęku, nie bałabym się śmierci. Cóż to jest śmierć, myślałabym, jedyne co ci mogą zrobić, to oderwać cię od ziemi, poszatkować, usmażyć i zjeść"; *Dom*, 69.
80 Paleczek, "Olga Tokarczuk's *House of Day, House of Night*," 48–49.

but perhaps most notably through the language itself. Using the grammatical properties of Polish as well as the stereotyping that is embedded in the lexicon, Tokarczuk reveals the deeply gendered construction of language; but unfortunately, some of her critique is lost in the English translation, as scholars have pointed out. Focusing on feminist translation practices, Paulina Gąsior argues that the English version omits the novel's feminist message, most importantly by leaving out an entire chapter on the gendered construction of language. Gąsior also notes that foregrounding the novel's focus on history in the paratexts further downplays the importance of gender.[81] Paleczek analyzes the novel's gendered language and draws attention to difficulties in the English translation, which "omits most of Tokarczuk's challenges to the patriarchal structures of the Polish language." The above-mentioned translation of "grzybość" is just one instance of such omissions. Furthermore, Paleczek points out that entire passages are missing from the English translation, which I also found to be true of the German translation.[82]

Comparing the original text of the sections I cited earlier, for example, shows that in Polish, the subjectless narrator uses the gender-neutral "it" in the formulation "I *was* like the cursor"—"jakbym *było* strzałką." As Polish verb endings in the past tense mark gender, "było" is the first-person singular subjunctive of the verb *to be* and the *o* ending marks the gender of the speaking "I" as neutral. A male narrator would have to say, "jakbym *był* strzałką" without an ending, while a female narrator would say, "jakbym *była* strzałką," with the feminine *a* verb ending. In assuming the nonidentity of a subjectless being, the narrator therefore also rejects being gendered in any way. Although this is the only instance of such grammatical play in the chapter, it is one of Tokarczuk's recurring narrative strategies. And at least within the dream described above, the narrator claims a pure, universal being, unbounded in every sense of the word—right down to the words themselves—and is open to perceive and contain each and every particular detail without preconceived notions. The "pure sight, without a body" wanders from one marginalized, Other, or queer perspective to the next, giving it a voice and narrating it into existence. Tokarczuk's borderland again reminds me of Anzaldúa's: It is a "constant state of transition" that belongs to the Other and marginalized. The fictional universe in *House* is occupied by individuals whose otherness is naturalized and valorized through mythology and fantastic elements that include alternative ways of knowing, but this universe reveals itself quietly to the reader: It is not

---

81   Gąsior, "Taming of the Eastern European Beast," 152–59. The missing chapter is titled "listy" (letters) in *Dom*, 143–44. Citing the translator of the English version, Antonia Lloyd-Jones, Gąsior explains that the chapter was omitted in agreement with the author. Still, Gąsior is highly critical of this decision by the publisher and the translator (153–54). The chapter is also omitted from the German translation.

82   Paleczek, "Olga Tokarczuk's *House of Day, House of Night*," 48, 47–59.

166 ♦ BELONGING: DEFOCALIZED NARRATIVES

dominated by a mean-spirited narrator like Oskar Matzerath nor a manipulative one like Kinga Mischa.

The following example from the novel illustrates how three different perspectives are interconnected, and how memories and emotions are conveyed across great temporal and spatial divides. The focus here is on the narrator's discovery of a book and the intertwined stories of a monk from the sixteenth century and a saint from the thirteenth century. The story begins in the narrative present and the narrator's visit to a famous pilgrimage site, the basilica in Wambierzyce (formerly Albendorf), a few miles south of Nowa Ruda. Walking its grounds, she comes across the crucifix of a bearded woman whose name was Saint Wilgefortis.[83] Later, in the tourist shop by the church, she discovers among the various brochures an old book that turns out to be the anonymous and unpaginated biography of Kummernis of Schonau ("Kümmernis von Schonau" in German), known also as Saint Wilgefortis. As a book within a book, this biography is presented to the reader in its entirety.

Together with the narrator, the reader learns of the unusual woman's life and suffering: After her mother dies, Kummernis grows up in a convent while her father, Baron Schonau, a Teutonic Knight, crusades through Europe. Kummernis finds fulfillment in devoting her life to God and is prepared to take her vows. When her father returns, however, he sees that his daughter has turned into a beautiful young woman, and he arranges her marriage to a fellow knight. When Kummernis refuses, her enraged father locks her in a cell. She does not relent and prays desperately for God to save her. Her prayers are answered when Kummernis grows a beard that makes her unattractive as a wife. Baron Schonau tries to punish his daughter further, but seeing that it has no effect on her, he murders her. To her father's dismay, many Christians see her as a martyr and revere her. While the story is focalized through Kummernis, additional information and commentary also seem to have been added to her biography. For the narrator of the main narrative, who is reading the old book, this biography poses a certain problem: Who was the author of this hagiography and how could they have known so much about Kummernis? To answer this question, the narrative perspective changes, and several episodes that are dispersed throughout the novel tell the story of Paschalis. Paschalis is a young monk who lived several centuries after Kummernis, presumably in the early to mid-sixteenth century. After delivering some goods to a convent, Paschalis falls ill and ends up staying with the nuns. He feels deeply connected to the women, and even though men are strictly forbidden from living among the sisters, he manages to come to an arrangement with the Reverend Mother: he may stay—if he agrees to write down the story of Kummernis. He painstakingly reconstructs the life and suffering of Kummernis and thereby also articulates his own story. He realizes that he feels tormented and trapped inside his male body and desires nothing more than to be a woman.

83 *House*, 50–51; *Dom*, 71–72.

BELONGING: DEFOCALIZED NARRATIVES ♦ 167

From an embodied transgender perspective, Paschalis tells the story of a woman (Kummernis) who has crossed the boundaries of gender to escape her socially prescribed role. Paschalis explores his own pain to find the right narrative and gradually blends the growing awareness of his own female gender identity with that of the saint. Upon reading his account, the Reverend Mother admiringly asks Paschalis how he knew all those things, and he thinks to himself: "How did he know it? He didn't know how. Such knowledge comes from under closed eyelids, from prayers, from dreams, from looking at the world around you, from everywhere. Maybe the saint herself was speaking to him, maybe the scenes from her life originated among the verses of her writings."[84] The paragraph that follows is omitted in the published English translation and begins with the words: "It seemed to him that it will not only be important to write about what happened and to name the whole configuration of events and deeds. It will be equally important and maybe even more important to leave space for that which never was, that which never actually occurred but what only could have occurred—it was enough that it had been imagined."[85] The stories of Paschalis and Kummernis require imagination in order to access and recover a different version of history. Paschalis must use his imagination to tell Kummernis's true story, but the narrator of the frame narrative herself must also use her imagination to understand how Paschalis knew what he knew. To do so, she assumes her subjectless position and retells and re-creates history. This history is told simultaneously from above and below, acknowledging alternative forms of knowing, and allowing for gaps and breaks to remain open for alternative and flexible interpretations. As Elżbieta Wiącek has shown, with this strategy the novel reflects the postmodern condition and makes clear that there is no singular form of privileged knowledge.[86] More importantly, however, it uses such gaps and breaks to make a case for mutual recognition and interconnectedness.

Through this and other plotlines, *House* creates spaces in which a specific place and particular moment become opportunities to explore other times and places that require multiple border crossings and imaginative transgressions. Thus, more universally relatable questions (such as those of gender identity) are made visible through their connection to the particular. Boundaries are

---

84   *House*, 116. The original reads, "Skąd wiedział? Nie wiedział skąd wie. Taka wiedza bierze się spod zamkniętych powiek, z modlitwy, ze snu, z patrzenia wokół, zewsząd. Może w ten sposób przemawiała do niego sama święta, może obrazy z jej życia rodziły się gdzieś między wierszami jej pism"; *Dom*, 157–58.

85   Paleczek, "Olga Tokarczuk's *House of Day, House of Night*," 50. Paleczek's translation modified. The original reads, "Wydawało mu się, że nie tylko będzie ważne, gdy napisze, jak było, nazwie tę całą konfigurację zdarzeń i czynów. Że równie ważne, a może nawet ważniejsze będzie pozostawienie miejsca i przestrzeni na to, czego nie było, co nigdy się nie zdarzyło, a co się tylko mogło zdarzyć—wystarczy, że zostało wyobrażone"; *Dom*, 158.

86   Wiącek, "The Works of Olga Tokarczuk," 143.

168　♦　Belonging: Defocalized Narratives

imagined as opportunities for contact and exchange across different time periods, a process that is also exemplified by the narrator's dissolution into a boundless being—albeit only in her dreams. The narrator's defocalized being puts her into temporary and flexible affiliations, thereby fostering a cosmopolitan imagination. The novel's title itself also provides an important point of orientation for this interpretation: The house of day is the space of the particular, the visible and tangible home that corresponds to lived reality. The house of night is the space of dreams and visions that are universally relatable and similarly structured in people throughout the world, as the narrator observes after sharing her own dreams on the internet (89). *House of Day, House of Night* thus combines the particular with the universal and creates a third home that can house a cosmopolitan imagination.

From Dislocation to Belonging

All three novels discussed here make clear how supernatural elements help express the fluidity and ambiguity of borders. Even more, the fantastic and its related modes of expression produce points of view, focalizations, and voices that bring locally lived border experiences into a framework of universally conceived human border experiences. Magical elements both serve to highlight and transgress the specificity of the experience and create productive intersections and entanglements. The movement across boundaries between dream and reality, life and death, or social and natural worlds does not dislocate the subject but rather relocates it in a new space created by a cosmopolitan imagination. This power to create new spaces also derives from the magical realist mode itself. As Zamora and Faris have argued, this mode effectuates "the fusion, or coexistence, of possible worlds, spaces, systems that would be irreconcilable in other modes of fiction." They continue that the "plurality of worlds" that is made possible by fantastic elements often places the texts themselves "on liminal territory between or among those worlds—in phenomenal and spiritual regions where transformation, metamorphosis, dissolution are common, where magic is a branch of naturalism, or pragmatism."[87] As we have seen in the examples discussed here, these texts are not detached from reality but rather help imagine alternatives in which existing boundaries and spaces are transformed into sites of interaction and exchange. In this understanding, magical realism can be understood to negotiate "between these normative oppositions and alternative structures with which they propose to destabilize and/or displace them."[88]

While such narratives rattle the very foundations of what Azade Seyhan has described as "officially sanctioned" discourses, the texts discussed here also generate universally relevant cosmopolitan spaces out of the historical

87　Zamora and Faris, *Magical Realism*, 6.
88　Zamora and Faris, *Magical Realism*, 6.

and the present conditions of the German-Polish borderland.[89] The world-formation through border poetics can therefore be read as a "mode of value creation," a term Ganguly uses to define an ideal of world literature that is more than an extension of reality.[90] Binaries such as life and death, dream and reality, and social and natural world are creatively negotiated, and the border between them is temporarily suspended. This world is a testing ground, a space of transdifference, in which to train the cosmopolitan imagination. The new spaces remain flexible and fluid (just like the subjects that inhabit it), and they do not insist on their own completeness. Anzaldúa has expressed this sentiment through her concept of the "third country," "a borderland is a vague and undetermined place created by the emotional residue of an unnatural boundary. It is a constant state of transition."[91] Its transitory nature is also always a question of perspective—and this perspective is not naturally or socially given: it is one that can be claimed through an open, creative process.

89   Seyhan, *Writing outside the Nation*, 31.
90   Ganguly, *This Thing Called the World*, 80.
91   Anzaldúa, *Borderlands/La Frontera*, 25.

Ends and Beginnings (Not a Conclusion)

CONVENTION DICTATES that a book requires a conclusion. It is my hope that this book's impending material end also signals an opening, however small, for new conversations, open networks, and further entanglements. In her reflections on world literature, Rebecca Walkowitz asks us to "imagine that the location of any literary work is achieved and unfinished, indebted to a network of past collaborations and contestations, and to collaborations and contestations that have not yet taken place."[1] I believe that the same applies to scholarship, and that a sense of process and exchange enables us to transcend our limited horizons and push against the boundaries of our subject positions. Ideally, our work as readers and scholars is always unfinished: it should connect us to larger, ever-growing networks and enrich ongoing discussions with questions, interjections, and new perspectives. In this study, I have attempted to put German literature, Polish literature, European literature, and world literature in productive conversation with one another—through both scholarship and literary texts. My goal was to write a book that would open new perspectives on the significance of borders in and for the literary imagination, and to contribute to a more entangled literary history that thrives on the crossings of borders between different fields. I hope that this book becomes part of the conversations on literature, borders, and cosmopolitanism that have also inspired it, and that it contributes to the work of pushing the boundaries of my own field, German studies, a little further. To bring it to a close, I have some thoughts and questions, but no conclusions or answers:

If literature is an unfinished process, then we as readers play a crucial role in its making. It is up to us to discover entanglements and create connections; we are responsible, at the very least, for those "collaborations and contestations that have not yet taken place," to repeat Walkowitz. Thinking about and through the borders in a text can help us articulate these entanglements across vast times and spaces, as in the following example. Early in this book, I offered a reflection on an episode from Olga Tokarczuk's novel *House of Day, House of Night*. It involved Peter Dieter, a German returning to the now Polish lands of his childhood, who dies an inconvenient death right on the Polish-Czech border. The border guards are unwilling to deal with the paperwork, and they keep moving Peter Dieter's body back and forth—out of their respective zones of responsibility—while his soul watches the events unfold from above. The violence of borders and their complete indifference toward those they entrap

1   Walkowitz, "The Location of Literature," 543.

ENDS AND BEGINNINGS (NOT A CONCLUSION) ♦ 171

is recounted in numerous other stories. By chance, I came across Saadat Hasan Manto's 1955 story "Toba Tek Singh" after reading Tokarczuk's novel, and I was struck by the radically different, yet similarly absurd border situation it describes. Manto is a Pakistani author who was born in British India in 1912. The story takes place a few years after India's partition, and Indian and Pakistani officials are planning to reallocate the populations of their "insane asylums" according to the new political order. The goal is to bring the Muslim patients to Pakistan, while all Sikh and Hindu patients are to be transferred to India. At the center of the story is a mental hospital in Lahore, which is preparing for the prescribed transfer of patients. The plans have triggered heated debates among the patients, including Toba Tek Singh, whose name is identical with that of his hometown. Nobody in his group is certain whether the little town is now part of India or of Pakistan, but regardless, Toba Tek Singh wants to go to the country to which his town now belongs. He cares more about the actual space that is his home than the political identity it has most recently acquired. At the end of the story, he learns that his hometown is now in Pakistan, but, because he is Sikh, he will be transferred to India. He tries to escape but collapses in the no-man's-land between the two states: "There, behind barbed wire, on one side, lay India and behind more barbed wire, on the other side, lay Pakistan. In between, on a bit of earth which had no name, lay Toba Tek Singh."[2]

Tokarczuk's and Manto's stories are only one node in the vast network of world literature, a point of connection in the human imagination that illuminates the shared nature of our border experiences and the cosmopolitan potential of borders—or, rather, the cosmopolitan potential that lies in critiquing their contingent nature and the disruption and violence they cause. Border poetics questions the possibility of belonging in light of such bordering, and it urges us to reconsider the primacy of the border over human dignity. It asks us to observe with tenderness and to recognize correspondences between ourselves and Peter Dieter, Toba Tek Singh, and many others. This does not mean that the traumas and injustices of the past can be overcome, but perhaps there is an opportunity to imagine a different future and create spaces for new senses of belonging.

This future requires effort and imaginative labor, as the poem to which I refer at the end of my introduction urges. In "The End and the Beginning," Polish poet and 1996 Nobel laureate Wisława Szymborska (1923–2012) suggests that with time, the devastation of war and violence can recede into the background, as long as someone is peacefully "gazing at the clouds."[3] This reorientation is preceded by the hard work of cleaning up and rebuilding, but the effort carries the possibility of imagining a future. This future is not fixed but transient and changeable like a cloud: it is neither tied to a particular space,

2   Manto, "Toba Tek Singh," 31.
3   Szymborska, "Koniec i początek/The End and the Beginning," 326–29, line 47.

172 ♦ Ends and Beginnings (Not a Conclusion)

nor is it constrained by rigid boundaries. Elsewhere, Szymborska observes that clouds are not only free of firm boundaries that manage their contours; they also traverse borders with ease: "Oh, the leaky boundaries of man-made-states! / How many clouds float past them with impunity."[4] Clouds simultaneously evoke fluidity of form and freedom of movement: their shapes are just as ambiguous as their positions in the sky. Clouds inspire the human imagination and foster alternative ways of seeing the world. And, as the lyrical "I" of the first poem notes, this refocusing from the past to the future is not an option, but an imperative: "Someone *must* be stretched out" and look toward the sky.[5] Nonetheless, borders, past or present, literal or figurative, have real and lasting effects; they may change over time, but they do not simply disappear. The borderland is still a literal ground—an actual space that is marked by rifts and breaks—upon which the (lyrical) "I" must stand, even when staring at the clouds. The implications of historical events can still be felt, and memories of the past continue to impact the present. The sentiment still resonates powerfully in the current political climate, and it is present in the literature of our time.

Border poetics derives from the tension between the reality of the borders that millions of people experience every day as well as the desire for borders to be less precarious and deadly—both in their literal and in their figurative iterations. Thinking through borders, critiquing them, and ultimately imagining them as sites of entanglement are acts of the social imagination, and as such, they can fuel social change. These narratives deserve our attention, not only because they can tell us something about our own border experiences and add new perspectives but also because this process draws attention to shared border experiences, and it makes visible our shared responsibility for the border experiences of others. Border narratives may be about local or individual concerns, but border poetics makes these particulars comprehensible in broader contexts. In the process of translating particulars into other contexts, narratives of border poetics participate in a cosmopolitan world-making. While things typically end at borders, border poetics demonstrates that borders can also be reclaimed for new beginnings—a process for which literature and art are indispensable.

There is a certain optimism here, one that is admittedly difficult to justify or maintain. It is based on an affirmative belief in narratives, and it resonates with the argument that Romance scholar Ottmar Ette makes about literature. He names among the most critical issues of our time the question of "how

---

4   Szymborska, "Psalm," 183, lines 1–2.

5   Szymborska, "Koniec i Początek/The End and the Beginning," 326–29, lines 45 and 47, emphasis mine. The poem was originally published in 1993, and Szymborska's insistence on an alternate perspective is informed by her own border experiences. The author, who lived from 1923 to 2012, survived the Second World War in occupied Poland, lived through the oppressions of the Communist period, and experienced the end of the Cold War (and later the enlargement of the European Union).

radically different cultures might live together with mutual respect for each other's differences." He emphasizes the crucial role played by the humanities, particularly literary studies, in answering this challenge.[6] Germany and Poland may not be the "radically different cultures" that Ette had in mind, but difference does not run neatly along "cultural" or "national" lines. Rather, it runs *through* "cultures," groups, and individuals as much as between them. These differences create the kinds of complex but unremarkable entanglements that Inga Iwasiów has described and that we could see in the texts I examined here: "Knots are knots. Nothing less, nothing more. Knots."[7] A cosmopolitan imagination may not be able to untangle these knots, but we can acknowledge, recognize, and try to understand their tangled ways. Elsewhere Ette has argued that the knowledge about life transmitted through literature ("Lebenswissen der Literatur") equals a knowledge required for the survival of humanity ("ÜberLebenswissen der Menschheit").[8] Ette's wordplay with "leben" (to live), "über" (about), and "überleben" (to survive) shows that he ascribes to literature both a practical and an ethical role: the literary imagination helps us shape the world we live in—and it is essential to our survival.

*　　*　　*

In this book, I have proposed that border poetics is an idiom of the cosmopolitan imagination that helps us rethink and reimagine the world from the perspective of multiply overlapping and entangled borders. Yet, for most people in the world today, borders are neither poetic nor a matter of the imagination—they are very real, often insurmountable, and frequently a matter of life and death. What can it mean in such a context to write about border poetics and to claim that a literary and cultural practice can advance a cosmopolitan imagination; that it can create new worlds in which difference is temporarily suspended? And what is the meaning of this cosmopolitan critique for those who are currently on the move? Is it even possible to provide a serious critique of borders from the safe distance of a text? Then again, it can hardly be claimed that texts offer safety—we need only consider the hundreds of writers suffering persecution and violence for what they have imagined and written.[9] I have no satisfying answers to these questions. In fact, there are many more questions to be asked. But it is precisely the persistence of these questions and the lack of answers that is the motor for border poetics. Border poetics reminds us to care and to build alliances and solidarities, to imagine a more equitable world, and finally to realize a "tenderness toward any being other than ourselves."[10]

6   Ette, "Knowledge for Living," 983.
7   Iwasiów, "Bambino," 148. For the original Polish, see Iwasiów, *Bambino*, 66.
8   Ette, *ÜberLebenswissen*.
9   PEN America, "Writers at Risk Database."
10   Tokarczuk, "Nobel Lecture," 25.

Bibliography

Ächtler, Norman. "Topographie eines Familiengedächtnisses: Polen als Raum des Gegengedächtnisses in Tanja Dückers' Roman *Himmelskörper*." *Seminar: A Journal of Germanic Studies* 45, no. 3 (2009): 276–98. https://doi.org/10.3138/seminar.45.3.276.

Adelson, Leslie. "Against Between: A Manifesto." In *Unpacking Europe: Towards a Critical Reading*, edited by Iftikhar Dadi and Salah Hassan, 244–55. Rotterdam: NAI, 2001.

Agier, Michel. *Borderlands: Towards an Anthropology of the Cosmopolitan Condition*. Translated by David Fernbach. Cambridge: Polity Press, 2016.

Albrecht, Dietmar, Bernd Neumann, and Andrzej Talarczyk, eds. *Literatur, Grenzen, Erinnerungsräume: Erkundungen des deutsch-polnisch-baltischen Ostseeraumes als einer Literaturlandschaft*. Würzburg: Königshausen & Neumann, 2004.

Alexander, Manfred. *Kleine Geschichte Polens*. Bonn: Bundeszentrale für politische Bildung, 2005.

American Association of Teachers of German (AATG). "Post from DERSTAN DARD.AT: Nobelpreis für Literatur geht an Peter Handke." Facebook, October 10, 2019. https://www.facebook.com/AATGHQ.

Andreas, Peter. *Border Games: Policing the U.S.-Mexico Divide*. Ithaca, NY: Cornell University Press, 2009.

Antor, Heinz. "Interculturality or Transculturality?" In *The Cambridge Handbook of Intercultural Communication*, edited by Guido Rings and Sebastian Rasinger, 68–82. Cambridge: Cambridge University Press, 2020. https://doi.org/10.1017/9781108555067.

Anzaldúa, Gloria. *Borderlands/La Frontera: The New Mestiza*. San Francisco: Aunt Lute Books, 2007.

Appadurai, Arjun. *Modernity at Large: Cultural Dimensions of Globalization*. Minneapolis: University of Minnesota Press, 2003.

Appiah, Kwame Anthony. *Cosmopolitanism: Ethics in a World of Strangers*. New York: W. W. Norton, 2007.

———. "Rooted Cosmopolitanism." In *The Ethics of Identity*, 213–372. Princeton, NJ: Princeton University Press, 2005.

Archiv Bürgerbewegung Leipzig e.V. "'Bazillus' Solidarność: Solidarität mit Polen." Accessed June 25, 2021. https://www.archiv-buergerbewegung.de/96-power-to-the-people/themenbloecke-polen/353-bazillus-solidarnosc-solidaritaet.

Arslan, Gizem, Brooke Kreitinger, Deniz Göktürk, David Gramling, B. Venkat Mani, Olivia Landry, Barbara Mennel, Scott Denham, Robin Ellis, and Roman

176 ◆ Bibliography

Utkin. "Forum: Migration Studies." *German Quarterly* 90, no. 2 (2017): 212–34. https://doi.org/10.1111/gequ.12033.

"Atak brukowców, spokój kibiców" News Website. Archiwum Rzeczpospolitej. June 5, 2008. https://archiwum.rp.pl/artykul/782231-Atak-brukowcow-spokoj-kibicow.html.

Aust, Martin, Krzysztof Ruchniewicz, and Stefan Troebst, eds. *Verflochtene Erinnerungen: Polen und seine Nachbarn im 19. und 20. Jahrhundert.* Cologne: Böhlau, 2009.

Bachmann, Klaus. "Die polnische Regierung missbraucht die Flüchtlingskrise." *Berliner Zeitung*, March 27, 2022. https://www.berliner-zeitung.de/wochenende/die-polnische-regierung-missbraucht-die-fluechtlingskrise-li.218994.

———. "Die Versöhnung muss von Polen ausgehen." *taz—die tageszeitung*, August 5, 1994. LexisNexisAcademic. www-lexisnexis-com.

Badura, Ute, dir. *Schlesiens wilder Westen.* Eigenverleih—Ute Badura, 2002.

Balibar, Étienne. "The Borders of Europe." In Cheah and Robbins, *Cosmopolitics*, 216–29.

———. "Europe as Borderland." *Environment and Planning D: Society and Space* 27, no. 2 (2009): 190–215. https://doi.org/10.1068/d13008.

———. *We, the People of Europe? Reflections on Transnational Citizenship.* Translated by James Swenson. Princeton, NJ: Princeton University Press, 2004.

Baran-Szołtys, Magdalena. "Gonzo, Ironic Nostalgia, Magical Realism, or, How to Re-Narrate Traumatic Transnational Borderland Stories: Examples from the Twenty-First Century Polish(-German) Literature." *Prace Filologiczne Literaturoznawstwo* 12, no. 9, part 1 (2019): 63–80.

Baran-Szołtys, Magdalena, Nino Gude, Olena Dvoretska, and Elisabeth Janik-Freis, eds. *Galizien in Bewegung: Wahrnehmungen—Begegnungen—Verflechtungen.* Wiener Galizien-Studien, Band 1. Göttingen: V&R unipress, Vienna University Press, 2018.

Barbian, Jan-Pieter, and Marek Zybura, eds. *Erlebte Nachbarschaft: Aspekte der Deutsch-Polnischen Beziehungen im 20. Jahrhundert.* Veröffentlichungen des Deutschen Polen-Instituts Darmstadt. Wiesbaden: Harrassowitz, 1999.

Baumbach, Sibylle. "Rooting 'New European Literature': A Reconsideration of the European Myth of the Postnational and Cynical Cosmopolitanism." In *Cosmopolitanism and the Postnational: Literature and the New Europe*, edited by César Domínguez and Theo D'haen, 55–74. Leiden: Brill Rodopi, 2015.

Beck, Ulrich. "The European Crisis in the Context of Cosmopolitization." Translated by Ciaran Cronin. *New Literary History* 43, no. 4 (Autumn 2012): 641–63. https://doi.org/10.1353/nlh.2012.0040.

———. "Re-Inventing Europe: A Cosmopolitan Vision." *Quaderns de la Mediterrània* 10 (2007): 109–16. https://www.iemed.org/publication/reinventing-europe-a-cosmopolitan-vision.

Beck, Ulrich, and Edgar Grande. *Cosmopolitan Europe.* Translated by Ciaran Cronin. Cambridge: Polity Press, 2007.

Beebee, Thomas O., ed. *German Literature as World Literature.* New York: Bloomsbury Academic, 2014.

Berger, Karina. *Heimat, Loss and Identity: Flight and Expulsion in German Literature from the 1950s to the Present*. Oxford: Peter Lang, 2015.

Berman, Jessica. "Toward a Regional Cosmopolitanism: The Case of Mulk Raj Anand." *Modern Fiction Studies* 55, no. 1 (2009): 142–62. https://doi.org/10.1353/mfs.0.1591.

Beßlich, Barbara, Katharina Grätz, and Olaf Hildebrand, eds. *Wende des Erinnerns? Geschichtskonstruktionen in der deutschen Literatur nach 1989*. Berlin: Erich Schmidt, 2006.

Bhabha, Homi. "Interview with Homi Bhabha: The Third Space." Interview by Jonathan Rutherford. In *Identity: Community, Culture, Difference*, edited by Jonathan Rutherford, 207–21. London: Lawrence & Wishart, 1990.

———. *The Location of Culture*. London: Routledge, 2004.

Bilczewski, Tomasz, Stanley Bill, and Magdalena Popiel, eds. *The Routledge World Companion to Polish Literature*. Abingdon, UK: Routledge, 2021.

Bingen, Dieter. "Deutschland und Polen." Bundeszentrale für politische Bildung, Dossier Deutsch-polnische Beziehungen, October 2, 2009. https://www.bpb.de/themen/europaeische-geschichte/deutsch-polnische-beziehungen/39755/deutschland-und-polen.

Borchers, Roland. "Kaschubei." Online-Lexikon zur Kultur und Geschichte der Deutschen im östlichen Europa, 2012. https://ome-lexikon.uni-oldenburg.de/55217.html.

"Border Poetics." Wikidot.com. Accessed November 13, 2023. http://borderpoetics.wikidot.com/border-poetics.

Borodziej, Włodzimierz. *Geschichte Polens im 20. Jahrhundert*. Munich: C. H. Beck, 2010.

———. "Der Zweite Weltkrieg." In Lawaty and Orłowski, *Deutsche und Polen*, 68–77.

Braun, Rebecca, and Benedict Schofield, eds. *Transnational German Studies*. Liverpool: Liverpool University Press, 2020.

Breinig, Helmbrecht, and Klaus Lösch. "Introduction: Difference and Transdifference." In *Multiculturalism in Contemporary Societies: Perspectives on Difference and Transdifference*, edited by Helmbrecht Breinig, Jürgen Gebhardt, and Klaus Lösch, 11–36. Erlangen: Universitätsbund Erlangen, 2002.

Brennan, Timothy. *At Home in the World: Cosmopolitanism Now*. Cambridge, MA: Harvard University Press, 1997.

———. "Cosmo-Theory." *South Atlantic Quarterly* 100, no. 3 (2001): 659–91.

Brubaker, Rogers. "Categories of Analysis and Categories of Practice: A Note on the Study of Muslims in European Countries of Immigration." *Ethnic and Racial Studies* 36, no. 1 (January 1, 2013): 1–8. https://doi.org/10.1080/01419870.2012.729674.

Brudzyńska-Němec, Gabriela. "Polenbegeisterung in Deutschland nach 1830." EGO—Europäische Geschichte Online, December 3, 2010, edited by Institut für Europäische Geschichte (IEG), Mainz 2010-12-03. URL: http://www.ieg-ego.eu/brudzynskanemecg-2010-de. URN: urn:nbn:de:0159-20100921148.

178 ♦ Bibliography

Cameron, Rob. "Poland 'Invades' Czech Republic in 'Misunderstanding.'" BBC News, Europe, June 13, 2020. https://www.bbc.com/news/world-europe-53034930.

Cantú, Norma E., ed. "Comparative Perspectives Symposium. Gloria E. Anzaldúa, an International Perspective." Special issue, *Signs* 37, no. 1 (2011). http://www.jstor.org/stable/10.1086/660484.

Chanady, Amaryll Beatrice. *Magical Realism and the Fantastic: Resolved versus Unresolved Antinomy*. New York: Garland, 1985.

Chatman, Seymour Benjamin. *Story and Discourse: Narrative Structure in Fiction and Film*. Ithaca, N.Y.: Cornell University Press, 1978.

Cheah, Pheng. "Grounds of Comparison: Around the Work of Benedict Anderson." *Diacritics* 29, no. 4 (1999): 3–18.

———. *What Is a World? On Postcolonial Literature as World Literature*. Durham, NC: Duke University Press, 2016.

Cheah, Pheng, and Bruce Robbins, eds. *Cosmopolitics: Thinking and Feeling beyond the Nation*. Minneapolis: University of Minnesota Press, 1998.

Chernilo, Daniel. "Cosmopolitanism and the Question of Universalism." In *Routledge Handbook of Cosmopolitanism Studies*, edited by Gerard Delanty, 47–59. Abingdon, UK: Routledge, 2012.

Chołuj, Bożena. "Grenzliteraturen und ihre subversiven Effekte: Fallbeispiele aus den deutsch-polnischen Grenzgebieten (Wirbitzky, Skowronnek, Bienek, Iwasiów)." *Internationales Archiv für Sozialgeschichte der deutschen Literatur* 28, no. 1 (2003): 57–87. https://doi.org/10.1515/IASL.2003.1.57.

Chwin, Stefan. "'Grenzlandliteratur' und das mitteleuropäische Dilemma/'Literatura pogranicza' a dylematy Europy Środkowej." German translation by R. U. Henning. *Transodra* 17 (1997): 5–13 (German translation) and 5–12 (Polish original).

Cichocka-Gula, Joanna. "Literaturfestival in Polen—mit Deutschland als Gastland." Interview by Martin Adam. Rbb24 Inforadio, August 20, 2023. https://www.inforadio.de/rubriken/kultur/beitraege/2023/08/festival-literacki-sopot-in-polen.html.

Clifford, James. *Routes: Travel and Translation in the Late Twentieth Century*. Cambridge, MA: Harvard University Press, 1997.

Cohen, Walter. "Introduction." In *A History of European Literature: The West and the World from Antiquity to the Present*, 1–13. Oxford: Oxford University Press, 2017.

Coleman, Nicole. *The Right to Difference: Interculturality and Human Rights in Contemporary German Literature*. Ann Arbor: University of Michigan Press. 2021.

Cöllen, Barbara. "Polsko-niemieckie tematy w literaturze: Rośnie zainteresowanie." Deutsche Welle, March 16, 2015.

Cornis-Pope, Marcel, and John Neubauer, eds. *History of the Literary Cultures of East-Central Europe: Junctures and Disjunctures in the 19th and 20th Centuries*. 4 vols. Amsterdam: John Benjamins, 2004.

Costabile-Heming, Carol Anne. "Imagining German Studies for the Future." In *Transverse Disciplines: Queer-Feminist, Anti-Racist, and Decolonial Approaches to the University*, 81–105. Toronto: University of Toronto Press, 2022.

Czaplejewicz, Eugeniusz. "Jakie kresy? Jaka literatura kresowa? (Perspektywa współczesna)." *Przegląd Humanistyczny* 405, no. 6 (2007): 1–15.

Czapliński, Przemysław "The 'Mythic Homeland' in Contemporary Polish Prose." Translated by Karen Underhill and Tomasz Tabako. Special issue, *Chicago Review: New Polish Writing* 46, no. 3/4 (2000): 357–65.

———. "Shifting Sands: History of Polish Prose, 1945–2015." In *Being Poland: A New History of Polish Literature and Culture since 1918*, 372–406. Toronto: University of Toronto Press, 2018.

Dabrowski, Patrice M. *Poland: The First Thousand Years.* DeKalb: Northern Illinois University Press, 2016.

Damrosch, David. *What Is World Literature?* Princeton, N.J: Princeton University Press, 2003.

Darnton, Robert. "Peasants Tell Tales: The Meaning of Mother Goose." In *The Great Cat Massacre and Other Episodes in French Cultural History*, 9–74. New York: Vintage Books, 1985.

Dedecius, Karl. *Deutsche und Polen in ihren literarischen Wechselbeziehungen.* Stuttgart: Reclam, 1973.

Delanty, Gerard. *The Cosmopolitan Imagination: The Renewal of Critical Social Theory.* New York: Cambridge University Press, 2009.

———. "The Idea of Critical Cosmopolitanism." In *Routledge Handbook of Cosmopolitan Studies*, edited by Gerard Delanty, 38–46. New York: Routledge, 2012.

Die Deutschen und die Polen: Geschichte einer Nachbarschaft, 4 parts, directed by Andrzej Klamt, Zofia Kunert and Gordian Maugg. Halbtotal Filmproduktion, 2016. https://halbtotalfilm.de/deutsche-polen-eu.

Deutsches Kulturforum östliches Europa e.V. "Stadtschreiber-Stipendium." Accessed May 29, 2022. https://kulturforum.info/de/preise-stipendien/stadtschreiber-stipendium.

Deutschlandfunk. "Nach der Millionen-Strafe des EuGH: Polens Verhältnis zur EU." Deutschlandfunk, October 28, 2021. https://www.deutschlandfunk.de/nach-der-millionen-strafe-des-eugh-polens-verhaeltnis-zur-eu-100.html.

Domínguez, César. "Local Rooms with a Cosmopolitan View? Novels in/on the Limits of European Convergence." In *Cosmopolitanism and the Postnational: Literature and the New Europe*, edited by Theo D'haen and César Domínguez, 27–53. Leiden: Brill Rodopi, 2015.

dpa and tsp. "Update/Scharfe Kritik auch an Merkel: Polen wirft Deutschland vor, Russland-Sanktionen zu behindern," *Tagesspiegel*, Politik, April 4, 2022. https://www.tagesspiegel.de/politik/scharfe-kritik-auch-an-merkel-polen-wirft-deutschland-vor-russland-sanktionen-zu-behindern/28225596.html.

Drozdowska-Broering, Izabela. *Topographien der Begegnung: Untersuchungen zur jüngeren deutschen und polnischen Prosa der Grenzräume nach 1989.* Frankfurt am Main: Peter Lang, 2013.

Dückers, Tanja. *Himmelskörper.* Berlin: Aufbau, 2003. Translated by Magdalena Jatowska as *Ciała Niebieskie.* Warsaw: Świat Książki, 2014.

180 ♦ BIBLIOGRAPHY

Dunin, Kinga. "Czytelnia Krytyki Politycznej (8): Tanja Dückers, Ciała niebieskie, przeł. Magdalena Jatowska, Świat Książki 2014." *Krytyka Polityczna*, October 17, 2014. http://www.krytykapolityczna.pl/artykuly/czytaj-dalej/20141017/czytelnia-krytyki-politycznej-8.

Egger, Sabine. "Magical Realism and Polish-German Postmemory: Reimagining Flight and Expulsion in Sabrina Janesch's 'Katzenberge' (2010)." In "Magical Realism as Narrative Strategy in the Recovery of Historical Traumata," edited by Eugene Arva and Hubert Roland. Special issue, *Interférences littéraires/Literaire interferenties* 14 (2014): 65–78.

Egger, Sabine, Stefan Hajduk, and Britta C. Jung, eds. *Sarmatien—Germania Slavica—Mitteleuropa/Sarmatia—Germania Slavica—Central Europe: Vom Grenzland im Osten über Bobrowskis Utopie zur Ästhetik des Grenzraums/From the Borderland in the East and Bobrowski's Utopia to a Border Aesthetics.* Göttingen: Vandenhoeck & Ruprecht, 2020.

Eigler, Friederike. *Heimat, Space, Narrative: Toward a Transnational Approach to Flight and Expulsion.* New York: Camden House, 2014.

———. "Introduction: Moving Forward. New Perspectives on German-Polish Relations in Contemporary Europe." In "German-Polish Border Regions in Contemporary Culture and Politics: Between Regionalism and Transnationalism," edited by Friederike Eigler and Astrid Weigert. Special issue, *German Politics and Society* 31, no. 109 (2013): 1–15.

Erll, Astrid. *Memory in Culture.* Translated by Sara B. Young. London: Palgrave Macmillan, 2011.

Eshel, Amir. *Futurity: Contemporary Literature and the Quest for the Past.* Chicago: University of Chicago Press, 2013.

———. *Poetic Thinking Today: An Essay.* Square One: First-Order Questions in the Humanities. Stanford, CA: Stanford University Press, 2020.

Ette, Ottmar. "Literature as Knowledge for Living, Literary Studies as Science for Living," edited and translated by Vera Kutzinski. *PMLA: Publications of the Modern Language Association of America* 125, no. 4 (2010): 977–93.

———. *ÜberLebenswissen.* Berlin: Kadmos, 2004.

European Commission. "Commission Staff Working Document: 2021 Rule of Law Report, Country Chapter on the Rule of Law Situation in Poland," Document 52021SC0722, July 20, 2021. https://eur-lex.europa.eu/legal-content/EN/TXT/?uri=CELEX%3A52021SC0722.

European Council and Council of the European Union. "EU Restrictive Measures against Belarus," June 7, 2022. https://www.consilium.europa.eu/en/policies/sanctions/restrictive-measures-against-belarus.

Faber, Richard, and Barbara Naumann, eds. *Literatur der Grenze, Theorie der Grenze.* Würzburg: Königshausen & Neumann, 1995.

Fachinger, Petra, and Werner Nell. "Introduction." *Seminar: A Journal of Germanic Studies* 45, no. 3 (2009): 189–95.

Faris, Wendy B. *Ordinary Enchantments: Magical Realism and the Remystification of Narrative.* Nashville, TN: Vanderbilt University Press, 2004.

FAZ.NET. "Schriftstellerinnen zu Belarus: 'Lasst uns unseren Blick nicht von der Tragödie abwenden!'" November 9, 2021. https://www.faz.net/aktuell/

feuilleton/debatten/literaturnobelpreistraegerinnen-zu-belarus-ein-appell-an-europa-17625389.html.

Felsch, Corinna, and Magdalena Latkowska. "Brief der (polnischen) Bischöfe und Willy Brandts Kniefall: Verfrühte Helden?" In Hahn and Traba, *Deutsch-Polnische Erinnerungsorte*, vol. 3: *Parallelen*, 396–414.

Felski, Rita, and Susan Stanford Friedman. "Introduction." In *Comparison: Theories, Approaches, Uses*, edited by Rita Felski and Susan Stanford Friedman, 1–12. Baltimore: Johns Hopkins University Press, 2013.

Fiut, Aleksander. "In the Shadow of Empires: Post-Colonialism in Central and Eastern Europe—Why Not?" In "Postcolonial or Postdependence Studies?" Special issue, *Teksty Drugie* 1, no. 5 (2014): 34–40. https://tekstydrugie.pl/wp-content/uploads/2016/06/t2en_2014_1webCOMB.pdf.

Florczyk, Piotr, and K. A. Wisniewski, eds. *Polish Literature as World Literature*. New York: Bloomsbury, 2023.

Frank, Søren. "Literary Studies and Entanglements beyond the Nation." *German Quarterly* 94, no. 3 (2021): 378–80.

———. "The Migrant Vision in Günter Grass's *The Tin Drum*." *Canadian Review of Comparative Literature/Revue Canadienne de Littérature Comparée* 42, no. 2 (2015): 156–70.

———. "Place and Placelessness in the Literature of Migration." In *Globalization in Literature*, edited by Per Thomas Andersen, 69–91. Acta Nordica: Studier i Språk- Og Litteraturvitenskap. Bergen: Fagbokforlaget, 2014.

Friedman, Susan Stanford. "'Border Talk,' Hybridity, and Performativity: Cultural Theory and Identity in the Spaces between Difference." *Eurozine*, June 7, 2002. https://www.eurozine.com/border-talk-hybridity-and-performativity/.

———. *Mappings: Feminism and the Cultural Geographies of Encounter*. Princeton, NJ: Princeton University Press, 1998.

———. "Migration, Diasporas, and Borders." In *Introduction to Scholarship in Modern Languages and Literatures*, edited by David Nicholls, 260–93. New York: Modern Language Association of America, 2007.

———. "Spatial Poetics and Arundhati Roy's 'The God of Small Things.'" In *A Companion to Narrative Theory*, edited by James Phelan and Peter J Rabinowitz, 192–205. Malden, MA: Blackwell, 2005.

Ganeva, Mila. "From West-German Väterliteratur to Post-Wall Enkelliteratur: The End of the Generation Conflict in Marcel Beyer's *Spione* and Tanja Dückers's *Himmelskörper*." *Seminar: A Journal of Germanic Studies* 43, no. 2 (2007): 149–62. https://doi.org/10.3138/seminar.43.2.149.

Ganguly, Debjani. *This Thing Called the World: The Contemporary Novel as Global Form*. Durham, NC: Duke University Press, 2016.

Garland, Henry B., and Mary Garland. "Grass, Günter." In *The Oxford Companion to German Literature*, 302–4. Oxford: Oxford University Press, 1997.

Gąsior, Paulina. "The Taming of the Eastern European Beast? A Case Study of the Translation of a Polish Novel into English." In *Translation Theory and Practice in Dialogue*, edited by Antoinette Fawcett, Karla Guadarrama, and Rebecca Hyde Parker, 147–63. London: Continuum, 2010.

182 ♦ Bibliography

Gelberg, Johanna M. *Poetik und Politik der Grenze: Die Literatur der deutsch-deutschen Teilung seit 1945*. Bielefeld: Transcript, 2018.

Gelbin, Cathy S., and Sander L. Gilman. *Cosmopolitanisms and the Jews*. Ann Arbor: University of Michigan Press, 2017. https://library.oapen.org/bitstream/handle/20.500.12657/23986/1006148.pdf.

Genest, Andrea. "Die Solidarność aus deutscher Perspektive." *Potsdamer Bulletin für Zeithistorische Studien*, no. 34–35 (2005): 17–22. https://zzf-potsdam.de/sites/default/files/publikation/Bulletin/genest_34.pdf.

Genette, Gérard. *Narrative Discourse: An Essay in Method*. Translated by Jane E. Lewin. Ithaca, N.Y.: Cornell University Press, 1980.

German Studies Association (GSA). "GSA Statement on Nobel Prize for Literature." Approved October 16, 2019. https://www.thegsa.org/blog/gsa-statement-nobel-prize-literature.

———. "This Year's Nobel Prize in Literature Goes to Two People." Facebook, October 10, 2019. https://www.facebook.com/GermanStudiesAssociation.

Gerst, Dominik, Maria Klessmann, and Hannes Krämer. "Einleitung." In *Grenzforschung: Handbuch für Wissenschaft und Studium*, edited by Gerst, Klessmann, and Krämer, 9–25. Baden-Baden: Nomos, 2021. https://www.nomos-elibrary.de/10.5771/9783845295305/grenzforschung.

Görner, Rüdiger. *Grenzen, Schwellen, Übergänge: Zur Poetik des Transitorischen*. Göttingen: Vandenhoeck & Ruprecht, 2001.

Gourgouris, S. "Poiesis." In *The Princeton Encyclopedia of Poetry and Poetics*, edited by Roland Greene, Stephen Cushman, Clare Cavanagh, Jahan Ramazani, and Paul Rouzer, 1070–72. Princeton, N.J: Princeton University Press, 2012.

Grass, Günter. *Die Blechtrommel*. Munich: Deutscher Taschenbuch Verlag, 2002. Translated by Breon Mitchell as *The Tin Drum*. Boston: Mariner Books, 2010.

———. *Hundejahre*. Neuwied am Rhein: Luchterhand, n.d. (1963). Translated by Ralph Manheim as *Dog Years*. New York: Harcourt, Brace & World, n.d. (1965).

Großmann, Viktoria, and Josef Kelnberger. "Justiz in Polen: Erfüllt Warschau wirklich die EU-Forderungen?" Süddeutsche.de. June 2, 2022. https://www.sueddeutsche.de/politik/polen-justiz-rechtsstaatlichkeit-eu-wiederaufbaufonds-1.5595845.

Grucza, Franciszek, ed. *Tausend Jahre polnisch-deutsche Beziehungen: Sprache—Literatur—Kultur—Politik, Materialien des Millennium-Kongresses, 5.–8. April 2000, Warszawa*, 157–69. Warsaw: Graf-Punkt, 2001.

Gutschker, Thomas. "Rechtsstaatsbericht: EU-Kommission rügt Polen und Ungarn." FAZ.NET, July 13, 2022. https://www.faz.net/aktuell/politik/ausland/eu-kommission-legt-rechtsstaatsbericht-vor-18170571.html.

Haberl, Tobias. "Tanja Dückers hat ein Buch zum selben Thema geschrieben wie Günter Grass: Meine Version ist die richtige." *Berliner Zeitung*, March 22, 2003. http://www.berliner-zeitung.de/archiv/tanja-dueckers-hat-ein-buch-zum-selben-thema-geschrieben-wie-guenter-grass-meine-version-ist-die-richtige,10810590,10074490.html.

Hage, Volker. "Die Enkel kommen." *Der Spiegel*, no. 41 (1999): 244–54. http://www.spiegel.de/spiegel/print/d-14906942.html.

———. "Kein Respekt." *Die Zeit*, September 18, 1987. https://www.zeit.de/1987/39/kein-respekt.

———. "Das tausendmalige Sterben." *Der Spiegel*, no. 6 (2002): 184–90. https://magazin.spiegel.de/EpubDelivery/spiegel/pdf/21362876.

Hahn, Hans Henning, and Robert Traba, eds. *Deutsch-Polnische Erinnerungsorte*. 5 vols. Paderborn; Munich: Schöningh, 2012.

———. "Wovon die deutsch-polnischen Erinnerungsorte (nicht) erzählen." In Hahn and Traba, *Deutsch-Polnische Erinnerungsorte*, vol. 2: *Geteilt/Gemeinsam*, 11–49.

Halicka, Beata. *Polens Wilder Westen: Erzwungene Migration und die kulturelle Aneignung des Oderraums 1945–1948*. Paderborn: Schöningh, 2013.

Halle, Randall. *The Europeanization of Cinema: Interzones and Imaginative Communities*. Urbana: University of Illinois Press, 2014.

———. *German Film after Germany: Toward a Transnational Aesthetic*. Urbana: University of Illinois Press, 2008.

———. "Views from the German-Polish Border: The Exploration of International Space in 'Halbe Treppe' and 'Lichter.'" *German Quarterly* 80, no. 1 (2007): 77–96. https://doi.org/10.1111/j.1756-1183.2007.tb00063.x.

Handke, Kwiryna. "Przedmowa." In *Kresy - pojęcie i rzeczywistość: zbiór studiów*, edited by Kwiryna Handke, 7. Warsaw: Slawistyczny Ośrodek Wydawniczy, 1997.

Hayot, Eric. *On Literary Worlds*. Oxford: Oxford University Press, 2012.

Heinze, Rüdiger. "Violations of Mimetic Epistemology in First-Person Narrative Fiction." *Narrative* 16, no. 3 (2008): 279–97. https://doi.org/10.1353/nar.0.0008.

Higgins, Andrew. "Live Updates: Crisis on Europe's Eastern Flank Deepens as Tension Escalates at Polish Border." *New York Times*. November 10, 2021. https://www.nytimes.com/live/2021/11/10/world/poland-belarus-border-migrants.

The Green Border, directed by Agnieszka Holland. Metro Films, 2023.

Holt, Alexander. "Cold War Crossings: Border Poetics in German and Polish Literature" PhD diss., Columbia University, 2020.

Huelle, Paweł. *Weiser Dawidek*. Gdańsk: Wydawnictwo Znak, 2011. Translated by Michael Kandel as *Who Was David Weiser?* London: Bloomsbury, 1991.

Iwasiów, Inga. *Bambino*. Warsaw: Świat Książki, 2008.

———. "Bambino (2008): Excerpts from the Novel." Translated by Karolina May-Chu and Karolina Hicke. *TRANSIT* 14, no. 1 (2023): 140–48. https://doi.org/10.5070/T714162203.

———. "Inga Iwasiów." Author's website. Accessed January 14, 2022, https://ingaiwasiow.info/the-author/.

———. "Ingeleine, du wirst groß sein." Translated by Joanna Manc. In Jordan and Wyrwoll, *Oder—Rhein*, 134–39.

———. "Die Ungeliebten." In *Stettin: Wiedergeburt einer Stadt. Essays über die Odermetropole*, edited by Basil Kerski, translated by Monika Satizabal Niemeyer, 45–64. Potsdam: Deutsches Kulturforum östliches Europa, 2017. https://kulturforum.info/de/publikationen-2/geschichte/7399-basil-kerski-hrsg-stettin-wiedergeburt-einer-stadt.

184 ♦ BIBLIOGRAPHY

Janesch, Sabrina. *Ambra*. Berlin: Aufbau, 2012.

———. "Interview mit Sabrina Janesch." Interview by Gunnar Cynybulk. Sabrina Janesch website. Accessed March 30, 2017. http://www.sabrinajanesch.de/autorin/interview-mit-sabrina-janesch/#_jmp0_.

———. *Katzenberge*. Berlin: Aufbau, 2010.

Janion, Maria, "Obraz poslkości u Grassa" [1985]. In *Günter Grass i polski Pan Kichot*, edited by Maria Janion, 59–74. Gdańsk: Wydawnictwo słowo/obraz terytoria, 1999.

Joachimsthaler, Jürgen. *Text-Ränder: Die kulturelle Vielfalt in Mitteleuropa als Darstellungsproblem deutscher Literatur*. 3 vols. Heidelberg: Universitätsverlag Winter, 2011.

Johnson, Corey, Reece Jones, Anssi Paasi, Louise Amoore, Alison Mountz, Mark Salter, and Chris Rumford. "Interventions on Rethinking 'the Border' in Border Studies." *Political Geography* 30, no. 2 (2011): 61–69. https://doi.org/10.1016/j.polgeo.2011.01.002.

Johnson, Laurie Ruth, ed. *Germany from the Outside: Rethinking German Cultural History in an Age of Displacement*. New York: Bloomsbury, 2022.

Jones, Ellen. *Literature in Motion: Translating Multilingualism across the Americas*. Literature Now. New York: Columbia University Press, 2021.

Jordan, Lothar, and Regina Wyrwoll, eds. *Oder—Rhein: Grenzen im Fluss. Eine Anthologie*. Frankfurt and der Oder and Düsseldorf: Kleist-Museum and Heinrich-Heine-Institut, 2007.

Karahasan, Dževad, and Markus Jaroschka, eds. *Poetik der Grenze: Über die Grenzen sprechen—literarische Brücken für Europa*. Graz: Steirische Verlagsgesellschaft, 2003.

Kearney, Richard. *Poetics of Imagining: Modern to Postmodern*. New York: Fordham University Press, 1998.

Kent, Eddy, and Terri Tomsky, eds. *Negative Cosmopolitanism*. Montreal: McGill-Queen's University Press, 2017.

Kim, David D. *Cosmopolitan Parables: Trauma and Responsibility in Contemporary Germany*. Evanston, IL: Northwestern University Press, 2017.

———. "German Studies and Cosmopolitanism." *German Quarterly* 94, no. 4 (2021): 427–43.

Kleingeld, Pauline, and Eric Brown. "Cosmopolitanism." In *The Stanford Encyclopedia of Philosophy*, edited by Edward N. Zalta, Fall 2014. Metaphysics Research Lab, Stanford University, 2014. https://plato.stanford.edu/archives/fall2014/entries/cosmopolitanism/.

Kołodziejczyk, Dorota. "Post-Colonial Transfer to Central-and-Eastern Europe." In "Postcolonial or Postdependence Studies?" Special issue, *Teksty Drugie* 1, no. 5 (2014): 124–42. https://tekstydrugie.pl/wp-content/uploads/2016/06/t2en_2014_1webCOMB.pdf.

———. "The Uncanny Space of 'Lesser' Europe: Trans-Border Corpses and Transnational Ghosts in Post-1989 Eastern European Fiction." *Postcolonial Text* 6, no. 2 (2011): 1–19. https://www.postcolonial.org/index.php/pct/article/view/1282/1154.

Kontje, Todd. *German Orientalisms*. Ann Arbor: University of Michigan Press, 2004.

———. *Imperial Fictions: German Literature before and beyond the Nation-State*. Ann Arbor: University of Michigan Press, 2018.

Kopp, Kristin. *Germany's Wild East: Constructing Poland as Colonial Space*. Ann Arbor: University of Michigan Press, 2012.

Krzemiński, Adam. *Deutsch-polnische Verspiegelung: Essays*. Vienna: Holzhausen, 2001.

———. "1959: Die Blechtrommel." *Die Zeit*, Kultur, July 19, 2012. http://www.zeit.de/2012/30/L-Kanon-Grass.

———. "Wie die Polen Günter Grass verteidigen." *Die Welt*, Literatur, August 27, 2008. http://www.welt.de/kultur/article2355339/Wie-die-Polen-Guenter-Grass-verteidigen.html.

Krzoska, Markus. "Die polnische Literatur zu Beginn eines neuen Jahrhunderts: Aktuelle Tendenzen und Probleme ihrer Rezeption in Deutschland." *Osteuropa* 50, no. 9 (2000): 1022–30.

Krzoska, Markus, and Paweł Zajas. "Posthumane Verflechtungen." In *Kontinuität und Umbruch: Deutsch-polnische Beziehungen nach dem Zweiten Weltkrieg*, 213–25. *Deutsch-polnische Geschichte*, Band 5. Darmstadt: WBG Academic, 2021.

Kuczyński, Krzysztof A., and Thomas Schneider, eds. *Das literarische Antlitz des Grenzlandes*. Vol. 11. Gießener Arbeiten zur neueren deutschen Literatur und Literaturwissenschaft. Frankfurt am Main: Peter Lang, 1991.

Kuszyk, Karolina. *Poniemieckie*. Wołowiec: Wydawnictwo Czarne, 2019. Translated by Bernhard Hartmann as *In den Häusern der anderen: Spuren deutscher Vergangenheit in Westpolen*. Berlin: Ch. Links, 2022.

Łada, Agnieszka. "Auf persönlicher Ebene sind die Beziehungen sehr gut." Interview with Manfred Götzke, Deutschlandfunk, June 17, 2021. https://www.deutschlandfunk.de/deutschland-und-polen-auf-persoenlicher-ebene-sind-die-100.html.

Łada-Konefał, Agnieszka, and Jacek Kucharczyk. *Der deutsche und der polnische Blick auf die russische Aggression gegen die Ukraine: Deutsch-polnisches Barometer 2023*. Institut für Öffentliche Angelegenheiten, Warschau and Deutsches Polen-Institut, Darmstadt, 2023. https://www.deutsches-polen-institut.de/assets/downloads/Barometer-DE-PL/Barometer-2023-Juni-f.pdf.

Laine, Jussi P. "A Historical View on the Study of Borders." In *Introduction to Border Studies*, edited by Sergei V. Sevastinow, Jussi P. Laine, and Anton A. Kireev, 14–32. Vladivostok: Far Eastern Federal University Vladivostok, 2015. https://absborderlands.org/wp-content/uploads/2013/04/Introduction-to-Border-Studies-2.pdf.

Lamping, Dieter. *Über Grenzen: Eine literarische Topographie*. Göttingen: Vandenhoeck & Ruprecht, 2001.

Lawaty, Andreas, and Hubert Orłowski, eds. *Deutsche und Polen: Geschichte, Kultur, Politik* Munich: C. H. Beck, 2003.

186 ♦ BIBLIOGRAPHY

Levy, Daniel, Max Pensky, and John Torpey. "Editors' Introduction." In *Old Europe, New Europe, Core Europe: Transatlantic Relations after the Iraq War*, edited by Daniel Levy, Max Pensky, and John Torpey, xi–xxix. London: Verso, 2005.

Levy, Daniel, and Natan Sznaider. "Cosmopolitan Memory." In *The Holocaust and Memory in the Global Age*, translated by Assenka Oksiloff, 23–37. Philadelphia: Temple University Press, 2006.

———. "Memory Unbound: The Holocaust and the Formation of Cosmopolitan Memory." *European Journal of Social Theory* 5, no. 1 (2002): 87–106.

Lewandowski, Tomasz. "Grass jako brakujące ogniwo literatury polskiej." In *Polskie pytania o Grassa*, edited by Maria Janion, 240–42. Warsaw: CKS UW Hybrydy, 1988.

The Living Handbook of Narratology. Hamburg: Interdisciplinary Center for Narratology, University of Hamburg, September 24, 2013. https://www-archiv.fdm. uni-hamburg.de/lhn/.

Loew, Peter Oliver. *Danzig: Biographie einer Stadt.* Munich: Beck, 2011.

———. "Trzy mity: Niemieckość, polskość, wielokulturowość (2002)." In *Gdańskie tożsamości: eseje o mieście*, edited by Basil Kerski, 129–41. Gdańsk: Instytut Kultury Miejskiej, 2014.

Lösch, Klaus. "Begriff und Phänomen der Transdifferenz: Zur Infragestellung binärer Differenzkonstrukte." In *Differenzen anders denken: Bausteine zu einer Kulturtheorie der Transdifferenz*, edited by Lars Allolio-Näcke, Britta Kalscheuer, and Arne Manzeschke, 26–49. Frankfurt am Main: Campus, 2005.

Lüdke, Steffen, and dpa. "Streit um Panzer-Ringtausch: Polens Präsident wirft Deutschland Wortbruch vor," *Der Spiegel*, Ausland, May 24, 2022. https://www. spiegel.de/ausland/panzer-ringtausch-polens-praesident-andrzej-duda-wirft-deutschland-wortbruch-vor-a-9d42ed34-9ebe-4519-a740-789afeec902a.

Makarska, Renata. "Übersetzen zwischen Deutschland und Polen: Wie wird die Literatur des Nachbarlandes übersetzt, vermarktet und gelesen (1989 bis 2020)." *Polen-Analysen: Literarische Übersetzungen zwischen Deutschland und Polen*, no. 281 (2021): 2–7. https://laender-analysen.de/polen-analysen/281.

Mani, B. Venkat. *Cosmopolitical Claims: Turkish-German Literatures from Nadolny to Pamuk.* Iowa City: University of Iowa Press, 2007.

———. *Recoding World Literature: Libraries, Print Culture, and Germany's Pact with Books.* New York: Fordham University Press, 2017.

Manto, Saadat Hasan. "Toba Tek Singh." Translated by Khalid Hasan. In *Mirrorwork: 50 Years of Indian Writing, 1947–1997*, edited by Salman Rushdie and Elizabeth West, 25–31. New York: Henry Holt and Company, 1997.

Marszałek, Magdalena, and Sylvia Sasse, eds. *Geopoetiken: Geographische Entwürfe in den mittel- und osteuropäischen Literaturen.* Kadmos, 2010.

Martinez, Matias, and Michael Scheffel. *Einführung in die Erzähltheorie.* Munich: Beck, 2009.

Mau, Steffen. *Sortiermaschinen: Die Neuentdeckung der Grenze im 21. Jahrhundert.* Munich: C. H. Beck, 2021.

May-Chu, Karolina. "Introduction to the Translation." In "German-Polish Borderlands in Contemporary Literature and Culture," edited by Karolina May-Chu and Paula Wojcik. Special section, *TRANSIT: A Journal of Travel, Migration, and Multiculturalism in the German-Speaking World*, 14, no. 1 (2024): 137–39. http://dx.doi.org/10.5070/T714162201.

———. "Measuring the Borderland in Sabrina Janesch's *Katzenberge* (2010)." In "Measuring the World," edited by B. Venkat Mani and Pamela Potter. Special issue, *Monatshefte* 108, no. 3 (2016): 350–61. https://doi.org/10.14361/zig-2016-0208.

———. "Reading Germany, Europe, and the World in Abbas Khider's Novel *Ohrfeige*." In "Europe in Contemporary German-Language Literature." Special issue, *Colloquia Germanica* 51, no. 3/4 (2020), 363–82.

———. "Reimagining the German-Polish Borderlands in *Nowa Amerika* and *Słubfurt*." In "German-Polish Borderlands in Contemporary Literature and Culture," edited by Karolina May-Chu and Paula Wojcik. Special section, *TRANSIT: A Journal of Travel, Migration, and Multiculturalism in the German-Speaking World*, 14, no. 1 (2024): 54–73. http://dx.doi.org/10.5070/T714162194.

———. "Von Grenzlandliteratur zur Poetik der Grenze: Deutsch-polnische Transiträume und die kosmopolitische Imagination," edited by Withold Bonner and Sabine Egger. *Zeitschrift für interkulturelle Germanistik* 7, no. 2 (2016): 85–99.

McManus, Darragh. "The Tin Drum Summarised the 20th Century in Three Words." *Guardian*, Books blog, October 7, 2009. http://www.theguardian.com/books/booksblog/2009/oct/07/the-tin-drum-gunter-grass.

Melas, Natalie. *All the Difference in the World: Postcoloniality and the Ends of Comparison*. Stanford, CA: Stanford University Press, 2007.

Messmer, Nicole. "Türen zu, die Polen kommen!" *Tagesspiegel*, December 20, 2007. http://www.tagesspiegel.de/politik/schengen-erweiterung-tueren-zu-die-polen-kommen/1126426.html.

Modrzejewski, Arkadiusz. "Die kaschubische Minderheit in einer veränderten Umwelt." Translated by Silke Plate. *Polen-Analysen: Die Kaschuben*, no. 95 (September 20, 2011): 2–8. https://laender-analysen.de/polen-analysen/95.

Mufti, Aamir R. *Forget English!* Cambridge, MA: Harvard University Press, 2016.

Müller, Michael G. "Polnische Geschichte von den staatlichen Anfängen im 10. Jahrhundert bis zum Ersten Weltkrieg." In *Länderbericht Polen*, edited by Dieter Bingen and Krzysztof Ruchniewicz, 17–40. Bonn: Bundeszentrale für politische Bildung, 2009.

Musekamp, Jan. *Zwischen Stettin und Szczecin: Metamorphosen einer Stadt von 1945 bis 2005*. Wiesbaden: Harrassowitz, 2010.

Namowicz, Tadeusz. "Deutsche Literatur in Polen." In Grucza, *Tausend Jahre polnisch-deutsche Beziehungen*, 171–86.

———. "Zwischen Historizität und rückwärtsgewandter Utopie. Ostpreußen als 'Heimat' in der deutschen Literatur nach 1945." In Orłowski, *Heimat und Heimatliteratur in Vergangenheit und Gegenwart*, 77–92.

Neumann, Birgit. "The Literary Representation of Memory." In *Cultural Memory Studies: An International and Interdisciplinary Handbook*, edited by Astrid Erll and Ansgar Nünning, 333–43. Berlin: Walter de Gruyter, 2008.

Niederhoff, Burkhard. "Focalization." In *The Living Handbook of Narratology*. http://www.lhn.uni-hamburg.de/article/focalization.

188 ♦ Bibliography

———. "Perspective—Point of View." In *The Living Handbook of Narratology*. http://www.lhn.uni-hamburg.de/node/26.html.

Nünning, Vera, and Ansgar Nünning. "'Multiperspektivität—Lego oder Playmobil, Malkasten oder Puzzle?' Grundlagen, Kategorien und Modelle zur Analyse der Perspektivenstruktur narrativer Texte, Teil I." *Literatur in Wissenschaft und Unterricht* 32, no. 4 (1999): 367–88.

Nussbaum, Martha. "Patriotism and Cosmopolitanism." *Boston Review*, October 1, 1994. http://bostonreview.net/martha-nussbaum-patriotism-and-cosmo politanism.

"Obok: Polska–Niemcy. 1000 lat historii w sztuce/Tür an Tür. Polen–Deutschland 1000 Jahre Kunst und Geschichte." Exhibit, Berliner Festspiele, curated by Anda Rottenberg, realized by Royal Castle in Warsaw and Martin-Gropius-Bau Berlin, September 23, 2011–January 9, 2012.

Oklińska, Katarzyna. "Czy czuły narrator istnieje? Debata wokół nowej książki Olgi Tokarczuk." Podcast. *Audycje Kulturalne: Podcast Narodowego Centrum Kultury*. December 27, 2020. https://audycjekulturalne.pl/czuly-narrator.

Olschowsky, Heinrich. "Polnische Literatur in Deutschland." In Grucza, *Tausend Jahre polnisch-deutsche Beziehungen*, 157–69.

Oltermann, Philip. "German Thinkers' War of Words over Ukraine Exposes Generational Divide." *Guardian*, World News, May 6, 2022. https://www. theguardian.com/world/2022/may/06/german-thinkers-war-of-words-over-ukraine-exposes-generational-divide.

Orłowski, Hubert. "Grenzlandliteratur: Zur Karriere eines Begriffs und Phänomens." In Orłowski, *Heimat und Heimatliteratur in Vergangenheit und Gegenwart*, 9–18.

———, ed. *Heimat und Heimatliteratur in Vergangenheit und Gegenwart*. Poznań: New Ton, 1993.

Paleczek, Urszula. "Olga Tokarczuk's *House of Day, House of Night*: Gendered Language in Feminist Translation." *Canadian Slavonic Papers* 52, no. 1–2 (2010): 47–59.

Palej, Agnieszka. *Fließende Identitäten: Die deutsch-polnischen Autoren mit Migrationshintergrund nach 1989*. Krakauer Studien zur germanistischen Literatur- und Kulturwissenschaft, vol. 5. Kraków: Wydawnictwo Uniwersytetu Jagiellońskiego, 2015.

Palm, Christian. "'Neuer deutscher Opferdiskurs'? Flucht und Vertreibung in Günter Grass' *Im Krebsgang* und Tanja Dückers' *Himmelskörper*." *Germanistische Mitteilungen*, no. 66 (2007): 45–62.

PEN America. "Statement: Deep Regret over the Choice of Peter Handke for the 2019 Nobel Prize in Literature," October 10, 2019. https://pen.org/press-release/statement-nobel-prize-for-literature-2019.

———. "Writers at Risk Database," April 28, 2020. https://pen.org/writers-at-risk-database/.

Peter, Stefanie. "Grenzlandliteratur: Der Stoff liegt auf der Straße." *Fluter: Magazin der Bundeszentrale für politische Bildung*, September 29, 2002. http://www.fluter.de/de/polen/literatur/1235.

Phillips, Ursula. "Generation, Transformation and Place in Inga Iwasiów's Novels *Bambino* (2008) and *Ku słońcu* (2010)." *Argument: Biannual Philosophical Journal* 2, no. 1 (2012): 17–35.

Pieper, Cornelia. "'Die deutsch-polnische Nachbarschaft ist heute beispielhaft für gelebte europäische Nachbarschaft!'" Interview by André Wannewitz. *Auswärtiges Amt*, December 2011. https://www.auswaertiges-amt.de/de/newsroom/111201-stm-p-mdw/248930.

Pinkas, Claudia. *Der phantastische Film: Instabile Narrationen und die Narration der Instabilität*. Narratologia. Berlin: Walter de Gruyter, 2010.

Platthaus, Andreas. "Zu Besuch bei Sabrina Janesch: Hinter den Fassaden von Danzig." *Frankfurter Allgemeine Zeitung*, Feuilleton, August 18, 2012. http://www.faz.net/aktuell/feuilleton/buecher/zu-besuch-bei-sabrina-janesch-hinter-den-fassaden-von-danzig-11855682.html.

Porter-Szűcs, Brian. *Poland in the Modern World: Beyond Martyrdom*. Chichester, UK: Wiley-Blackwell, 2014.

Pratt, Mary Louise. "Arts of the Contact Zone." *MLA Profession* (1991): 33–40.

Puchner, Martin. "Teaching Worldly Literature." In *The Routledge Companion to World Literature*, edited by Theo L. D'haen, David Damrosch, and Djelal Kadir, 255–63. Abingdon, UK: Routledge, 2012.

Raabe, Katharina. "As the Fog Lifted—Literature in Eastern Central Europe since 1989." *Eurozine*, October 8, 2009. https://www.eurozine.com/as-the-fog-lifted.

Redkult. "Günter Grass nie żyje: Noblista miał 87 lat." *Gazeta Wyborcza*, Kultura, April 13, 2015. http://wyborcza.pl/1,75410,17744558,Gunter_Grass_nie_zyje__Noblista_mial_87_lat.html.

Reich-Ranicki, Marcel. *Mein Leben*. Munich: Deutscher Taschenbuch Verlag, 2000.

Richter, Sandra. *Eine Weltgeschichte der deutschsprachigen Literatur*. Munich: C. Bertelsmann, 2017.

Rinas, Karsten. "Die andere Grenzlandliteratur: Zu einigen tschechischen Romanen mit antideutscher Tendenz." *brücken – Germanistisches Jahrbuch Tschechien – Slowakei*, no. 16 (2008): 115–63.

Robbins, Bruce. "Introduction Part I: Actually Existing Cosmopolitanism." In Cheah and Robbins, *Cosmopolitics*, 1–19.

Rogge, Florian. "Galizien: Trauma und Tabu in S. Janeschs 'Katzenberge.'" In *Galizien als Kultur- und Gedächtnislandschaft im kultur- und sprachwissenschaftlichen Diskurs*, edited by Anna Hanus and Ruth Büttner, 283–98. Frankfurt am Main: Peter Lang, 2015.

Rothberg, Michael. *Multidirectional Memory: Remembering the Holocaust in the Age of Decolonization*. Stanford, CA: Stanford University Press, 2009.

Różycki, Tomasz. "PEN America—Guest Post: Tomasz Rozycki on 'Scorched Maps.'" Translated by Mira Rosenthal. PEN America, July 13, 2009. https://penamerica.blogspot.com/2009/07/guest-post-tomasz-rozycki-on-scorched.html.

———. "Scorched Maps." Translated by Mira Rosenthal. PEN America, April 7, 2009. https://pen.org/scorched-maps/.

———. "Zapomniane Mapy." In *Scorched Maps* (trilingual publication in Polish, English, and Chinese), edited by Bei Dao et al., 27. 2013 International Poetry

190 ◆ Bibliography

Nights in Hong Kong, Hong Kong: Chinese University of Hong Kong Press, 2014.

Ruchniewicz, Krzysztof. "Die DDR." In Lawaty and Orłowski, eds., *Deutsche und Polen*, 193–205.

Rumford, Chris. *Cosmopolitan Borders*. London: Palgrave Macmillan, 2014.

———. "Does Europe Have Cosmopolitan Borders?" *Globalizations* 4, no. 3 (September 2007): 327–39. https://doi.org/10.1080/14747730701532419.

Rushdie, Salman. "On Günter Grass." *Granta* 15 (Autumn 1985). https://granta.com/on-gunter-grass/.

Rybicka, Elżbieta. *Geopoetyka: Prestrzeń i miejsce we współczesnych teoriach i praktykach literackich*. Kraków: Universitas, 2014.

Said, Edward W. *Orientalism: Twenty-Fifth Anniversary Edition*. New York: Vintage Books, 2003.

Sasser, Kim. *Magical Realism and Cosmopolitanism: Strategizing Belonging*. Houndmills, UK: Palgrave Macmillan, 2014.

Sauerland, Karol. "Europäische Literatur als Begriff." In *Die kulturelle Eigenart Europas*, edited by Günter Buchstab and Konrad Adenauer-Stiftung e.V., 165–77. Munich: Herder, 2010. https://www.kas.de/verlagspublikationen/detail/-/content/die-kulturelle-eigenart-europas.

Schimanski, Johan. "Border Aesthetics." *International Lexicon of Aesthetics* (Autumn 2019). https://doi.org/10.7413/18258630068.

———. *Grenzungen: Versuche zu einer Poetik der Grenze*. Vienna: Turia + Kant, 2020.

———. "Reading Borders and Reading as Crossing Borders." In *Borders and the Changing Boundaries of Knowledge*, edited by Inga Brandell, Marie Carlson, and Önver A. Çetrez, 91–107. Transactions/Swedish Research Institute in Istanbul 22. Istanbul: Svenska forskningsinstitutet, 2015. https://www.srii.org/transaction/vol22.

Schimanski, Johan, and Stephen Wolfe, eds. *Border Poetics De-Limited*. Hanover: Wehrhahn, 2007.

———. "Cultural Production and Negotiation of Borders: Introduction to the Dossier." *Journal of Borderlands Studies* 25, no. 1 (2010): 38–49. https://doi.org/10.1080/08865655.2010.9695749.

Schimsheimer, Christof. "Galizien und die Kresy als polnische Erinnerungsorte im Vergleich." In Baran-Szołtys, Gude, Dvoretska, and Janik-Freis, eds., *Galizien in Bewegung*, 37–55.

Schmidgall, Renate. "Die Macht des Genius loci: Danzig in der Prosa von Stefan Chwin und Paweł Huelle." *Ansichten: Jahrbuch des deutschen Polen-Instituts Darmstadt* 7 (1996): 97–115.

Schoene, Berthold. "Cosmo-Kitsch vs. Cosmopoetics." *Review of Contemporary Fiction* 32, no. 3 (2012): 105–13.

science.ORF.at. "Streit um Sobieski-Denkmal." *Österreichischer Rundfunk*, Science, September 6, 2018. https://science.orf.at/v2/stories/2934421/.

Serrier, Thomas. "Formen kultureller Aneignung: Städtische Meistererzählungen in Nordosteuropa zwischen Nationalisierung und Pluralisierung." In *Die Aneignung fremder Vergangenheiten in Nordosteuropa am Beispiel plurikultureller Städte (20. Jahrhundert)*, edited by Thomas Serrier, 13–23. Nordost-Archiv 2006. Lüneburg: Nordost-Institut, 2007. https://www.ikgn. de/publikationen/band-xv-2006.html.

———. "Gedächtnistransfer und kulturelle Aneignung: Der deutsch-polnische Erinnerungsraum 1945–200. . . ." In *Europäische Erinnerungsräume*, edited by Kirstin Buchinger, Claire Gantet, and Jakob Vogel, 154–63. Frankfurt am Main: Campus, 2009.

Seyhan, Azade. *Writing outside the Nation*. Princeton, NJ: Princeton University Press, 2001.

Stan, Corina. "Novels in the Translation Zone: Abbas Khider, Weltliteratur, and the Ethics of the Passerby." *Comparative Literature Studies* 55, no. 2 (2018): 285–302.

Stelmaszyk, Natasza. "Die neue Situation der polnischen Literatur im deutschsprachigen Raum." *Zarys* 8 (2009): 153–66.

Stüben, Jens. "Erfragte Erinnerung–entsorgte Familiengeschichte: Tanja Dückers' 'Wilhelm-Gustloff'-Roman 'Himmelskörper.'" In Beßlich, Grätz, and Hildebrand, *Wende des Erinnerns?*, 169–89.

Surynt, Izabela, and Mirosława Zielińska. "Der polnisch-polnische Krieg um Günter Grass: Imponderabilien und Mythen. Streifzüge durch die wichtigsten polnischen Grass-Debatten 1963–2007." In *Amicus Poloniae: Teksty ofiarowane Profesorowi Heinrichowi Kunstmannowi w osiemdziesiątą piątą rocznicę urodzin*, edited by Krzysztof Ruchniewicz and Marek Zybura, 393–418. Wrocław: Via Nova, 2009. https://depot.ceon.pl/handle/123456789/3264.

Światłowski, Zbigniew. "Die Neue 'Ostlandliteratur' oder die Kunst des Abschiednehmens." In Orłowski, *Heimat und Heimatliteratur in Vergangenheit und Gegenwart*, 93–99.

Sywenky, Irene. "Representations of German-Polish Border Regions in Contemporary Polish Fiction: Space, Memory Identity." *German Politics and Society* 31, no. 4 (2013): 59–84.

Szymborska, Wisława. "Psalm" and "Koniec i początek/The End and the Beginning." In *Nothing Twice: Selected Poems/Nic dwa razy: Wybór wierszy*, translated by Stanisław Barańczak and Clare Cavanagh, 182–83, 326–29. Kraków: Wydawnictwo Literackie, 1997.

Taberner, Stuart. *Transnationalism and German-Language Literature in the Twenty-First Century*. London: Palgrave Macmillan, 2017.

"Tanja Dückers: Himmelskörper: Roman." *Perlentaucher: Das Kulturmagazin.* Accessed July 27, 2023. https://www.perlentaucher.de/buch/tanja-dueckers/himmelskoerper.html.

Ther, Philipp. *Deutsche und polnische Vertriebene: Gesellschaft und Vertriebenenpolitik in der SBZ/DDR und in Polen 1945–1956*. Göttingen: Vandenhoeck & Ruprecht, 1998.

Thum, Gregor. *Die fremde Stadt: Breslau 1945*. Berlin: Siedler, 2003. Translated by Tom Lampert and Allison Brown as *Uprooted: How Breslau Became Wrocław during the Century of Expulsions*. Princeton, NJ: Princeton University Press, 2011.

192 ♦ Bibliography

Todorov, Tzvetan. *The Fantastic: A Structural Approach to a Literary Genre.* Translated by Richard Howard. Ithaca, N.Y.: Cornell University Press, 1975.

Tokarczuk, Olga. *Czuły narrator.* Kraków: Wydawnictwo Literackie, 2020. Translated by Bernhard Hartmann, Lisa Palmes, and Lothar Quinkenstein as *Übungen im Fremdsein: Essays und Reden.* Zurich: Kampa, 2021.

———. *Dom dzienny, dom nocny.* Wałbrzych: RUTA, 1998. Translated by Antonia Lloyd-Jones as *House of Day, House of Night.* Evanston, IL: Northwestern University Press, 2003. Translated by Esther Kinsky as *Taghaus, Nachthaus.* Berlin: Deutscher Taschenbuch Verlag, 2004.

———. "Palec Stalina." *Kafka: kwartalnik środkowoeuropejski*, no. 3 (2001): 46–51.

———. "Przemowa noblowska Olgi Tokarczuk," Nobel Lecture Presented at the Swedish Academy, Stockholm, December 7, 2019. 1–26. https://www. nobelprize.org/uploads/2019/12/tokarczuk-lecture-polish-2.pdf. Translated by Jennifer Croft and Antonia Lloyd Jones as "Nobel Lecture: The Tender Narrator." 1–26. https://www.nobelprize.org/uploads/2019/12/tokarczuk-lecture-english-2.pdf.

———. "Syndrom Królewny Śnieżki i inne sny dolnośląskie/Das Schneewittchensyndrom und andere niederschlesische Träume." In Marek Hałub and Matthias Weber, eds., *Mein Schlesien-meine Schlesier: Zugänge und Sichtweisen/ Mój Śląsk-moi Ślązacy: Eksploracje i obserwacje.* Leipzig: Leipziger Universitätsverlag, 2014, 157–66 (Polish original), 164–75 (German translation).

Traba, Robert. "Gra w 'Niemca—wiecznego wroga': Trzy strategie polityczne." *Kultura Liberalna* 46, no. 671 (November 16, 2021). https://kulturaliberalna. pl/2021/11/16/gra-w-niemca-wiecznego-wroga-trzy-strategie-polityczne/.

Traba, Robert, and Peter Oliver Loew. "Die Identität des Ortes: Polnische Erfahrungen mit der Region." In *Jahrbuch Polen 2012: Regionen*, edited by Andrzej Kaluza and Jutta Wierczimok. Deutsches Polen-Institut Darmstadt. Wiesbaden: Otto Harrassowitz, 2012.

Trepte, Hans-Christian. "Zur niederschlesischen Identität in der polnischen Literatur." In *Identität Niederschlesien—Dolny Śląsk*, edited by Hans-Christian Trepte and Karoline Gil, 91–105. Westostpassagen—Slawistische Forschungen und Texte. Hildesheim: Olms, 2007.

Tzanelli, Rodanthi. *Magical Realist Sociologies of Belonging and Becoming.* Abingdon, UK: Routledge, 2020.

UiT/The Arctic University of Norway. "Border Poetics/Border Culture." Accessed November 13, 2023. https://en.uit.no/forskning/forskningsgrupper/gruppe? p_document_id=344750.

UNHCR. "Global Trends: Forced Displacement in 2022." UNHCR: The UN Refugee Agency. June 14, 2023. https://www.unhcr.org/global-trends-report-2022.

United Nations Development Programme (UNDP) "Human Development Index." Human Development Reports. Accessed March 25, 2022. http://hdr.undp.org/ en/indicators/137506.

Upstone, Sara. "Magical Realism and Postcolonial Studies: Twenty-First Century Perspectives." *Journal of Commonwealth and Postcolonial Studies* 17, no. 1 (2011): 153–63.

Vertretung in Deutschland. "Rechtsstaatlichkeit: EU-Kommission leitet Vertrags-verletzungsverfahren gegen Polen ein," June 8, 2023. https://germany. representation.ec.europa.eu/news/rechtsstaatlichkeit-eu-kommission-leitet-vertragsverletzungsverfahren-gegen-polen-ein-2023-06-08_de.

Volkmann-Schluck, Sonja. "Im Osten geht die Grenze auf." *Der Tagesspiegel*, December 2, 2007. http://www.tagesspiegel.de/berlin/brandenburgi/schengen-abkommen-im-osten-geht-die-grenze-auf/1110478.html.

Wagner, Winfried. "Literarische Grenzüberschreitungen im 'unheimlichen' deutsch-polnischen Raum: Untersuchungen zu Sabrina Janesch, Andrzej Stasiuk und Artur Becker." Diss., Technische Universität Dresden, 2017.

Walkowitz, Rebecca L. *Born Translated: The Contemporary Novel in an Age of World Literature.* New York: Columbia University Press, 2015.

———. "Comparison Literature." *New Literary History* 40, no. 3 (2009): 567–82. https://www.jstor.org/stable/27760276.

———. *Cosmopolitan Style: Modernism beyond the Nation.* New York: Columbia University Press, 2006.

———. "The Location of Literature: The Transnational Book and the Migrant Writer." *Contemporary Literature* 47, no. 4 (2006): 527–45. https://www.jstor. org/stable/4489178.

Wampuszyc, Ewa V. "Magical Realism in Olga Tokarczuk's *Primeval* and *Other Times* and *House of Day, House of Night.*" *East European Politics & Societies and Cultures* 28, no. 2 (2014): 366–85. https://doi.org/10.1177/0888325413519471.

Wanat, Zosia. "Poland's Persistent Forbidden Zone on the Border with Belarus." POLITICO, December 1, 2021. https://www.politico.eu/article/polands-persistent-forbidden-zone-on-the-border-with-belarus/.

Weber, Piere-Frédéric. "Angst in der polnischen Deutschlandpolitik nach 1945." In *Angst in den internationalen Beziehungen*, edited by Patrick Bormann, Thomas Freiberger, and Judith Michael, 131–47. Göttingen: V&R unipress, 2010.

Weiß, Christian. "Aufreger um Pinkelpause." *Stern*, June 6, 2008. https://www. stern.de/sport/fussball/em-2008/analyse/deutschland-gegen-polen-aufreger-um-pinkelpause-3856716.html.

Welzer, Harald. "Schön unscharf: Über die Konjunktur der Familien-und Generationenromane." *Mittelweg* 36, no. 1 (2004): 53–64.

Werberger, Annette. "Überlegungen zu einer Literaturgeschichte als Verflech-tungsgeschichte." In *Kulturen in Bewegung: Beiträge zur Theorie und Praxis der Transkulturalität*, edited by Dorothee Kimmich and Schamma Schahadat, 109–41. Bielefeld: transcript, 2012.

Wetenkamp, Lena. *Europa erzählt, verortet, erinnert: Europa-Diskurse in der deutschsprachigen Gegenwart.* Würzburg: Königshausen & Neumann, 2017.

Wiącek, Elżbieta. "The Works of Olga Tokarczuk: Postmodern Aesthetics, Myths, Archetypes, and the Feminine Touch." *Women's Writing Online*, no. 1 (2009): 134–55. https://web.archive.org/web/20141021112511/http://womenswriting. fi/files/2009/11/10_wiacek.pdf.

Wienroeder-Skinner, Dagmar. "Attempts at (Re)Conciliation: Polish-German Relations in Literary Texts by Stefan Chwin, Paweł Huelle, and Olga Tokar-czuk." In *Victims and Perpetrators: 1933–1945: (Re)Presenting the Past in*

194 ◆ Bibliography

Post-Unification Culture, edited by Laurel Cohen-Pfister and Dagmar Wienroeder-Skinner, 262–84. Berlin: Walter de Gruyter, 2006.

Winkler, Claudia. "A Third-Generation Perspective on German-Polish Flight and Expulsion: Discursive and Spatial Practices in Sabrina Janesch's Novel Katzenberge (2010)." *German Politics and Society* 31, no. 4 (2013): 85–101. https://doi.org/10.3167/gps.2013.310405.

Winkler, Heinrich August. "Im Schatten von Versailles: Das deutsch-polnische Verhältnis während der Weimarer Republik." In Lawaty and Orłowski, *Deutsche und Polen*, 60–68.

Wolf, Christa. *Kindheitsmuster*. Munich: dtv, 1994.

Wozniak, Paweł C. "Günter Grass and Paweł Huelle: Pilenz and Mahlke in Post-War Poland." In *Changing the Nation: Günter Grass in International Perspective*, edited by Rebecca Braun and Frank Brunssen, 119–31. Würzburg: Königshausen & Neumann, 2008.

Zamora, Lois Parkinson, and Wendy B. Faris. "Introduction: Daiguiri Birds and Flaubertian Parrot(ie)s." In *Magical Realism: Theory, History, Community*, edited by Lois Parkinson Zamora and Wendy B. Faris, 1–11. Durham, NC: Duke University Press, 1995.

Zduniak-Wiktorowicz, Małgorzata. "Philologie im Kontakt: Das Beispiel Migrationsliteratur." *Studia Germanica Gedanensia* 42 (2020): 35–44. https://doi.org/10.26881/sgg.2020.42.04.

Zernack, Klaus. "Deutsch-polnische Beziehungen im historischen Überblick." In Grucza, *Tausend Jahre polnisch-deutsche Beziehungen*, 88–102.

Zessin-Jurek, Lidia. "Real Refugees, Fake Refugees." *Eurozine*, March 28, 2022. https://www.eurozine.com/real-refugees-fake-refugees/.

Zybura, Marek. *Querdenker, Vermittler, Grenzüberschreiter: Beiträge zur deutschen und polnischen Literatur- und Kulturgeschichte*. Dresden: Neisse, 2007.

Zygadło, Grażyna. "'Where the Third World Grates against the First': Teaching Gloria Anzaldúa from a Polish Perspective." *Signs: Journal of Women in Culture and Society* 37, no. 1 (2011): 29–34. https://doi.org/10.1086/660288.

Index

Ächtler Norman, 118n49, 122, 125–26, 127n67
Adelson, Leslie, 18n54, 76
Agier, Michel, 18n52, 73, 89
Alexander, Manfred, 39
American Association of Teachers of German (AATG), 19n57
Andreas, Peter, 89n89
antisemitism, 3–4, 69n23, 105
Antor, Heinz, 7n17
Anzaldúa, Gloria, 10–11, 53, 87–89, 134, 139, 159, 165, 169
Appadurai, Arjun, 65, 69
Appiah, Kwame Anthony, 69n23, 71n31
appropriation, 79–81, 85–86, 106, 142, 154; as distinct from cosmopolitical claim-making, 82–83; types of, 82–83
Arens, Hiltrud, 18n54
Arslan, Gizem, 18n54
Aust, Martin, 15n46

Bachmann, Klaus, 3n8, 24, 119
Badura, Ute, 81n64
Balibar, Étienne, 1n1, 72–73, 75
Baran-Szołtys, Magdalena, 113
Baumbach, Sibylle, 14n42, 21
Beck, Ulrich, 20–21, 114, 116n45
Beebee, Thomas O., 19
belonging, 10, 13–15, 64, 70–71, 73, 75–76, 94, 108, 130–31, 171; and cosmopolitan/cosmopolitical claim-making, 76–78, 81–83; and disruption, 10–11, 16–17, 25, 27–28, 64–65, 68, 78–82, 135–38, 164; and entanglement, 33–34; and "impermanence syndrome" (concept of Gregor Thum), 101, 106; and magical realism, 134–38; and motif of soil, 112–16, 164; and Snow White syndrome, 79–81, 83, 111, 160

Berger, Karina, 17n50
Berlin, 36n5, 38–39, 47n53, 105, 109, 117, 119, 121
Berlin Wall, fall of as threshold, 1, 5–6, 8–10, 34–35, 44–45, 48, 51, 54–56, 58–61, 82, 161n66, 162
Berman, Jessica, 71n31
Beßlich, Barbara, 60n99, 60n100
betweenness, 16, 21, 27, 59, 76–77, 88, 136, 155, 171. *See also* "interzone" (concept of Randall Halle)
Bhabha, Homi, 11, 87–88
Biendarra, Anke, 18n54
Bilczewski, Tomasz, 19n55
Bill, Stanley, 19n55
Bingen, Dieter, 42
body, 110, 113, 130, 138, 146n45, 164, 166–67; as crossed by borders, 102–3; as trapped at a border, 6–7, 170–71
Borchers, Roland, 140
border poetics, characteristics of, 4–5, 10, 12–15, 17, 21, 24–25, 26, 27–28, 67–69; emergence of, 5–6, 8–10, 17, 21, 26, 34, 62, 169, 171–72; previous uses of, 4–5, 12–13, 68–69; in relation to the universal and the particular, 4–5, 7, 20–23, 26, 64–65, 68–72, 84, 88, 96, 168, 172; and resistance/ subversion, 27–28, 58–59, 74, 82–83, 131, 136–37, 141
border regime, 10, 73; English as, 25
border studies, 8–9, 11
border/borderlands literature, 54, 58, 59–60, 86–87; as *Grenzlandliteratur*, 34–35, 53–62, 86, 133–34; as *Heimatliteratur*, 58; as *literatura kresowa*, 53–54, 56, 59
borders/borderlands, 6–7, 16, 25–26, 29, 53–57, 59–60, 64–65, 75, 88–89; ambiguity of, 7–9, 76–77, 168; and cosmopolitanism, 18, 24, 69, 72–75,

196 ♦ INDEX

borders/borderlands (*continued*):
78, 89, 115; as conceptualized by
Gloria Anzaldúa, 11, 87–88, 134,
139, 165, 169; as in-between spaces,
76–77, 136; and memory, 27, 83, 85;
terminology for, 53–59
borders/borderlands, German-Polish,
40–45, 51, 55, 78–81, 84, 89n89, 99,
101–2, 109, 160; Europe as, 73; Oder-
Neisse border, 43, 51, 101
Borodziej, Włodzimierz, 39–40, 42–45
Brandt, Marion, 16
Brandt, Willy, 35, 42–43
Braun, Rebecca, 18n54
Breinig, Helmbrecht, 21n65, 27n87, 72,
75n48, 96, 136
Brennan, Timothy, 69n23, 71n30
Breslau (Polish: Wrocław), 15n46, 40,
41n28, 101
Brown, Eric, 69n23
Brubaker, Rogers, 13n39
Brudzyńska-Němec, Gabriela, 39n18
Bug River, 57, 111, 114–15

Chanady, Amaryll Beatrice, 135
Chatman, Seymour Benjamin, 27n88
Cheah, Pheng, 23–24, 29n92, 64n3,
69n23
Chernilo, Daniel, 70
Chołuj, Bożena, 16, 58–59
Chwin, Stefan, 26, 41, 52, 54–58, 60,
78n57, 86n81, 133–35
Cichocka-Gula, Joanna, 53n78
Clifford, James, 71n30, 112–13
clouds, as motif, 29, 119, 121–22, 171–72
Cohen, Walter, 22n69
Cold War, 12, 41–44, 46–47, 49, 54, 141;
changes following the end of, 1–2,
5–6, 10, 15–16, 22, 35, 47–48, 50, 52,
60, 70, 78, 84. *See also* Berlin Wall, fall
of as threshold
Coleman, Nicole, 16–17, 18n54, 100n14,
112n35, 115n42
Cöllen, Barbara, 86n79
comparison, 20, 28–29, 61–62;
"comparison literature" (concept of
Rebecca Walkowitz), 13–15
contact zone, 7–8, 56, 73

Cornis-Pope, Marcel, 16n48
cosmo-kitsch, 24, 95–96, 119. *See also*
kitsch
cosmopolitan/cosmopolitical claim-
making, 65, 76–78, 81–85, 137–38;
as distinct from appropriation,
82–85
cosmopolitan imagination/vision, 4–5,
11, 18, 23–24, 34, 67–69, 72, 75, 85,
88–89, 108, 114, 116–17, 135–36, 138,
168–69
cosmopolitan style; as defined by
Rebecca Walkowitz, 33–34, 66–67
"cosmopolitan workshops," borders as
(concept of Chris Rumford), 24, 27,
72, 74–75, 77
cosmopolitanism, definitions of, 4, 9–10,
20–21, 67–72, 74, 78; and borders, 11,
15, 17–18, 24, 72–73, 139, 170; and
open regionalism, 71–72; and relation
to the universal and the particular, 5,
20–21, 26, 64–65, 68–72, 84, 88, 96,
168, 172
Costabile-Heming, Carol Anne, 19n57
Croft, Jennifer, 66n10
Czaplejewicz, Eugeniusz, 56n84, 56n85
Czapliński, Przemysław, 16, 56n84, 60,
63–64, 162n69

Dabrowski, Patrice, 36–40, 43n36
Damrosch, David, 14n42, 22–23
Danzig (Polish: Gdańsk), 1, 39–40,
50–52, 138–43, 145–46, 149–50,
153–54, 158n62, 161
Darnton, Robert, 80n61
Dedecius, Karl, 38–39, 47, 49n58
defocalization, 28, 54–55, 131, 133–36,
138–39, 143, 145, 150, 153, 156; and
blurriness, 133–34; of gender, 164–68;
in magical realism, 133, 135
Delanty, Gerard, 4, 20, 68, 71, 73
disruption, 35, 41, 72, 76, 78–81,
94, 96–67, 99–103, 106, 128; and
belonging, 10–11, 16–17, 25, 27–28,
64–65, 68, 78–82, 135–38, 164. *See
also* belonging
Domínguez, César, 21n66
Drozdowska-Broering, Izabela, 127

Dückers, Tanja, 58, 84, 86, 97, 98n12, 117; and Günter Grass, 117–18
Dückers, Tanja, works by: *Himmelskörper*, 118–28; reception of in Poland, 127
Dunin, Kinga, 127

Egger, Sabine, 12n29, 16, 108
Eigler, Friederike, 16, 17n50, 45n46, 60n98, 108–9, 116n46, 122, 127, 162
entanglement, 5, 8–9, 24–27, 51, 71, 78–79, 118, 142–43, 155, 168, 170, 172–73; and (literary) history, 14, 46, 52–54, 170; and the motif of the knot, 33–34, 99–101, 107, 173; and the motif of the mushroom, 163–64; and the motif of the spiderweb, 158–59; and the "tender narrator" (concept of Olga Tokarczuk), 67–68, 159
Erll, Astrid, 118n50
Eshel, Amir, 74, 116
Ette, Ottmar, 172–73
Europe, 15–16, 20–21, 35–39, 46, 60, 71, 73, 84–85, 102, 108; as cosmopolitan, 20–21, 114, 116
European literature, notion of, 21–22, 54–58, 170; and poetics of Europeanness, 21; and world literature, 14, 20–22, 25, 52
European Union, 2–4, 36, 46, 89n89; accession of Poland to, 5, 45, 84
expellees, 6, 40, 44, 57, 78–81, 111, 145, 160

Fachinger, Petra, 60–61
fantastic. *See* magical realism
Faris, Wendy B., 133, 135, 137, 168
Felsch, Corinna, 42n33, 43n34
Felski, Rita, 28n91
fictions of memory, 27–28, 93–96, 128
First World War, 1, 39–40
Fiut, Aleksander, 17n51
Florczyk, Piotr, 19n55
Frank, Søren, 20, 25, 143, 144n39, 147, 152
Frankfurt an der Oder, 84, 101
Frankfurt Book Fair, 48

Friedman, Susan Stanford, 8–9, 28, 63, 68n18, 77, 84n72, 87; and ambiguity of borders, 9; and notion of betweenness, 77
futurity, 72, 74, 116

Galicia, 57n86, 74, 105, 109, 111–16
Ganeva, Mila, 119
Ganguly, Debjani, 9–10, 24–25, 64n3, 142, 169
Gąsior, Paulina, 165
Gdańsk (German: Danzig), 1, 39–40, 50–52, 138–43, 145–46, 149–50, 153–54, 158n62, 161
Gdynia (German: Gotenhafen), 40, 119–21, 123–25
Gelbin, Cathy S., 69n23
gender, 97, 107, 121–22, 127, 159, 164–67
Genest, Andrea, 43
Genette, Gérard, 27, 87, 93, 131–32, 143n38
Genius loci, 141–42, 153–54
geopoetics, 11, 60n101
German Studies Association (GSA), 19n57
Gerst, Dominik, 8n18, 11n27
Gilman, Sander L., 69n23
Goethe, Johann Wolfgang von, 48; and world literature, 73n42
Göktürk, Deniz, 18n54
Gotenhafen (Polish: Gdynia), 40, 119–21, 123–25
Gourgouris, S., 65n5
Grande, Edgar, 20–21, 114
Grass, Günter, 47n53, 49–52, 78, 139–40, 148; and world literature, 142–43
Grass, Günter, works by: *Die Blechtrommel* (English: *The Tin Drum*), 28, 93, 51–52, 132, 137–51; publication history of, 49–50; film adaptation of, 50; *Hundejahre* (English: *Dog Years*), 142–43, 149; *Im Krebsgang* (English: *Crab Walk*), 117–18, 120n54; *Katz und Maus* (English: *Cat and Mouse*), 142n33, 149, 150n51, 151
Grätz, Katharina, 60n99, 60n100

198 ♦ INDEX

Grenzlandliteratur. See border/
borderlands literature

Hage, Volker, 50n66, 61, 120n54
Hahn, Hans Henning, 15n46, 85
Halicka, Beata, 57n87, 81n64, 82
Halle, Randall, 16n47, 20n59, 65n4, 76,
83, 88
Handke, Kwiryna, 57n88
Handke, Peter, 19
Heimat (English: homeland), 16–17, 26,
40, 44, 58, 108, 115n43, 162; *See also*
small fatherlands
Heimatliteratur, 58. *See also* border/
borderlands literature
Heinze, Rüdiger, 144n40, 151n54,
162n72
Helbig, Brygida, 16
Hicke, Karolina, 98n11
Hildebrand, Olaf, 60n99, 60n100
Holland, Agnieszka, 2n4
Holocaust, 9, 18, 47n53, 60n99, 85,
105–7
Holt, Xan (Alexander), 12, 35n2
Huelle, Paweł, 41n28, 52, 78n57, 86n81
Huelle, Paweł, works by: *Weiser Dawidek*
(English: *Who Was David Weiser?*),
142n33, 150–51

"impermanence syndrome" (concept of
Gregor Thum), 101, 106
"interzone" (concept of Randall Halle),
76, 83
Iwasiów, Inga, 33–34, 67, 84, 97–98
Iwasiów, Inga, works by: *Bambino*, 57,
75–76, 98–108, 117, 173; "Ingeleine,
du wirst groß sein," 102–3; "Die
Ungeliebten," 78n57, 98n11

Janesch, Sabrina, 108, 113, 158n62
Janesch, Sabrina, works by: *Ambra*, 1, 67,
108, 137–38, 141n30, 144n33, 150–59;
Katzenberge, 17n50, 41, 57, 58, 67, 74,
108–17, 162
Janion, Maria, 51, 139n23
Joachimsthaler, Jürgen, 16, 57–58
Johnson, Laurie Ruth, 18n54
Jones, Ellen, 23

Kafka (journal), 79n58
Kantner, Katarzyna, 66n12
Kashubia, 139–41, 145
Kearney, Richard, 65
Kent, Eddy, 69n23
Kim, David, 9, 18, 60n99, 67, 70n25,
116n44
kitsch, 51, 127; "cosmo-kitsch" (concept
of Berthold Schoene), 24, 95–96, 119;
"Versöhnungskitsch," (concept of Klaus
Bachmann, English: reconciliation
kitsch), 24, 102, 119, 127
Kleingeld, Pauline, 69n23
Klessmann, Maria, 8n18, 11n27
knot, as motif, 33–34, 47, 51, 99–101,
103–5, 107, 173
Koehler, Krzysztof, 66n12
Kołodziejczyk, Dorota, 17n51, 161n67
Königsberg (Russian: Kaliningrad), 123
Kontje, Todd, 15–17
Kopp, Kristin, 16–17, 45n46
Krämer, Hannes, 8n18, 11n27
kresy, 26, 53, 56–57, 61, 110. *See also*
borders/borderlands, terminology for
Krzemiński, Adam, 41n28, 50–51
Krzoska, Markus, 22n70, 48n54, 155n61
Kuszyk, Karolina, 41n30, 81n65

Łada, Agnieszka, 2n5, 46n49
Laine, Jussi P., 8n18, 11n27
Lamping, Dieter, 12n29, 59
Langfuhr (Polish: Wrzeszcz), 142–43,
161
Latkowska, Magdalena, 42n33, 43n34
Levy, Daniel, 20n60, 85n76
Lewandowski, Tomasz, 51, 146n45,
146n46
Literacki Sopot (festival), 53
Lloyd Jones, Antonia, 66n10, 98n11,
165n81
Loew, Peter Oliver, 50n64, 50n67, 52,
139n25, 141, 143n36, 154
Lösch, Klaus, 21n65, 27n87, 72, 75n48,
96, 136

magical realism/fantastic, 28, 76n49,
108–9, 111–12, 116n46, 131–38, 150,
155, 161, 168; and belonging, 136;

and defocalization, 131, 133–35; and resistance/subversion, 136–37
Makarska, Renata, 48, 52–53, 84n73
Mani, B. Venkat, 18n54, 19, 81–83, 137n21
Manto, Saadat Hasan, works by: "Toba Tek Singh," 171
Martinez, Matias, 132
Marszałek, Magdalena, 11
Mau, Steffen, 73
May-Chu, Karolina, 84n75, 98n11
Melas, Natalie, 29n92
memory, 16–17, 60–61, 78–79, 83–86, 99, 107–9, 110n33, 116, 118–22, 127–28, 162; as border phenomenon, 83–84, 93; fictions of, 27–28, 93–96, 128; as "multidirectional" (concept of Michael Rothberg), 85, 95
Miłosz, Czesław, 57n87
Modrzejewski, Arkadiusz, 140n27
Mufti, Aamir, 25, 104
Müller, Michael, 38
Musekamp, Jan, 101

Namowicz, Tadeusz, 48–49, 52, 58
narrative, definition of, 94; and distinction between story and discourse, 27, 87, 93
narrative perspective, and point of view, 66–67; relation to focalization and point of view, 130–33, 139, 143, 168; and voice, 132
narrator, 66–68, 96, 130–33, 138, 144; "tender narrator" (Polish: "czuły narrator," concept of Olga Tokarczuk), 66–69, 141n30, 159, 162–64, 171, 173
Nell, Werner, 60–61
Neubauer, John, 16n48
Neumann, Birgit, 28n90, 95–96
Niederhoff, Burkhard, 131–32
1989/fall of Berlin Wall as threshold, 1, 5–6, 8–10, 34–35, 44–45, 48, 51, 54–56, 58–61, 82, 161n66, 162
Nobel Prize in Literature, 4, 19, 29, 37, 48, 171
Nosbers, Hedwig, 52n75
Nowa Ruda (German: Neurode), 160–61
Nünning, Ansgar, 131n3

Nünning, Vera, 131n3
Nussbaum, Martha, 69n23, 71n30

Oder River, 101, 111
Oder-Neisse border, 43, 51, 101
Oder-Rhine literary cruise, 84, 102
Olschowsky, Heinrich, 46–48
Orłowski, Hubert, 16, 56n84, 57–58
Ostpolitik, 35, 42–43

Paleczek, Urszula, 164–65, 167
Palej, Agnieszka, 41n29
Palm, Christian, 117n47, 120n54
Partition, of Poland, 34, 38–39, 105; of India, 171
PEN America, 113, 173; on the 2019 Nobel prize, 19
Pensky, Max, 20n60
Phillips, Ursula, 99
Pinkas, Claudia, 132–33
PiS (Prawo i Sprawiedliwość, English: Law and Justice Party), 2, 3n9, 46, 53n78
poetics, definition of, 65; of Europeanness, 21. See also border poetics
Pogranicze (journal), 97
Polenfreundschaft/ Polenschwärmerei (English: friendship/infatuation with Poland), 38–39
Polish-Lithuanian Commonwealth, 37–38
Popiel, Magdalena, 19n55
Porter-Szűcs, Brian, 49, 55n82
post-German (Polish: poniemieckie), 41, 81
Poznań (German: Posen), 39, 104
Pratt, Mary Louise, 7–8
Prussia, 35–39, 42, 41n27, 45n46, 58, 139–41, 160
Puchner, Martin, 64n3, 73n42

Raabe, Katharina, 84n73
reconciliation, between Germany and Poland, 42–43, 45–46, and Border Treaty of 1990, 45; and Treaty on Good Neighborly Relations, 45–46
Reich-Ranicki, Marcel, 47

200 ♦ INDEX

Richter, Sandra, 19
Rinas, Karsten, 57–58
Robbins, Bruce, 69n23, 71n31
Rogge, Florian, 110n32, 112n35
Rothberg, Michael, 85, 95
Różycki, Tomasz, 113–15, 57n87
Ruchniewicz, Krzysztof, 15n46, 43–44
Rumford, Chris, 18n52, 24, 27n87,
    72–75, 77, 85
Rushdie, Salman, 144n39
Rybicka, Elżbieta, 11

Said, Edward, 11, 63–64
Sasse, Sylvia, 11
Sasser, Kim Anderson, 136
Sauerland, Karol, 22n69
Scheffel, Michael, 132
Schimanski, Johan, 4, 12–13, 68–69,
    75n47
Schlesien (Polish: Śląsk; English: Silesia),
    6, 39, 41, 55, 109, 111–12, 115–16,
    125, 160
Schlöndorff, Volker, 50
Schmidgall, Renate, 41n28
Schoene, Berthold, 24, 95, 119
Schofield, Benedict, 18n54
Second World War, 1, 5–6, 16–17, 28,
    33–34, 40, 78, 85, 125, 138–39, 145,
    154, 158, 160, 172n5; postwar period
    and effects of, 1, 6, 16, 33–34, 40–42,
    44, 46–47, 54–55, 57, 75–76, 78–81,
    98–99, 104, 109, 125
Serrier, Thomas, 82
Seyhan, Azade, 18n54, 27, 78n56, 83–84,
    93–94, 96, 168–69
Silesia (Polish: Śląsk; German: Schlesien),
    6, 39, 41, 55, 109, 111–12, 115–16, 125
small fatherlands, 16, 161–62. *See also*
    Heimat
Snow White syndrome (Polish: syndrom
    Królewny Śnieżki), 79–81, 83, 111,
    160; and "impermanence syndrome"
    (concept of Gregor Thum), 101, 106
soil, as motif, 109, 112–16, 164
Solidarność/Solidarity (movement),
    43–44, 50, 98
Stan, Corina, 24n79
Stasiuk, Andrzej, 57n87

Stelmaszyk, Natasza, 22–23, 47–48, 52
Stettin (Polish Szczecin), 33, 40, 97–99,
    101–3, 106, 108
storytelling, as border crossing, 68; as
    existential act, 65, 147, 157, 165
Stüben, Jens, 121n55, 127n67
Surynt, Izabela, 50n65
Światłowski, Zbigniew, 58
Sywenky, Irene, 161
Szczecin (German Stettin), 33, 40, 97–99,
    101–3, 106, 108
Sznaider, Natan, 85n76
Szymborska, Wisława, 29, 171–72

Taberner, Stuart, 18n54
"tender narrator" (Polish: "czuły
    narrator," concept of Olga Tokarczuk),
    66–69, 141n30, 159, 162–64, 171, 173
Teutonic knights, 36–37, 166; as
    stereotype, 37
Ther, Philipp, 44n41, 57n87
Thum, Gregor, 81n64, 101
Todorov, Tzvetan, 134–35, 137
Tokarczuk, Olga, 4, 84, 86, 160; as
    recipient of the Nobel Prize in
    Literature, 19, 48
Tokarczuk, Olga, works by: *Dom dzienny,
    dom nocny* (English: *House of Day,
    House of Night*), 6–7, 36, 41, 81,
    131, 138, 141n30, 142n33, 155n61,
    159–68, 170–71; "Nobel Lecture" 2,
    65n4, 66–69, 130, 173; "Palec Stalina,"
    (English: Stalin's Finger), 79; and
    Syndrom Królewny Śnieżki (English:
    Snow White syndrome), 79–80
Tomsky, Terri, 69n23
Torpey, John, 20n60
Traba, Robert, 15n46, 46n48, 71–72, 85
transdifference, 21–22, 27, 51n70, 59, 72,
    75–77, 83, 88, 96, 108, 136, 157, 162,
    169
Treaty of Versailles, 39–40
Treaty on Good Neighborly Relations,
    45–46
Trepte, Hans-Christian, 7n14, 16
Troebst, Stefan, 15n46
Tür an Tür (Polish: Obok Polska, exhibit),
    36n5

Twardoch, Szczepan, 141n30
Tzanelli, Rodanthi, 136n16

Ukraine, 3n8, 56–57, 74, 104, 109–11, 113, 115–16
underground press, in Poland during Cold War, 49–50
Upstone, Sara, 137n18

Verflechtungsgeschichte. See entanglement, and (literary) history
Versöhnungskitsch. See kitsch

Wagner, Winfried, 7n14, 41n28, 150n51, 151n55
Walkowitz, Rebecca L., 13–15, 23, 33, 66–67, 131, 138n22, 170; and "born translated," 14, 23, 131; and "comparison literature," 13–15; and "cosmopolitan style," 33, 66–67; and ethical discomfort, 33, 138n22
Wambierzyce (German: Albendorf), 166
Wampuszyc, Ewa V., 161–62
Warsaw, 36n5, 38, 47n53, 50, 105–6, 121, 123–26; Book Fair, 52–53; and 1970 visit by Willy Brandt; 42–43
Weber, Piere-Frédéric, 44n43, 45n44, 80n62, 101n16
Welzer, Harald, 119, 127n67
Werberger, Annette, 14
Wetenkamp, Lena, 20–21
Wiącek, Elżbieta, 162n73, 167

Wienroeder-Skinner, Dagmar, 122, 127n70, 162
Winkler, Claudia, 115
Winkler, Heinrich August, 40n23
Wisniewski, K. A., 19n55
Wolf, Christa, 78, 86n82, 110n33
Wolf, Christa, works by: *Kindheitsmuster* (English: *Patterns of Childhood*), 44
Wolfe, Stephen, 12–13, 68–69
Wolff, Kurt, 142–43
Wolting, Monika, 16
world literature, 9–10, 14, 17–22, 49, 51–52, 64, 73–74, 161, 169, 170; definitions of, 22–25
worlding, 22–24, 52n75, 97, 108, 161n66
world-making, 17, 23–24, 26–27, 64–65, 69, 75, 77, 97, 143, 157, 172
Wozniak, Paweł C., 150n51
Wrocław (German: Breslau), 15n46, 40, 41n28, 101
Wrzeszcz (German: Langfuhr), 142–43, 161

Zagajewski, Adam, 57n87
Zamora, Lois Parkinson, 137, 168
Zduniak-Wiktorowicz, Małgorzata, 16
Zernack, Klaus, 35–36, 38, 41n27, 42n32, 44
Zielińska, Mirosława, 50n65
Zybura, Marek, 16
Zygadło, Grażyna, 89n89

Printed in the United States
by Baker & Taylor Publisher Services